Of Latitudes Unknown

Of Latitudes Unknown

James Baldwin's Radical Imagination

Edited by
Alice Mikal Craven
and William E. Dow

Associate Editor: Yoko Nakamura

BLOOMSBURY ACADEMIC

NEW YORK · LONDON · OXFORD · NEW DELHI · SYDNEY

BLOOMSBURY ACADEMIC
Bloomsbury Publishing Inc
1385 Broadway, New York, NY 10018, USA
50 Bedford Square, London, WC1B 3DP, UK

BLOOMSBURY, BLOOMSBURY ACADEMIC and the Diana logo are trademarks of
Bloomsbury Publishing Plc

First published in the United States of America 2019
Paperback edition first published 2020

A catalog record for this book is available from the Library of Congress.

Library of Congress Cataloging-in-Publication Data
Names: Craven, Alice Mikal, editor. | Dow, William (William E.), editor. |
Nakamura, Yoko, editor.
Title: Of latitudes unknown: James Baldwin's radical imagination / edited by
Alice Mikal Craven, William E. Dow, and Yoko Nakamura.
Description: New York, NY: Bloomsbury Academic, 2019. | Includes
bibliographical references and index.
Identifiers: LCCN 2018059679 (print) | LCCN 2019002702 (ebook) |
ISBN 9781501337727 (ePub) | ISBN 9781501337734 (ePDF) | ISBN 9781501337741
(xml-platform) | ISBN 9781501337710 (hardback:alk. paper)
Subjects: LCSH: Baldwin, James, 1924-1987—Political and social views. |
Baldwin, James, 1924-1987—Criticism and interpretation.
Classification: LCC PS3552.A45 (ebook) | LCC PS3552.A45 Z843 2019 (print) |
DDC 818/.5409—dc23
LC record available at https://lccn.loc.gov/2018059679

ISBN: HB: 978-1-5013-3771-0
PB: 978-1-5013-6757-1
ePDF: 978-1-5013-3773-4
eBook: 978-1-5013-3772-7

Typeset by Integra Software Services Pvt. Ltd.

To find out more about our authors and books visit www.bloomsbury.com
and sign up for our newsletters.

CONTENTS

FOREWORD: THE DEATH OF THE PROPHET

Douglas Field

It is said that the camera cannot lie, but rarely do we allow it to do anything else, since the camera sees what you point it at: the camera sees what you want it to see. The language of the camera is the language of our dreams.

—JAMES BALDWIN, *THE DEVIL FINDS WORK*

In an article for *Esquire*, first published in 1960 as "The Precarious Vogue of Ingmar Bergman" and later with the title "The Northern Protestant," James Baldwin recounted the outline of a film that he wanted to make: "My film would begin with slaves boarding the good ship *Jesus* ... There would be one intransigent slave, an eternal figure, destined to appear, and to be put to death in every generation." This eternal figure, Baldwin explained, would first be a witch doctor, singer, or prince, then a politician murdered during Reconstruction, later a soldier returning from the First World War, and finally, in an echo of Rufus Scott, the tragic protagonist of his third novel, *Another Country*, "a jazz musician [who would] go mad" ("Northern Protestant" 245).

Baldwin never made that film; however, his outline, structured around the recurring murder of "an eternal figure, destined to appear, and to be put to death in every generation," haunts *I Am Not Your Negro* (2016), Raoul Peck's award-winning documentary, which begins with the author's appearance on *The Dick Cavett Show* in 1968. Asked why African Americans aren't optimistic, even though "There are Negro mayors, there are Negroes in all of sports, there are Negroes in politics, they're even accorded the ultimate accolade of being in television commercials now," Baldwin's reply was unequivocal: "the real question is what's going to happen to this country? I have to repeat that." As Peck intimates through footage of Black Lives Matter activists in the wake of contemporary racial violence, Baldwin's question, posed to Dick Cavett fifty years ago, remains vital and perhaps unanswerable.

In "The White Man's Guilt," Baldwin reminded readers that the present is always haunted by the past: "The great force of history comes from the fact that we carry it within us, are unconsciously controlled by it in many ways, and history is literally *present* in all that we do" (723). The roll call of assassinations has changed, Peck suggests, from Medgar Evers, Malcolm X, and Martin Luther King Jr. to Amadou Diallo, Manuel Loggins Jr., Ronald Madison, Kendra James, Sean Bell, Eric Garner, Trayvon Martin, Michael Brown, and Alton Sterling. Some journeys are too difficult to recount; Baldwin's proposed book—*Remember This House*, an account of the lives and assassinations of Evers, King, and Malcolm X—remained in note form, its tragic subject matter resisting narrative and sense.

Although Baldwin did not finish his biography of the assassinated activists, he managed to complete a film script of *Giovanni's Room* sometime in the 1980s. While the film treatment is a largely faithful adaptation, the unnamed transvestite in the novel who "looked like a mummy or a zombie," whose "face is white and thoroughly bloodless," is transformed in the film script into "Princess," an African American transvestite and former dancer (41). Princess becomes a haunting reminder of the absence of black queer figures in American culture, including Baldwin's 1956 version of *Giovanni's Room*. In *I Am Not Your Negro*, there is one fleeting reference to Baldwin's sexuality shown to us through an FBI memorandum, which haunts the film through the conspicuous absence of any other references to his sexuality. Some stories are still too difficult to be told.

As the essays assembled in this collection attest, Baldwin's radical imagination remains vital and urgent in this so-called post-racial era. His career, spanning four decades across different continents, is a reminder that difficult stories must be told in the "post-truth" West. "There are, have been, and no doubt will be numerous James Baldwins," the editors of this volume remind us; indeed, there are "multiple forms of Baldwin's voice," many of which are reflected in this thought-provoking collection of essays. They remind the reader of the author's vitality across different media and genres, including his contributions to film and television, and his relationship with the painter Beauford Delaney. Several essays in this collection explore Baldwin's contribution to literary journalism, while others explore his position as a transnational writer, including his relationships to Africa and to the Arab world.

The editors and contributors avoid the trap of describing Baldwin as "prophetic," which has long been a tendency in Baldwin scholarship and wider commentary on the author. Entrepreneurs are even selling a "James Baldwin Secular Saint Candle" online, enabling consumers to "Show [their] devotion to James Baldwin, patron saint of poets, uncles, and exiles." Baldwin was a singularly perceptive cultural and political commentator, but to describe him as "prophetic" sanitizes the author and his work; it not only airbrushes out his flaws and contradictions, but it also covers up his body, rather than acknowledging what Ta-Nehisi Coates has described as "the sanctity of the black body" (35).

As Baldwin explored in *Go Tell It on the Mountain* (1953), holy vestments cover the body but cannot contain it. Elisha's "thighs moved terribly against the cloth of his suit," while Ella Mae's "white robes now seemed to be the merest, thinnest covering for the nakedness of breasts and insistent thighs" (17, 19). In his work, Baldwin celebrates the body, describing Jesus as a "disreputable sun-baked Jew" (*Fire Next Time* 312) and reminding readers that even holy men go the way their blood beats: "Nowhere, in the brief and extraordinary passage of the man known as Jesus Christ, is it recorded that he ever upbraided his disciples concerning their carnality. These were rough, hard-working fishermen on the Sea of Galilee" ("To Crush a Serpent" 161).

In "Rendezvous with Life: Reading Early and Later Baldwin," Robert Reid-Pharr warns against scholarship that has become "settled and static" (127). As the editors of this present collection rightly observe, "Baldwin scholarship has become too celebratory, passive," which is a useful reminder of the author's insistence on the need to remain critical and alert: "I love America more than any other country in the world, and, exactly for this reason, I insist on the right to criticize her perpetually" ("Autobiographical Notes" 9). Over the last two decades, renewed interest in Baldwin has recuperated the author as a major force in twentieth-century letters, but there is a danger, as the editors attest, that criticism is reluctant to point out the writer's flaws and contradictions and that it focuses on themes at the expense of an examination of form and style. "Too often in the criticism," the editors remind us, "Baldwin's writing techniques and style have been neglected in favor of his political vision."

In "The Price of the Ticket" (1985), Baldwin reminded his readers of the importance of going back and inward, rather than trying to prophesy the future: "To do your first works over," Baldwin explains "means to reexamine everything. Go back to where you started, or as far back as you can, examine all of it, travel your road again and tell the truth about it. Sing or shout or testify or keep it to yourself: but *know whence you came*" (841).

Works Cited

Baldwin, James. "Autobiographical Notes." 1955. Baldwin, *Collected Essays*, pp. 5–9.

Baldwin, James. *Collected Essays*. Edited by Toni Morrison, Library of America, 1998.

Baldwin, James. *The Devil Finds Work*. 1976. Baldwin, *Collected Essays*, pp. 479–572.

Baldwin, James. *The Fire Next Time*. 1963. Baldwin, *Collected Essays*, pp. 291–347.

Baldwin, James. *Giovanni's Room*. 1956. Penguin, 1990.

Baldwin, James. *Go Tell It on the Mountain*. 1953. Penguin, 1991.

Baldwin, James. "The Northern Protestant." 1960. Baldwin, *Collected Essays*, pp. 236–46.

Baldwin, James. "The Price of the Ticket." 1985. Baldwin, *Collected Essays*, pp. 830–42.

Baldwin, James. "To Crush a Serpent." 1987. *The Cross of Redemption: Uncollected Writings*, edited and introduced by Randall Kenan, Pantheon, 2010, pp. 158–65.

Baldwin, James. "The White Man's Guilt." 1965. Baldwin, *Collected Essays*, pp. 722–27.

Coates, Ta-Nehisi. *Between the World and Me*. Text Publishing Company, 2015.

Reid-Pharr, Robert. "Rendezvous with Life: Reading Early and Later Baldwin." *James Baldwin: America and Beyond*, edited by Cora Kaplan and Bill Schwarz, U of Michigan P, 2011, pp. 126–40.

ACKNOWLEDGMENTS

We would like to thank the American University of Paris for its support in the completion of this volume. We acknowledge our many Baldwin scholar colleagues and the creative artists with whom we have collaborated since 2011 in the preparation of this book, such as Rich Blint, James Campbell, Anna Everett, Cora Kaplan, Jake Lamar, D. Quentin Miller, Samuel Price, Bill Schwarz, amongst many others.

We thank our colleague Mark Ennis who worked with author Claudine Raynaud on the translations of French passages into English in her chapter "French Baldwin (on Screen): '*le criminel artiste.*'"

Though all chapters included here are previously unpublished, it should be noted that Kathy Roberts Forde's chapter draws roughly from an earlier version entitled "The Fire Next Time in the Civil Sphere: Literary Journalism and Justice in America 1963," *Journalism* (15.6), pp. 573–88, copyright © 2014 by Kathy Roberts Forde. Reprinted by Permission of SAGE Publications, Ltd.

Permission has been granted to cite the film illustration captured in Professor Raynaud's chapter from "James Baldwin et l'émission PostScriptum" réalisateur Maurice Dugouson, prod. ORH, 21/10/1970, archive INA.

Permission for illustrations cited in Tyler T. Schmidt's chapter "Lessons in Light: Beauford Delaney's and James Baldwin's 'Unnameable Objects'" is granted by the Michael Rosenfeld Gallery.

We are most grateful to our publisher Bloomsbury, for its commitment to working with us on this critical volume. We wish to express our special thanks for the encouragement and support of Harris Naqvi, Editorial Director, Bloomsbury Academic USA.

Introduction: Baldwin's Radical Imagination

There are, have been, and no doubt will be numerous James Baldwins. Many of the scholars and artists to whom the current volume owes tribute knew James Baldwin personally. His television interviews around the world and the numerous groundbreaking documentaries based on his life and his writings, such as *The Price of the Ticket* (1989) and the recent *I Am Not Your Negro* (2016) have led many to feel that they also knew him personally, due to the force of his media presence. His experimentation with multiple forms such as literary journalism, essays, novels, poetry, and even a children's book suggests that his imagination was in many ways unbounded. Varied collaborations with others during his lifetime have made his presence on the American and the international (transnational) cultural scene an enduring and ever more vital force.

The present volume explores the multiple forms of Baldwin's voice and his impact on pressing social, political, and cultural issues over the span of his lifetime and beyond. Baldwin attests in his 1962 essay "The Creative Process" that "Society must accept some things as real; but [the artist] must always know that the visible reality hides a deeper one, and that all our action and all our achievement rests on things unseen" (670). Despite the many Baldwins that we encounter, his adherence to his own integrity as an artist and human being was reflected through this fundamental observation. *Of Latitudes Unknown* could not have been written without having recourse to the impressive body of texts dedicated to chronicling the critical reception of his life and work. Conseula Francis's bibliographical essay, "Reading and Theorizing James Baldwin: A Bibliographic Essay," traces in particular the writings of scholars who have argued that placing Baldwin intellectually is complex due to his resistance to being categorized (179). In this connection, Baldwin's ability to think innovatively and reflectively about the social world fueled his approach to aesthetic and political resistance. "To the different constituencies that composed [Baldwin's] native land," Cora Kaplan and Bill Schwarz have recently acknowledged, "his was an imagination that was too wayward, too given to detours, parentheses, and complexity, and never straight enough" (2).

Francis, Kaplan, and Schwarz all emphasize the renaissance in Baldwin scholarship in the late 1990s and early twenty-first century with publications such as Dwight A. McBride's *James Baldwin Now* (1998) and D. Quentin Miller's *Re-Viewing James Baldwin: Things Not Seen* (2000) as well as more recent contributions to the study of Baldwin's rhizomatic imagination. We are pleased to have our foreword written by Douglas Field, a guiding force in cultivating the critical and intellectual renaissance of Baldwin studies. Relying on the chronology offered by Francis concerning the various turning points in appreciations of Baldwin's legacy, this volume builds upon the many strides which have already been made in Baldwin criticism since the late 1990s.

According to D. Quentin Miller, it is largely Baldwin's resistance to being categorized that has led to his being underappreciated at certain points in his career. It is equally this resistance to categorization that has, according to the analyses offered by contributors to this volume, assured his enduring influence on many racial and social problems that define our contemporary world. In the interest of illuminating Baldwin's impact on literary and journalistic forms, contemporary political and social issues, and visual imaginaries, we frame the chapters that follow in terms of the concept of the "radical imagination" as articulated in recent critical works. By using this concept, we by no means intend to categorize Baldwin. Rather, we hope to exhibit the many ways in which he anticipated trends in literary, journalistic, and social critique, primarily by refusing to be trapped within already existing categories.

In the past several years, the term "radical imagination" has been defined in many ways. In their work *The Radical Imagination: Social Movement Research in the Age of Austerity*, Max Haiven and Alex Khasnabish argue how "the imagination is an intimate part of how we empathize with others, the way we gain some sense of the forces that impact our lives, and the way we project ourselves into the future and gain inspiration and direction from the past" (4). As Haiven and Khasnabish make clear, the "radical" in radical imagination does not necessarily occupy a particular position on the political spectrum nor is it a "value judgement" (6). Rather, radical imagination is a "force that resists the present order" (6) and the authors see racial and social problems "as deeply rooted in social institutions and, importantly, believe these institutions can and should be changed" (7). Creating a racialized version of the term, Robin D. G. Kelley's *Freedom Dreams: The Black Radical Imagination* outlines a history of "black radical imagination" (6) through the lens of postcolonial perspectives, African American social movements, and Marxist methodologies. Kelley examines how alternative visions and social imaginations emerge out of political engagements and historical conditions to envision and work toward creating a new, alternative world. He argues that "any revolution must begin with thought, with how we imagine a New World, with how we reconstruct our social and individual relationships, with unleashing our desire and building a new future on the basis of love and creativity rather than rationality" (193). Crucially, through his historical narrative, Kelley emphasizes that the dreams and articulations of the black radical imagination are not conceived within academia or social institutions but rather are derived from social movements and cultural productions.

Relatedly, Charles Taylor underscores the political implications of "our modern social imaginaries" that demonstrate "the ways people imagine their social existence, how they fit together with others, how things go on between them and their fellows, the expectations that are normally met, and the deeper normative notions and images that underline these expectations" (23). Similarly, Jessica Berman contends that "the social imaginary can be the place where the demands of the world become configured, contested, and refigured and where new situations, relationships, and attitudes are created, tested, and put into play" (13). Variously conceptualized and defined, "radical imagination," the overarching term applicable to these positions, can hold the power to change existing social orders and subvert dominant racial mythologies.[1]

In anticipating such perspectives, Baldwin's radical imagination inaugurates new forms of collective knowledge and coexistences. At the same time, his work insists that narrative is at the core of any created process of imagination. As Berman argues, "narratives ... can operate as ... nodal points, generating models of association and accountability that order our social and political relationships" (14). The encounter between the reader and the text in Baldwin's work thus becomes historically and politically positioned, encouraging the reader and even the spectator to move "beyond the individual ethical encounter [and] to play an active role in the imaginative construction of a common justice within the political domain" (Berman 14). From this position of profound intersubjectivity, Baldwin's narrative process provides a means of self-disclosure while eliciting an engagement with others. It gives form to the expression of a relational selfhood.

Baldwin's radical imagination, however fraught with historical interpretive difficulties, can perhaps best be understood through his hybridity—the conjunctions between his American and transnational self, his political and aesthetic perspectives, and the rich relationships between his fiction and his nonfiction. It is an imagination that marked him from the very beginning of his career, carried him through his literary productions in New York, and continued to distinguish him through his expatriate writings in France, Switzerland, and Turkey. Both a personal possession and a collective appeal, his radical imagination has always assured his relevance. It forces the critic to expand her understanding of his writings and to break with conventional narrative as well as with identity boundaries. Through this imagination, Baldwin insists on the personal stakes of race consciousness and on the dangers and virtues of antagonistic and rejectionist social perspectives.

Of Latitudes Unknown: James Baldwin's Radical Imagination joins such recent critical collections as *A Historical Guide to James Baldwin* (2009), *James Baldwin: America and Beyond* (2011), and *The Cambridge Companion to James Baldwin* (2015) in "un-fragmenting" Baldwin studies and establishing further "conjunctions" in his work: between the essay and the novel, as well as the polemical and the aesthetic. His participation in visual forms and the negotiation of his American and international identities are also of vital concern. But the volume hopes to go beyond these studies by focusing on new entities of Baldwin's radical imagination. Most explicitly, it covers such subjects as Baldwin's English and French language selves, his late encounters with Africa, his appearances on French television and his interviews by French journalists, his unrecognized literary journalism, his relations with the Arab world, his anticipation of contemporary film and media studies, and his paradoxical public intellectualism.

This latter concern, Baldwin's role as a public intellectual, parallels Robert Reid-Pharr's recent challenge that Baldwin scholarship has become too celebratory, passive, "settled and static" (127). While acknowledging the significant accomplishments of recent Baldwin scholarship, *Of Latitudes Unknown* calls for taking Baldwin scholarship into an active reexamination of Baldwin's hitherto *unquestioned* celebrity. We propose a volume that is substantive, critical, and inclusive. Still a rarity in Baldwin studies, the volume provides a sustained formal attention to Baldwin's fiction and nonfiction. As it reassesses Baldwin's contributions to and influences on world literary history, *Of Latitudes Unknown* addresses the question of why the critical appreciation of Baldwin's writing continues to flourish, and why it remains a vast territory for deeper exploration.

Part One: James Baldwin: Film, photography, and the visual arts

Too often in the criticism, Baldwin's writing techniques and style have been neglected in favor of his political vision. This section does not omit the political elements of Baldwin's writing but rather shows how they can be seen as being linked to a visual ontology and aesthetic. Alice Mikal Craven's opening chapter, "Black Bodies on Screen, White Privilege in Hollywood: James Baldwin on Lang and Preminger," explores other codes and protocols: namely, how Baldwin's film criticism in *The Devil Finds Work* and his articles "Carmen: The Dark is Light Enough" (published in *Notes of a Native Son*, 1955) and "On Catfish Row" deconstruct "the white supremacist mythologies controlling the Hollywood film industry." Baldwin's contrasting assessments of Otto Preminger's *Carmen* and *Porgy and Bess* with Fritz Lang's early American films, Craven argues, create new ways for understanding the impact of these German *émigré* directors on American cinema.

That Baldwin finds a deep and disturbing divergence in Lang's and Preminger's views of Hollywood and of the American mythologies upon which its studio productions are dependent introduces questions concerning their intentions as observers of American racial conflict. Baldwin's own sense of purpose in writing about the cinema is sharpened through this analysis. Craven's chapter evaluates "alien or other perspectives on American culture." In *The Devil Finds Work*, Baldwin, in the interest of rendering white supremacist codes more visible, links his film analysis to conflicts in American public life (e.g., the Scottsboro case, the Spanish civil war) and to his own life story. Configuring himself as a young moviegoer slowly coming of age, Baldwin's book-length essay anticipates contemporary theories of the ethnic spectator such as in the work of Manthia Diawara or Jacqueline Stewart.

In "Picturing Jimmy, Picturing Self: James Baldwin, Beauford Delaney, and the Color of Light," James Smalls explores various images of Baldwin that have taken form since his death to contribute to his status as an iconic writer. "Through his own writings and need to seek recognition from the public," Smalls argues, "Baldwin encouraged the production of images of himself as a public figure represented in alternating circumstances of extroversion and introspection." In this way, Baldwin perpetuated a relationship between his writing and visual ways of knowing. As Smalls demonstrates, this process became a way for Baldwin to better understand himself in relation to his visual world and to consolidate his major obsessions with race, poverty, social class, sexuality, and gender. Smalls combines an interpretation of Baldwin's visual ontology with that of his "visual representation by others" to reveal a pictorial and photographic side to Baldwin's radical imagination.

In the final chapter of this section, Tyler T. Schmidt argues that though much attention has been given to the importance of Beauford Delaney for Baldwin, Delaney's civil rights portraits, and in particular his Rosa Parks series, merit deeper scholarly analysis—especially in relation to their influence on Baldwin's writings on America's racial struggles. Centering on Delaney's *Street Sweeper* (1968), Schmidt explores "the intellectual/aesthetic exchanges between Baldwin and Delaney [that] invite us to think more expansively about how certain kinds of coexistences redefine activism." Baldwin's tributes to Delaney allow us to discover "unexpected visual forms of Civil Rights activism [that] offe[r] a useful theory for reading Delaney's politically slippery portraits of the 1960s." In this regard, the Delaney–Baldwin connection adds to the revaluation of Baldwin's radical *visual* imagination that does not offer naïve hope but rather challenges us to look at the American civil rights movement in new ways.

Part Two: Baldwin's journalism and literary journalism

Baldwin's radical imagination has an impressive flexibility. Not only is it in harmony with his visual representations, which can be seen as providing a fresh ethico-political articulation of the world, but it also shows itself in the particularities of his literary journalism. To say the least, the silence around Baldwin's central connection to journalism and literary/narrative journalism is both conspicuous and surprising. It is therefore revealing that the American literary establishment has increasingly been reassessing the relationship of fiction to nonfiction. As Randall Kenan has recently remarked, "James Baldwin's legacy seems tailor-made for this debate" (59). And yet Baldwin scholarship has largely not responded to this call.

Addressing such an oversight, this section begins with Kathy Roberts Forde's chapter, "'To End the Racial Nightmare, and Achieve Our Country': James Baldwin and the US Civil Rights Movement." A literary-journalistic mainstay, empathy, as expressed in *The Fire Next Time* (1963), was Baldwin's "sharp-edged commitment," a "tool for social and political change … rooted in historical awareness and the recognition of contemporary institutional and personal oppression." Forde demonstrates how in this text Baldwin's literary journalism can be particularly effective in communicating struggles for social justice. Indeed, *The Fire Next Time* "offered a forceful interpretation, in the terms of the period's white and black racial dualism, of what it would mean for the United States to become a truly civil society that actually embraced and enacted democracy, equality, freedom, and justice." Forde's essay is the volume's first step in exploring the nature and function of Baldwin's literary-journalistic talents.

Isabelle Meuret's chapter, "The Documentary Tradition in Baldwin's *Écriture Vérité*," expands the scope of Baldwin's literary journalism and documentary modes to highlight his writing as a form of *écriture vérité*. Like Richard Wright and other African American literary journalists, Baldwin created various mixtures of genres and techniques, incorporating sermonizing traditions, jeremiads, documentary film, photojournalistic techniques, memoir, and fiction. But Meuret proposes that Baldwin's literary journalism should be seen as *écriture vérité*, "a conceptual proposition that posits Baldwin's oeuvre as a series of sequence shots that exceed the frame of his written production." Connecting this approach to *cinéma vérité*, defined by Edgar Morin as a dual technique resting on "*distanciation* and *fraternization*," Meuret's chapter also reveals innovative and valuable ties between the exploration of visual forms elaborated in Part One and the journalistic forms at the center of Part Two of the volume.

Baldwin's *écriture vérité* foregrounds the issues of cosmopolitan and diasporic narratives, as well as national and comparative models for narrative studies. It provides further questioning of concepts such as colonialism and postcolonialism, interculturalism, hybridity, cultural traffic, and transculturation. Building on the recent research about African American literary journalism (Dow, Foley, Forde, Roiland, Maguire), Meuret argues for a reexamination of Baldwin's "essays" in light of the many documentary modes he employed and the hybrid forms upon which he depended. Her chapter focuses on Baldwin's *Nothing Personal* (1964), *A Rap on Race* (1970), and *The Evidence of Things Not Seen* (1985) as comparative pillars for her discussions of *cinema vérité* (e.g., *I Heard It through the Grapevine*, 1982; *The Price of the Ticket*, 1989) and Baldwin's distinctive *écriture vérité*.

The final chapter in this section, William E. Dow's "Journeys of the 'I' in James Baldwin's Literary-Journalistic Essays," argues that James Baldwin's "I" "prompts us to understand his function as a writer bringing together or *pairing* literature and journalism—in ways and under a certain African American literary journalistic tradition that have gone largely unrecognized by Baldwin critics." Baldwin's first-person literary journalism, Dow contends, makes us think about what it means to read ourselves into history. Tracking the conditions of his first-person journeys constitutes a certain historical enterprise: "Baldwin constantly proclaims the necessity of his readers to understand the historical forces at work behind the racial conflicts he exposes." *Notes of a Native Son* (1955), *Nobody Knows My Name* (1961), *The Fire Next Time* (1963), *No Name in the Street* (1972), *The Devil Finds Work* (1976)—all insist on the importance of their first-person historicity. At the same time, the internal perspectives of these literary-journalistic texts, achieved through first-person narrations, best promotes narrator identification and reader empathy. By focusing on *The Evidence of Things Not Seen* as well as other essays by Baldwin, Dow shapes yet another crucial link between Parts One and Two of this volume.

Part Three: Baldwin re-sighted transnationally

Part Three explores Baldwin's transatlantic circuitry in relation to his inexhaustible radical imagination. Claudine Raynaud's "French Baldwin (on Screen): '*le criminel artiste*'" examines Baldwin's appearances on French television. Raynaud focuses on Baldwin interviews with French journalists such as Pierre Desgraupes, Pierre Dumayet, Michel Polac, and Danièle Guilbert. French television programs featured in this chapter include "James

Baldwin à propos de *Les Elus du Seigneur*" as well as *Lectures pour tous*, and "James Baldwin sur la situation des Noirs américains," amongst others. Raynaud's analysis addresses a largely unexplored dimension of Baldwin's forty-year relationship with France.

Raynaud claims that "reassessing Baldwin's presence on French television ... means understanding how the creative writer—'Baldwin the author'— was more readily apprehended in France" than in the United States. When presenting his work as a writer to a French audience, Baldwin's intention is to inform viewers and listeners about the reality of growing up black in America. One vital discovery that Raynaud brings attention to is Baldwin's pedagogical abilities to help the French in understanding what it means to be American and black. Perhaps the most fascinating revelation of Raynaud's chapter, however, is the French-language Baldwin. Hearing Baldwin "in Molière's language with a strong American accent" reinforces Raynaud's principal argument that context—and Baldwin's way of cultivating human connections across races and cultures, which serves as a blueprint of his writing—is essential to understanding the American versus expatriate Baldwin.

The second chapter in this section, Timothy McGinnis's "The Terror Within: *Giovanni's Room, L'Étranger*, and the Possibility of an Absurd Heroism," argues how "*Giovanni's Room* inverts, recycles, and eclipses [Camus's] *L'Étranger* and the 'absurd' heroism depicted therein." In their respective works, McGinnis argues, both Baldwin and Camus suggest how self-questioning can create an individual's orientation in which current and long-held beliefs are displaced, inducing a trajectory of discovering one's relation to social and racial forces. A central concern for both writers is that all human beings are products of a shared history. Baldwin's conception of heroism is dependent on historical memory in which each individual is inescapably committed to all others. For McGinnis, this is ultimately "Baldwin's project for America."

The last chapter in this section, James Miller's "James Baldwin's Black Power: *No Name in the Street*, Fanon, Camus, and the Black Panthers," looks at Baldwin's global imagination through an examination of Baldwin's intellectual engagement with the concept of Black Power. Focusing on the extent to which Baldwin's *No Name in the Street* (1972) mediates Frantz Fanon's ideas in *The Wretched of the Earth* (1961), Miller argues that Baldwin adopts Fanon's anti-Western, anti-humanist perspective to condemn white, Euro-American culture and forges a symbolic moral allegiance between third world freedom fighters and African Americans. Miller demonstrates how Baldwin, in "articulating his sense of Black Power ... returns to the problems of whiteness that inform his early work." Underscoring the collaborative and social engagements of Baldwin's craft and imaginative vision, Miller shows Baldwin as a negotiator of the positions of Fanon and Black Power activists. He also claims that Baldwin is a writer who "articulates his own version of Black Power, an ideology which, by this point, had largely replaced the integrationist ethic of the first stage of Civil Rights."

Part Four: James Baldwin and changing communities: Recontextualizing Baldwin's legacy

A focus on Baldwin's radical imagination leads to conclusions that potentially open Baldwin scholarship to innovative horizons and to the tributaries of his thoughts and writings. Part Four expands on these conclusions in relation to the consequences upon which earlier parts have elaborated. This section specifically explores how Baldwin's writing continually functions to project his readers beyond their temporal and physical limits in order to envision an alternative racial and social future. Marcus Bruce's "Continuing a Legacy: James Baldwin, Ta-Nehisi Coates, and the African American Witness" argues that Baldwin's *The Fire Next Time* and Ta-Nehisi Coates's *Between the World and Me* (2015) "bear witness" to "living in a black body in the United States of America." Using Toni Morrison's comments on Coates in her "James Baldwin: His Voice Remembered; Life in His Language," Bruce concludes that both texts elucidate versions of freedom that offer unique forms of subjectivity. In contrast to mainstream political theory, Bruce shows how the fiery prose of Baldwin and Coates, in their creation of witnessing and spirituality, exposes the submerged complexities of contemporary American life. Bruce asserts that Baldwin's and Coates's rhetoric readily lends itself to being gathered as explanation and evidence of both historical and contemporary racial tensions. Their rhetorical flourishes equally serve as powerful testimony with respect to the racially inflected problems currently besieging the United States.

Bill V. Mullen's "Baldwin, the 'Arab,' and the End of the West" argues for the vital role played by "the Arab," and the Arab world, in Baldwin's "evolving comprehension of race, colonialism, and ... Western empire under capitalist modernity." Mullen contends that the Arab was essential to Baldwin's understanding of what Baldwin called in 1968 "'the very last form of imperialism—Western imperialism.'" Mullen's new focus illuminates Baldwin's "complex disidentification with Europe and the West as ... 'a frame of reference, a standard-bearer, the classic model for literature and civilization.'" In light of what Edward Said termed "Zionism from the standpoint of its victims" (Zionism understood in Mullen's argument as the process of European and Western colonial rule), Mullen argues that Baldwin's later writings, particularly *The Welcome Table*, "should be understood as fables of affiliation to this perspective." These later writings reveal how

Baldwin discovered "historical analogue, and apotheosis, of Afro-Arab subordination and deterritorialization, and a vehicle for expressing ... the terminal geopolitical drama in his journey out of the West." Mullen asserts here that Baldwin's conceptualization of "statelessness" and imperialism is part of his complex artistry and worldview.

Robert F. Reid-Pharr's concluding essay, "Effective/Defective James Baldwin," responds to Giorgio Agamben's philosophical theory of the "anthropophorous," by focusing on Baldwin as a celebrity during the US civil rights movement (1954–70). Reid-Pharr appraises how Baldwin understood that "progressive intellectuals needed to hail and defend the structural changes then taking place in the country while also modeling new forms of subjectivity and *inter*-subjectivity for individuals and communities with no clear understanding of how they might continue to operate in a world in which basic social protocols were being called into question." Yet, according to Reid-Pharr, despite his writerly eloquence and vision, Baldwin "was never fully in control of the protocols of celebrity that helped to establish and maintain his career."

Reid-Pharr's chapter proposes that Baldwin's celebrity, which should be treated "as a script," "was itself yet another example of the fretful nature in which American culture continuously announces, consumes, discards, and recycles presumably new versions of black subjectivity." What Reid-Pharr calls the "New Negrohood" of the 1954–75 period contributed to a form of celebrity that contained both specialized American forms of modernity and progressive thinking. But it also rejected radical infringements on hegemonic ideas and limited "commonsensical notions" of the individual and the communal.

Establishing the interconnections between Baldwin's projections for America and the socio-racial realities of this nation, *Of Latitudes Unknown* builds a ground for realizing what his imagination sought to create in concrete terms. Baldwin's radical imagination is about drawing on the past as well as on the present, recounting various stories about how the world came to be, and remembering the importance of past struggles. The willingness to dissent and the capacity to hold power accountable constitute Baldwin's vision, a vision that urges us to have a more imaginative grasp on the future while still taking seriously the present demands of justice, equity, and civic courage. As this volume contends, Baldwin's imagination lays the groundwork for a more vital and productive vision of race relations in the United States.

Note

1   The ideas of social and radical imaginations can be approached from varied directions. See for example Cornell; Fraser; Brick and Phelps; Rancière; Keulen; Rickford; Frazier; and Laibman.

Works Cited

Baldwin, James. "The Creative Process." Baldwin, *Collected Essays*, pp. 669–72.

Berman, Jessica. *Modernist Commitments: Ethics, Politics, and Transnational Modernism*. Columbia UP, 2012.

Brick, Howard, and Christopher Phelps. *Radicals in America: The U.S. Left since the Second World War*. Cambridge UP, 2015.

Cornell, Drucilla. *At the Heart of Freedom: Feminism, Sex, and Equality*. Princeton UP, 1998.

Delaney, Beauford. *Street Sweeper/Le Balayeur*. 1968, private collection. "Beauford at the International James Baldwin Conference in Paris," *Les Amis de Beauford Delaney*, 4 June 2016, lesamisdebeauforddelaney.blogspot.com/2016/06/beauford-at-international-james-baldwin.html. Accessed 25 Aug. 2018.

Francis, Conseula. "Reading and Theorizing James Baldwin: A Bibliographic Essay." *James Baldwin Review*, vol. 1, 2015, pp. 179–97.

Fraser, Nancy. *Scales of Justice: Reimagining Political Space in a Globalizing World*. Columbia UP, 2008.

Frazier, Robeson Taj. *The East Is Black: Cold War China in the Black Radical Imagination*. Duke UP, 2015.

Haiven, Max, and Alex Khasnabish. *The Radical Imagination: Social Movement Research in the Age of Austerity*. Zed Books, 2014.

I Am Not Your Negro. Directed by Raoul Peck. Velvet Film and Velvet Film SAS, 2016.

I Heard It through the Grapevine. Directed by Dick Fontaine and Pat Hartley. Living Archives, 1982.

Kaplan, Cora, and Bill Schwarz. Introduction. *James Baldwin: America and Beyond*, edited by Kaplan and Schwarz, U of Michigan P, 2011, pp. 1–32.

Kelley, Robin D. G. *Freedom Dreams: The Black Radical Imagination*. Beacon Press, 2002.

Kenan, Randall. "James Baldwin, 1924–1987: A Brief Biography." *A Historical Guide to James Baldwin*, edited by Douglas Field, Oxford UP, 2009, pp. 21–60.

Keulen, Margarete. *Radical Imagination: Feminist Conceptions of the Future in Ursula Le Guin, Marge Piercy and Sally Miller Gearhart*. Peter Lang, 1991.

Laibman, David. *Political Economy after Economics: Scientific Method and Radical Imagination*. Routledge, 2012.

The Price of the Ticket. Directed and produced by Karen Thorsen and Douglas K. Dempsey. DKDmedia, 1989.

Rancière, Jacques. *Dissensus: On Politics and Aesthetics*. Edited and translated by Steven Corcoran, Continuum, 2010.

Reid-Pharr, Robert. "Rendezvous with Life: Reading Early and Later Baldwin." *James Baldwin: America and Beyond*, edited by Cora Kaplan and Bill Schwarz, U of Michigan P, 2011, pp. 126–40.

Rickford, Russell. *We Are an African People: Independent Education, Black Power, and the Radical Imagination*. Oxford UP, 2016.

Taylor, Charles. *Modern Social Imaginaries*. Duke UP, 2004.

PART ONE

James Baldwin: Film, Photography, and the Visual Arts

1

Black Bodies on Screen, White Privilege in Hollywood: James Baldwin on Lang and Preminger

Alice Mikal Craven

Condescension towards black American actors and actresses has long been attributed to the unconscious patronage and sense of white privilege that grounded the early filmmaking techniques of classical Hollywood cinema.[1] Blacks were systematically discriminated against and relegated to the category of the "Other." James Baldwin's study of the *émigré* directors Fritz Lang and Otto Preminger is therefore an intriguing experiment in providing a new form of "Other," namely, the *émigré* directors and their alien perspectives on Hollywood's depictions of black American lives. By analyzing these directors' responses to their assimilation into Hollywood studio filmmaking, Baldwin explores the gratuitous nature of American racism in the film industry.[2] On one hand, Baldwin views Lang as having initially used American narratives and genres as exploratory allegories of the German racial tensions from which he had fled (*Devil* 27). On the other hand, Baldwin argues that Preminger fundamentally underestimated the prejudices against American blacks when making his films *Carmen Jones* (1954) and *Porgy and Bess* (1959). I focus in this chapter on the *émigré* directors' purported intentions in their American work and the place of Baldwin's interpretations of their work in his innovative film criticism. *The Devil Finds Work* (1976), "*Carmen Jones*: The Dark Is Light Enough"

(1955), and "On Catfish Row" (1959) are revelatory examples of Baldwin's critique of Hollywood.[3] The "othered" perspective offered by Lang and Preminger is not lost on Baldwin, and it allows him to nuance his critique of the American film industry's use of white supremacist mythologies and its abuse of black performers. The time span between the early essays and the later publication of *Devil* is also noteworthy. Baldwin's writings on film matured between 1955 and 1976. The parallels between his film critique and the positions he takes up in his more politically charged works such as "Many Thousands Gone" and *The Fire Next Time* are important concerns for this chapter as well.

Lang and Preminger both came to Hollywood in the 1930s shortly after the rise of the Hitler regime.[4] Unlike directors such as Jean Renoir, their films engaged with American settings and themes from the outset. Renoir was initially hired in Hollywood to make films about French culture for American audiences until he rebelled and insisted that he was more interested in engaging with the narratives and genres of his newly adopted country.[5] Of the three, Lang was the least constrained by his studio contracts and had even formed his own production company, Diana Productions, by 1945 (Gunning 286).

Hollywood cinematic language was routinely placed in opposition to the European art house techniques in which these *émigré* directors were trained, as Thomas Elsaesser has argued in *European Cinema: Face to Face with Hollywood.* Producers in Hollywood contradicted their own filmmaking preferences when they welcomed renowned European directors to America. In their view, directors such as Lang added a cultural veneer to their studios, though their art house techniques were still frowned upon as ultimately unsuitable for an industry driven by box office results. Production studios tended to favor techniques that reinforced the supremacist myths so endemic to the Hollywood system. Ironically, this was done at times in order to adhere to the moral guides of the Hays Code. As Gunning points out in particular, the ending of Lang's *You Only Live Once* was "demanded by the Production Code which would not have permitted the criminals to reach their refuge across the border" (258). Studios also had control over which films would be made and what their final cuts would yield. Filmmakers working in America and certainly in Hollywood usually worked under contract. It is therefore crucial to distinguish how each of these directors adapted their European filmmaking techniques when addressing American material and to gauge how they intuited the privilege of whiteness informing the studio world to which they were being introduced.

Émigré directors were often faulted for their inauthentic portraits of American life or for their failure to adhere to the moral demands of Hollywood filmmaking according to the directives of the Hays Code, such as the interdiction to portray interracial relationships on screen.[6] Prominent African American film director Charles Burnett nonetheless praised Renoir for his film *The Southerner* due to its balanced representation of blacks and whites. Though the film was banned in Memphis as an inauthentic and damaging portrait of the South, Burnett considered it to be a rare and honest portrayal of southern poverty for both blacks and whites (Finger; Kapsis 157). In a similar manner, Lang was recognized by Baldwin as a careful student of American identity politics in *You Only Live Once*. Preminger, though lauded by many for his direct challenges to the Hays Code and for other aspects of his Hollywood films, was by contrast condemned by Baldwin for his seeming lack of concern about the realities of black life in America (Champlin).

Fairly or not, Baldwin portrays Preminger as a foreigner on vacation unperturbed by how his films misrepresented the lives of African Americans, which intensifies the need to distinguish Preminger's own intent from his need to adhere to studio demands. The production histories of both *Carmen* and *Porgy and Bess* make it difficult to entirely condone Baldwin's negative views of Preminger's involvement in the filmmaking processes. At times, his work was controlled by the conditions of his studio contract, and in the case of *Porgy and Bess*, he was brought in as director very late when many of the decisions about the production had already been made by others. Producer Samuel Goldwyn gave his permission for Preminger to make some changes but a lot of details, such as casting, had already been determined (Preminger 151).

In Baldwin's defense, there *has* been much discussion of the racist leanings of the films in question. According to Chris Fujiwara, Sidney Poitier tried to avoid being cast in *Porgy and Bess* because he considered it to be a racist script, but he gave in so that he could also later be considered for a role in Stanley Kramer's 1958 film *The Defiant Ones* (Fujiwara, location 4147). Yet, despite the claims about the racist tendencies of *Porgy and Bess*, Baldwin ultimately seemed more interested in exploring how *émigré* directors might embrace white privilege without being fully aware that they were doing so. A careful study of Baldwin's essays suggests that the real culprit was the system itself rather than the perspectives of one individual director. Did these foreign directors fully perceive the embedded supremacist myths of their newly adopted country and its culture industry?[7]

According to Baldwin, Preminger was simply not interested in deconstructing the racially inflected meanings beneath the surface of his source material. In "On Catfish Row," Baldwin argues that Preminger, along with Goldwyn and the film's white audience, was not concerned with the fates of the *real* inhabitants of Catfish Row. Preminger did, however, see these films as star vehicles for Dorothy Dandridge, to whom he played a strong and disciplined Pygmalion (Boyd 235). Dandridge, who plays Carmen in *Carmen Jones* and also Bess in *Porgy and Bess*, was the first African American actress to grace the cover of *Life* magazine and to be nominated for an Academy Award for Best Actress (Bogle 242). Many, including Dandridge herself, attributed her star status to her willingness to be allied with Preminger's all-black cast filmmaking (246). Her rapid ascent to fame was quickly extinguished when she was found in 1965, at the age of forty-one, victim of an overdose and equally of the negative press that ensued (248). Donald Bogle's book-length biography of Dandridge has thankfully restored her reputation in a way that is worthy of her beauty and her talent. Though Preminger was never faulted for her early demise, he was the one who triggered her rise to stardom. As Bogle points out, her eventual inability to distinguish between her real life and the tragic but erotic mulatto she had been hired to play on screen no doubt precipitated her fall (247).

Preminger seemed mesmerized by the impact of black bodies on screen and thus Dandridge was a perfect foil for his filmmaking plans. But since he was not particularly invested in a study of racism in the United States, these tensions functioned as inconveniences or obstacles to his filmmaking vision more than anything else. According to Baldwin, Preminger's failure to recognize the depth of American racism made him less aware of how endemic the condescension toward blacks in Hollywood was. As Baldwin remarks about *Carmen*, "The fact that one is watching a Negro cast interpreting *Carmen* is used to justify their remarkable vacuity, their complete improbability, their total divorce from anything suggestive of Negro life" ("*Carmen Jones*" 49).

Preminger was nonetheless instrumental in challenging the dictates of the Hays Code and its racist tendencies, and therefore Baldwin's condemnation of his films needs to be considered in light of his overall legacy (Champlin). Baldwin's critique of Preminger is not an entirely balanced judgment of Preminger's talents as an *émigré* director in Hollywood, but it does raise the specter of white appropriation of black suffering in ways that Lang's work does not. In the final analysis, however, Baldwin's condemnation of Preminger is rooted in Baldwin's own sense of purpose when considering how Hollywood narratives maintain their stronghold on white privilege and on the white supremacist mythologies that ground American cinematic language. It is in the contrast between Baldwin's positive assessment of Lang and his overwhelmingly negative assessment of Preminger that Baldwin's critique of Hollywood's ethical practices can be made more precise.

The American justice system and black life

Due to Lang's close attention to the mechanics of the American justice system and to how it functioned within the gangster genre, the director serves Baldwin's larger purpose well. Though he praises the director for his astute grasp of the realities of American life, Baldwin nonetheless claims in *Devil* that Lang did not really "find his American feet" until he made the film *You Only Live Once* in 1937 (27). Baldwin argues that Lang's first film in America, *Fury* (1936), was still focused on trying to use American genres and plotlines to deconstruct the racial tensions of his native Germany. As Baldwin notes on the subject of *Fury*: "Lang's is the fury of the film: but his grasp of the texture of American life is still extremely weak: he has not yet really left Germany" (*Devil* 27). Preminger's grasp of American culture is a much more complicated affair, according to Baldwin. Baldwin's assessment of American identity politics in Preminger's films makes him unwilling to afford the filmmaker the time to find American feet. Baldwin's critique of *Carmen Jones* nonetheless targets Twentieth-Century Fox rather than Preminger, who is directly evoked only twice in the essay. Baldwin's later critique of *Porgy and Bess* targets Preminger more directly and more harshly.

Baldwin condemns *Carmen*'s abuse of African American identities and black bodies and suggests that Preminger is implicated in this film's unfortunate representation of black lives. He argues that if the Negroes in *Carmen* are to be taken as ciphers of American sexual mores, then all is lost since "when people have become this empty they are not ciphers any longer, but monsters" ("*Carmen Jones*" 54). This seemingly throwaway line suggests that Baldwin's critique of *Carmen* is in line with his earlier works, including the essay "Many Thousands Gone" where he suggests that Richard Wright's novel *Native Son* has shown its readers the monster created by the American Republic, that is, the characterization of the Negro who lives inside each and every black American (41). Baldwin's objections to Wright's characterization of Bigger derives from a similar argument: Bigger is finally a symbolic monster, representative of America's abuse of blacks and of its white guilt rather than a depiction of an authentic human being.

That Baldwin places his critique of *Carmen* in the same section of *Notes of a Native Son* as his essay "Everybody's Protest Novel" and "Many Thousands Gone" is telling if read in this light. The placement suggests that Baldwin's critique of Hollywood is linked in complex ways to his critique of racial politics from the beginning, and this critique becomes fully realized in *Devil*. Highlighting the steps he takes along the way helps in contextualizing *Devil*. By the time he writes "On Catfish Row" in 1959, Baldwin has been wounded by the untimely death of Billie Holiday, and he is therefore more eager to chastise filmmakers coming from outside of black American life for their romanticizing of the miserable lives of the black Americans they depict. As Baldwin remarks, "Out of one Catfish Row or another came the murdered Bessie Smith and the dead Billie Holiday and virtually every Negro performer this country has produced" ("On Catfish Row").

Baldwin thus approaches the work of the foreign directors at different stages in his own career and uses these analyses in order to evaluate alien or "othered" perspectives on American culture. Baldwin is concerned with how the American mythologies that he explores throughout his works have

been absorbed differently by these outsiders. On another level, his essay on
Carmen is in keeping with his youthful book reviews written around the
same time. These early reviews were directed against authors such as James
M. Cain and Wright, and were unsparingly harsh. As David Leeming notes,
Baldwin was still approaching "his subject with the insensitivity of a young
writer determined to shock" in his early career (64). His essay on *Carmen*
displays this youthful bravado as well. His later film critique is written with
more genuine concern about Hollywood's ability to divide and conquer
black and white audiences in America.

In the interim, Baldwin intensifies his critique of Preminger's work in his
1959 review of *Porgy and Bess*, which appeared a few years before he wrote
and published *The Fire Next Time* (1963). At this later point in his career,
Baldwin's fears about Hollywood's insensitivity to black American life have
deepened. His critique of America's inability to use its own past to confront
its racial conflicts will control his message in *Fire*, and we see that same
critique applied to the Hollywood industry thirteen years later in *Devil*. In
many ways, the death of Billie Holiday just one month before the opening of
Porgy and Bess in theaters serves as a pivotal moment in Baldwin's decision
to link American sociopolitical concerns with his analysis of the American
moviegoer.

Baldwin remarks that it was precisely the *real-life version* of *Porgy and
Bess*'s cardboard and romanticized ghetto setting that was the cause of Billie
Holiday's demise. Leeming suggests that Preminger's blithe comparison of
Hollywood lies to the reality of black Americans deeply angered Baldwin
(164). Leeming also notes that Baldwin's essay "On Catfish Row" began as
a critique of *Porgy and Bess* but was deliberately transformed by Baldwin
into a lament about the tragic life and death of Billie Holiday (164). Baldwin
does not fault the material of the opera itself, since he claims that the vitality
of the narrative is owed to the author of the original source material, DuBose
Heyward. Heyward was a white southerner who "loved the people he was
writing about" ("On Catfish Row").

Baldwin hastens to add that he does not want to imply that Heyward
loved all Negroes ("he was a better man than that") but rather that once
Preminger got his hands on the material, he turned it into a more gratuitous
"white man's vision of Negro life" ("On Catfish Row"). One can equally
imply, though Baldwin does not state it, that *Porgy and Bess* was a white
European man's vision of Negro life. At the very least, Heyward was
writing from his own experience in Charleston, South Carolina, whereas
Preminger was seeing it all from the outside or one might even argue
through the lens of early Hollywood films and their depictions of blacks.
For Baldwin, the worst offense on the part of Preminger was his insistence
that the world depicted in his film could be excused since it was essentially
a "world that does not really exist" ("On Catfish Row"). Baldwin asserts
that the contrast between Billie Holiday's death and Preminger's dismissive

conversion of hers and other black Americans' harsh living conditions into a screen space replete with melodrama and exoticism was too painful for him to bear.

This pivotal moment of comparison between the real Holiday and the fictional Porgy eventually leads to Baldwin's analyses of Lang's filmmaking, which were written much later in 1976. These analyses provide a stark contrast to his assault on Preminger and are more mature and tempered. Baldwin nuances his critiques in order to speak to the deeper issues in his exploration of how to read Hollywood films and their entrenched links to the privileging of whiteness. In this later work, Baldwin speaks to American spectators and readers about the cultural stakes of moviegoing in America in his lifetime and beyond. For example, in *Devil*, Baldwin expresses deep concern for what the audiences of the film *The Exorcist* (1973) "were seeing and what it meant to them" (140). His remarks on *The Exorcist*, which form part of the conclusion of *Devil*, suggest that he had become just as worried about white audiences as he had been about black audiences in earlier sections of *Devil* and in earlier periods of his career.

Baldwin's concern about racial tensions and audience reception is consistent with the lines of thought developed in *Fire* when he states that "we, the black and the white, deeply need each other if we really are to become a nation—if we are really, that is, to achieve our identity, our maturity, as men and women" (97). *Devil* transforms much of what is developed in Baldwin's arguments about black and white American life and identity politics in *Fire* into critical observations on the racially integrated movie audience of the 1970s. In another chapter of this volume, Kathy Roberts Forde argues that literary journalism "can play a constitutive role in the social and political struggles for justice and freedom in democratic societies." Similarly, Baldwin's analysis of how Hollywood cinematic language affects American spectators, whether black or white, comments on social and political struggles for justice and freedom and serves as a plea to spectators to resist Hollywood's divisive forces.

In short, Baldwin's remark that the film *Carmen* belies more about the interior lives of black *and* white Americans than it does about the true representation of black Americans argues that his goal is not simply to combat misrepresentations of "Negroes" on the screen so much as it is to see how those representations affect American audiences. More importantly, he asserts that Hollywood technique dictates and perpetuates mythologies of white privilege and enables the white spectator just as D. W. Griffith's *The Birth of a Nation* empowered both white spectators and the KKK. As suggested, Susan Courtney has traced the ways in which white spectators were empowered by the film. Additionally, as Melvyn Stokes and Ron Stallworth have both indicated, Griffith's film was used as a recruiting tool for prospective KKK members from 1915 until at least as late as the 1970s in various state chapters. Stallworth recounts that in his undercover investigation of the Colorado chapter of the KKK, he was often informed of scheduled viewings of the film for new members of the KKK.

In this respect, Baldwin implicitly relies upon much of what is central to *Fire* when fleshing out his goals in *Devil*. As Baldwin states, again in *Fire*, "The Negroes of this country may never be able to rise to power, but they are very well placed to precipitate chaos and *ring down the curtain* on the American dream" (88; emphasis added). Given that the American dream is indeed the fodder of Hollywood, the use of the metaphor "ring down the curtain" evokes the importance of exploring white privilege not simply through the politics of American social life but equally and perhaps even more importantly through its cultural life. Hollywood has of course long served as a vital center of that culture.

Though Baldwin approaches white guilt and privilege from a broader perspective in *Fire*, his claim in *Devil* is that the ugly truths of American white supremacy and its mythologies that undergird Hollywood's construction of fantasy worlds are truths that Hollywood either blindly accepts in a form of unconscious patronage or actively promotes. In cases where white privilege is directly called out by critics, Hollywood strives to repress or to deny that *such critiques are valid*. As Baldwin says of *Carmen Jones*, "the tone is stifling: a wedding of the blank, lofty solemnity with which Hollywood so often approaches 'works of art' and the really quite helpless condescension with which Hollywood has always handled Negroes" (49). Baldwin views Preminger as complicit in perpetuating white supremacist myths and argues that Lang's filmmaking, by contrast, seems more intent on deconstructing the narrative and generic frameworks that preserve the privileging of whiteness.

In order to argue this contrast, Baldwin gives attention not only to Lang's narratives but also to his casting decisions as well as to his engagement with the deeper meanings of Hollywood genres. All of these tactics contribute to an understanding of just how anticipatory and radically imagined Baldwin's film critique is for film studies. Debates about affronts to the civil rights of black Americans played themselves out vehemently and at times violently in the 1960s and in certain sections of *Fire*. With *Devil*, Baldwin lays the groundwork for the ethnic or resistant spectator, which becomes a crucial concept for film theory from the 1970s onward and still resonates today.[8] Baldwin's contrasting readings of directors Lang and Preminger provide astute observations on how American white supremacy has controlled and still continues to control Hollywood's cinematic language. These analyses also show how easily this language influences the filmmaking practices of non-American directors, unschooled in the nuances of American racially inflected material. More importantly, Baldwin's revelatory approach to Lang's early Hollywood filmmaking is grasped more precisely when weighed against his despairing reactions to Preminger's all-black cast musicals, *Carmen Jones* as well as *Porgy and Bess*.

Baldwin argues that Lang avoids being caught in a naïve position on American racial issues by studying rather than simply absorbing Hollywood's cinematic language. Lang scrutinizes it as a language *in and of itself* and as one that perpetuates white privilege. Baldwin's observation that Lang had "found his American feet" with the filming of *You Only Live Once* indeed depends upon his estimation that Lang's casting as well as his understanding of the American gangster genre were legitimate explorations into the ability of selected Hollywood genres to visualize the American victim.[9] For Baldwin, this included the victimization of American blacks as well. Both Henry Fonda and Sylvia Sidney were highly praised by Baldwin in *You Only Live Once* because they reminded Baldwin of *his* reality, the harsh reality of a young black man in America. As Baldwin claims in *Devil*, "The only actor of the era with whom I identified was Henry Fonda and I was not alone. A black friend of mine, after seeing Henry Fonda in *The Grapes of Wrath*, swore that he [Fonda] had colored blood" (25).

In essence, Baldwin claims that Fonda was the only actor with whom he could identify in his early moviegoing days. This is high praise from the celebrated black writer, whose tough attitudes toward Hollywood in *Devil* are never lost on the reader. Of Sidney, Baldwin claims that she was "the only American film actress who reminded me of a colored girl, or woman" (24). Baldwin praises Lang not only for his realistic portrayal of the ways in which the justice system is stacked against the reformed criminal in the gangster genre but equally for Lang's ability, through casting, to link the injustice of that system to black American life, *albeit* indirectly.

Baldwin's anticipation of the resistant spectator

Whether or not Lang's intention was to tie racially inflected arguments to the injustice of the American criminal reform system is immaterial if one appeals to the premises of spectator theory. As Tom Gunning points out, following the lead of Frieda Grafe, Lang was "not interested in a reproduction of reality one has already seen. He wants to reveal, with his instrument, the real power of forms" (235). Gunning suggests that Lang was interested in providing the audience with a "visionary moment, an act of seeing that tears away the fabric of reality" (236). In this sense, what Baldwin saw in his first viewing of *You Only Live Once* was a reality with which he could identify and find "the other scene of ultimate significance" (236). Lang sought to elucidate the deeper connotations of the screen space he created, which is consistent with the premises of structuralism that are so fundamental to film theory, in particular the concept of cinematic excess as articulated by Kristin Thompson.

Thompson's articulation of cinematic excess stresses that watching a film or reading a text that incorporates myths or layered meanings which go against the grain of the central narrative must be deciphered rather than taken *at surface value*. In this vein, Lang must be considered as a careful student of Hollywood cinematic language, and Baldwin's *Devil* anticipates the concept of cinematic excess, providing lessons in how black spectators should become more reflective about what they are seeing on the screen. In like manner, a fundamental principle of spectator theory is that the spectator must be willing to suspend his or her disbelief in the narrative's principal message. To refuse to do so, particularly when watching classical Hollywood narratives, is essentially to resist the film's entreaty to have the spectator identify with the characters on the screen in a way that is consistent with the narrative invoked. The spectator must cede his or her own identity and put themselves in the place of the protagonist or some other character on the screen. Having done so, they have essentially acquiesced to whatever ideologies or mythologies that are implicit in the film's narrative. Manthia Diawara, in "Black Spectatorship: Problems of Identification and Resistance," gives an overview of different forms of spectator theory in the 1970s and applies these theories to the case of the black spectator (767). Ryan Jay Friedman also provides innovative perspectives on links between Baldwin's work and spectator theory (385).

Thus while Lang's film does not put black actors and actresses on the screen, he does weave their pressing social conflicts into his narrative. Baldwin argues that this is an astute move and one that Lang seems to have learned through his careful study of the American justice system, which is, by extension, commensurate with the white supremacist myths from which it originally derived. The narrative of *You Only Live Once* is therefore a narrative with which Baldwin can identify because he is able to recognize that what is implicit in the film is applicable to his own life as a black man in America. It is by understanding the premises of spectator theory that one can fully appreciate Baldwin's embrace of the film.

Baldwin's contrasting critique of *Carmen* is not only about the abysmal casting of the film and Preminger's use of black actors on the screen representing inauthentic black characters. It is also and more importantly about the power the screen space holds over the diegetic space of the film. This is especially the case for a film that was first lauded for its use of an all-black cast in Technicolor (Boyd 214). Baldwin points out that *Carmen* is "one of the first and most explicit—and far and away the most self-conscious—weddings of sex and color which Hollywood has yet turned out" ("*Carmen Jones*" 50). Black actors and actresses therefore serve primarily as ornaments for an elaborate display of Hollywood's technological advances.

In short, the attraction of this film in the 1950s was not about how the narrative commented on the authentic lives of the black characters on the screen. Its real appeal was that black actors and actresses were adorning the screen with their erotic and colorful bodies while performing a musical opera based on a work of high culture, a "classic" ("*Carmen Jones*" 47). This separation of screen meaning from narrative meaning is crucial for many influential film theories such as the deconstruction of the privileged white male gaze so central to the work of feminist scholars Mary Ann Doane, Laura Mulvey, and Kaja Silverman, amongst others. Those theories lay the groundwork for later scholarly work on spectator response and the concept of the resistant spectator, notably, that of Diawara and Jacqueline Stewart. Susan Courtney uses the gender and racial intersectionality of these theories in an expert manner in her chapter on the birth of the great white spectator in *Hollywood Fantasies of Miscegenation: Spectacular Narratives of Gender and Race, 1903–1967*.

With a focus on Griffith's *The Birth of a Nation*, Courtney traces how the white (male) gaze becomes the controlling factor in Griffith's cinematic language to the detriment of all other forms of seeing in the film. Her strategies parallel those of Baldwin's cinema critique. She argues that Griffith's film attributes the empowering gaze only to white men and, additionally, that black characters can only look and be looked at but their acts of seeing do not give them agency. The camera itself controls what the spectator sees and entreats the spectator to identify with the white man's gaze. The narrative and what actually appears on the screen are split. Though Baldwin's arguments on these issues are linked back rhetorically to his autobiographical "I," William E. Dow has suggested in one of the articles of this volume that Baldwin's self-personification is complex, innovative, and in need of deeper exploration. Indeed, the role of the empowered gaze in film theory is linked to the writings on the literary journalistic "I" evoked by several authors in another section of this volume.

Gunning points to Lang's challenge to unconscious patronage in *You Only Live Once* through his analysis of the frog scene in the film. Lang's techniques are indeed inherited from Griffith in part, but the ideological message of his camera is completely different. The frog scene shows a stark schism between what the narrative dialogue conveys and how the camera language comments on that dialogue in an oblique manner. In this scene, the two lovers, Eddie and Jo, observe two frogs mating in a lily pond and they discuss the mating habits of frogs. Eddie tells Jo that frogs mate for life and if one of them dies then the other does too. At this point in the dialogue, Lang's camera "cuts to a reflection of the lovers upside down as in a *camera obscura*. This figure of the reversed vision becomes more complex as one of the frogs leaps into the water and the image of the couple melts into obscurity in the rippling water" (Gunning 237).

The rippling effects suggest that like the frogs, if either Eddie or Jo dies, then the other will as well. The meaning is conveyed not through narrative dialogue but, rather, through a metaphorical surface created by the camera. According to Baldwin, Preminger's films are a series of images that rely upon only the surface, though the myth of white supremacy is clearly lurking underneath as a result of the film language he inherits from Hollywood. This is in complete contradistinction to Lang as the example of the frog scene suggests. As Baldwin states, "A movie is, literally, a series of images, and what one sees in a movie can really be taken, beyond its stammering or misleading dialogue, as the key to what the movie is actually involved in saying" ("*Carmen Jones*" 50). With respect to his critique of *Porgy and Bess*, Baldwin notes that because Preminger understands nothing of the life that produced the actors he has on the screen, the actors know they will be ill-used and "they resign themselves to it with as much sardonic good humor as they can muster. They are working at least, and they will be *seen*" ("On Catfish Row"; emphasis added).

Baldwin does not fault Preminger for his casting of blacks per se. He does, however, criticize him for his inability to use the actors and actresses in an authentic way. Baldwin prefaces his scathing critique of Preminger's *Carmen* by providing a color wheel and meticulously color-coding the actors and actresses as either "taffy-colored", i.e., light enough as the title of the article suggests, or as in the case of Pearl Bailey, "quite dark and she plays, in effect, a floozie" ("*Carmen Jones*" 51). In the case of *Porgy and Bess*, he suggests that Preminger has an excellent cast in front of the camera but that he just does not know what to do with them. In essence, Baldwin accuses Preminger of having cast his film as all-black but denigrates the *émigré* director for privileging light-skinned "Negroes" over dark-skinned ones. Baldwin argues that such a move inadvertently reinforces myths of white privilege. As Richard Dyer argues in his chapter "Coloured White, Not Coloured," different levels of skin tints ranging from white to black can be invoked visually to create a hierarchy of privilege for characters on screen (62).

Baldwin is also disturbed by Preminger's decision to impose a dialogue characterized by "black English" and claims that *Carmen* is difficult to watch given that "everyone appears to undergo a tiny, strangling death before resolutely substituting 'de' for 'the'" (50). In his essay "Black English: A Dishonest Argument" Baldwin refers specifically to *Porgy and Bess* when he notes that the idea of black English is essentially rooted in a defense of the white man's right to distinguish the Negro from himself through linguistic forms, that is, through a simple substitution of "de" for "the." As Baldwin states, "We the blacks, can be described by others, but we are forbidden to describe ourselves" ("Black English" 128). Baldwin asserts that the use of black English in Preminger's film could be construed as a form of condescending control over how black characters are portrayed.

The all-black cast in the age of integration

On the surface, Preminger's use of an all-black cast for both films might initially be seen as progressive in 1950s Hollywood with respect to race and American identity politics. Both Baldwin and Preminger were no doubt aware of the vogue for all-black casts in the wake of integration. Jeffrey Paul Smith nonetheless points out that the critiques of said films have largely suggested that they were attempts to prolong segregation through the creation of imaginary black worlds. The implication here was that these worlds were to be interpreted as "separate but equal" in nature. Smith's intriguing article provides background on this topic but also asserts that the singing voices of the characters in *Carmen* are dubbed with white operatic voices, which is the only form of integration one finds in the film. He equally claims that the separation of black bodies and black voices in the film compounded the affront to an integrationist politic, which was already in place when the film was made (31).

Baldwin deems Preminger's films to be violence against black bodies on screen and by extension against real-life black Americans. He is therefore also indirectly commenting upon the concerns raised by this Hollywood vogue of all-black casts at the time. Baldwin does mention the films *Stormy Weather* (1959) and *Cabin in the Sky* (1943) as entertaining examples of this phenomenon while still faulting *Carmen* for its lack of authenticity ("*Carmen Jones*" 48). In contrast to these accusations by Baldwin, contemporary critics see a certain charm in Preminger's musicals and thus potentially belie the harshness of Baldwin's critique.

Jonathan Rosenbaum remarks that the film is "ideologically intolerable yet often fascinating and intermittently pungent" (*Carmen Jones*, Review). David Melville, while acknowledging that Baldwin was right to call out Preminger for the film's distressing use of blacks to capitalize on the public's association of black bodies with eroticism nonetheless argues that it is "one of the defining film melodramas of the 50s" ("Kissin' the Breeze Goodbye: Otto Preminger and *Carmen Jones*"). Courtney Small literally suggests that "there is a vibrant charm to the film that still resonates today" ("Blind Spot: *Carmen Jones*"). The real value of Baldwin's contrasting critique, however, is its contribution to film theory and in particular to spectator theory through the use of specific examples.

For example, as noted by Stewart, "black spectators will still seek moments of identification ('something out of which we come') in Hollywood films, even as they reject the classical positioning of the spectator as silent, engrossed recipient" (676). Baldwin's film analysis approximates the use of what Stewart refers to as the reconstructive strategies of the black spectator. His reading of Lang's film culminates in his observation that "in the American context, there being no way for him to get to the n***er, [Lang] could only use that other American prototype, the criminal, *le gangster*" ("Many Thousands Gone" 28). In Baldwin's imagination, Lang pinpointed the undeniable obstacles to progress for the "n***er" though his structural application of the gangster genre.

Baldwin read the internal contradictions of the film through his reconstructive strategies. Though *You Only Live Once* does not take up racial injustice as a specific theme, Baldwin asserts that Lang's representations of *American* injustice resonated with Baldwin's feelings about the racial injustices from which he suffered in his everyday life.[10] Lang's need to work through his own demons— those imposed by his precipitate exit from Germany at the beginning of the Third Reich—was the point of departure for his Hollywood career (Eisner 8).

Billie, Eddie, and Porgy: Looking through the eyes of the protagonist

You Only Live Once therefore felt more authentic with respect to Baldwin's own reality than did *Fury* and certainly than did *Carmen* or *Porgy and Bess*. As Baldwin concludes on the subject of *Porgy and Bess*: "If the day ever comes when the survivors of the place [Catfish Row] can be fooled into believing that the Hollywood cardboard even faintly resembles, or is intended to resemble, what it was like to be there, all our terrible and beautiful history will be gone for nothing and will all be doomed to an unimaginable reality" ("On Catfish Row"). Baldwin stresses his discomfort by claiming that Poitier's Porgy is a character with whom he finds it difficult for a black man to identify.

However, Baldwin picks up on Lang's protagonist, Eddie, as epitomizing the suffering of the authentic black man in twentieth-century America because he captures the essence of Lang's "obsession," which was "the fact and the effect of human loneliness, and the ways in which we are all responsible for the creation, and the fate, of the isolated monster: whom we isolate because we recognize him as living within us" ("Many Thousands Gone" 27). There are echoes here of Baldwin's "monster" "created by the American republic" that we find lurking in his earlier essay "Many Thousands Gone" (*Notes of a Native Son* 41). By the time of *Devil*, that monster, based on Baldwin's reading of Wright's character Bigger Thomas in *Native Son*, had become symbolic both in social terms as argued in "Many Thousands Gone" as well as in cinematic terms, as asserted by *Devil*.

Baldwin's conclusion, based on his understanding of Lang's protagonists, was that "we were all n***ers in the thirties [in America]" ("Many Thousands Gone" 29), and "Lang's indictment of the small faceless people ... who are society" (28) articulates American guilt and communicates its relevance for victims of racism. Of Eddie's question about why should *he* not try to kill *them* before *they* try to kill *him*, Baldwin says, "I understood that: it was a real question. I was living with that question" (30). For if there was one truth for the 1930s black man, it was that the American dream was unattainable, and happiness as an implicit outcome of attaining the American dream was a key component for the gangster genre.

As Gunning points out, Eddie's unsuccessful attempt to reintegrate into the life of the American dream upon leaving prison ends in the violent death of himself and his wife Jo, his sole supporter. At the close of the film, as they try to escape across the US border, Eddie and Jo are pursued and shot, first Eddie's wife and then he himself shortly afterward. She claims before dying that she would gladly do it all over again. As Eddie holds his dead wife in his arms, he looks up into a forest landscape and hears the voice-over of Father Dolan (the priest who served first as his friend and accomplice but whom he had to kill in order to go free) saying, "Eddie, Eddie. You're free, Eddie! The gates are open."

This line eerily echoes Baldwin's comparative reading of Billie Holiday's death when Baldwin claims that Holiday's life was one where she "had escaped all of their definitions by becoming herself ... Now Billie Holiday [upon her death] has escaped forever from managers, landlords, locked hotels, fear, poverty, illness and the watchdogs of morality and the law" ("On Catfish Row"). Like Eddie, she was free. I draw this comparison to argue that though Eddie is a fictional protagonist, the depiction of his death rings true with respect to the real-life death of Billie Holiday, according to Baldwin's own understanding of both Eddie and Billie.

Lang essentially articulates about the gangster what Baldwin claimed about the life of blacks in 1930s America: death is about release rather than redemption. As a character in a melodramatic and tragic opera, Carmen will also die, but her triumph is that she has always looked life "straight in de eye." Baldwin does not make this comparison in any of his writings on the two directors, though he indirectly rejects the authenticity of Carmen's death as comparable to Eddie's or Billie Holiday's when he suggests that "the movie-makers have dreamed up some sort of mumbo jumbo about buzzards' wings, signs of the zodiac" ("*Carmen Jones*" 52). Baldwin argues that the sexual mores of American filmmaking that were dictated by the Hays Code would not allow for an authentic presentation of the cause for Carmen's fall. In the original source material, Carmen's fall is caused by her indecorous sexual attraction to men (51), a narrative detail which would not have been allowed in 1950s Hollywood.

In short, Carmen's death is arbitrary in the film adaptation. It is a *deus ex machina* and does nothing to reflect on the authentic lives of black Americans, whereas hopeless dread awaits Eddie no matter which way he might turn. As Baldwin attests: "This dread is underscored by the film's last line, delivered (in the dying prisoner's memory) by the priest: *the gates are open*. I knew damn well that the gates were not open and by this time, in any case, the lovers were dead" ("Many Thousands Gone" 31). Baldwin recognizes that Lang's exiled vision succeeded in giving truth to the lie of American mythic structures, particularly those that purportedly guaranteed justice and equality to all.[11]

For Baldwin, reading the cinema in an authentic way depends upon not being trapped into reductive readings of Hollywood films or being duped by films that are there to victimize the spectator. As he puts it, "The victim who is able to articulate the situation of the victim has ceased to be a victim: he, or she, has become a threat" (*Devil* 134). The film viewer *can* make a difference. This is reminiscent of Baldwin's suggestion in *Fire* that "To accept one's past—one's history—is not the same thing as drowning in it; it is learning how to use it" (81). Baldwin's reading of Lang's film indirectly suggests that Lang has learned how to use his past in his new American environment, something he ultimately judges Preminger was unwilling or unable to do.

In short, Baldwin's radical imagination with respect to spectator response, particularly the reconstructive strategies of African American audiences when watching Hollywood films in this period, anticipates much of what is considered to be central to the works of scholars such as Diawara and Stewart in later film studies. More importantly, contrasting Baldwin's critiques of Lang and Preminger as "othered" directors using American narratives, we can see that Baldwin provides us with perspectives on how American mythologies have influenced Hollywood filmmaking practices. Those mythologies perpetuate the privileging of whiteness in Hollywood narratives and genres and on Hollywood screens. Indeed, according to Baldwin's critiques, Lang came close to understanding the truth of America and the constraining force of white privilege in Hollywood whereas Preminger found and helped shape Hollywood's embrace of said white privilege and its cardboard lies through his seemingly gratuitous use of black bodies on the screen.

Notes

1 Classical Hollywood cinema is to be understood as defined by David Bordwell, Janet Staiger, and Kristin Thompson in *The Classical Hollywood Cinema: Film Style and Mode of Production to 1960*. The style of classical Hollywood cinema privileges seamless narratives intended to lull the spectator into the fictional worlds presented as well as full closure with "happy" endings and strong viewer identification with the gaze of the protagonist. Most often, the protagonist is a white male with the exception of the melodramas that came to the fore in the 1930s to 1950s. It must also be noted that the problems of white supremacy in Hollywood is still a pressing issue to be addressed but that is not within the scope of this chapter.

2 For more on the role of the *émigré* directors in Hollywood, cf. Nick Smedley's *A Divided World: Hollywood and the Émigré Directors in the Era of Roosevelt and Hitler, 1933–1948*.

3 "*Carmen Jones*: The Dark Is Light Enough" appears in *Notes of a Native Son*, and was first published as "Life Straight in de Eye" in *Commentary*, January 1955. Page numbers for this essay are referenced from the "*Carmen Jones*: The Dark Is Light Enough" article throughout the chapter.

4 Preminger referred in his autobiography to his arrival in America as a rebirth. Lang arrived in America, according to many, as an *émigré deluxe* (Gunning 203).

5 As Renoir recounts, though he was welcomed with open arms, Darryl F. Zanuck quickly made it clear that he proposed "to get me to film French stories, which was the very last thing I wanted" (193). Renoir eventually persuaded Zanuck "with some difficulty" (194) for the right to do location shooting with American landscapes, notably in his films *Swamp Water* (1941) and *The Southerner* (1945).

6 The Hays Code was a self-imposed set of rules concerning moral conduct in Hollywood filmmaking and was in effect from 1930 to 1968. The code was ostensibly used to ensure basic principles such as the refusal to reward gratuitous violence, a ban on miscegenation, and other ethical issues, but it suffered from its myopic vision and unconscious patronage with regard to sexual and racial mores. For more on this topic, cf. Geltzer. Renoir's *The Southerner*, for example, which was banned in Memphis by censor Lloyd T. Binford for its purportedly negative portrayal of poor white southerners. The banning was justified by Binford on the basis of the Hays Code.

7 Preminger seemed intent on many things in his filming of *Carmen, Porgy and Bess*, and his later film *Hurry Sundown* (1967), but racism was not consistent with his actions off set. In fact, when filming *Hurry Sundown*, the cast and crew encountered blatant racism in the South when one of their black actors jumped into a swimming pool at the hotel where they were staying. When Preminger saw the town's overwhelmingly racist response, he solved the problem by renting out the entire hotel so that his black actors and actresses would not be bothered by the locals (Fujiwara, location 6449).

8 The recent debates about films such as Quentin Tarantino's *Django Unchained* (2012), Steve McQueen's *12 Years a Slave* (2013), and, in particular, Nate Parker's *The Birth of a Nation* (2016) amongst many others suggest that the new wave of debate on how white supremacy structures Hollywood filmmaking has not yet reached solutions on this pressing concern.

9 The Hays Code was very specific about its condemnation of graphic or gratuitous violence. As a result, the gangster genre was very closely scrutinized.

10 Of the white heroes Baldwin regarded on the screen, he remarked that he "despised and feared them because they *did* take vengeance into their own hands." He speculates that he was introduced to the film *You Only Live Once* as a way of being compensated for having to experience such fear in his viewing experiences (*Devil* 22).

11 Baldwin cites a brief incident in the film where Fonda stops his pacing and stands by the window of the flop house in which he is staying to listen to the Salvation Army singing, "if you love your mother, meet her in the skies" (*Devil* 29). Of this scene Baldwin remarks, "I cannot imagine any native-born white American daring to use, so laconically, a banality so nearly comic in order to capture so deep a distress" (29). The stress on the adjective native-born indicates that the alienated gaze Lang brings to the representation of *American* suffering is not lost on Baldwin.

Works Cited

Baldwin, James. "Black English: A Dishonest Argument." *The Cross of Redemption: Uncollected Writings*, edited by Randall Kenan, Pantheon, 2010, pp. 125–30.

Baldwin, James. "*Carmen Jones*: The Dark Is Light Enough." *Notes of a Native Son*. Beacon Press, 1955, pp. 46–56.

Baldwin, James. *The Devil Finds Work*. Laurel, 1976.

Baldwin, James. *The Fire Next Time*. Vintage, 1963.

Baldwin, James. "Many Thousands Gone." *Notes of a Native Son*. Beacon Press, 1955, pp. 24–45.

Baldwin, James. "On Catfish Row." *Commentary*, 1 Sept. 1959. commentarymagazine.com/articles/on-the-horizon-on-catfish-row/. Accessed 3 Sept. 2018.

Bogle, Donald. *Toms, Coons, Mulattoes, Mammies, and Bucks: An Interpretive History of Blacks in American Films*. Bantam, 1974.

Bordwell, David, Janet Staiger, and Kristin Thompson. *The Classical Hollywood Cinema: Film Style and Mode of Production to 1960*. Columbia UP, 1985.

Boyd, Melinda. "The Politics of Color in Oscar Hammerstein's *Carmen Jones*." *Blackness in Opera: Carmen Jones from Silent Film to MTV*, edited by Naomi André, Karen M. Bryan, and Eric Saylor, U of Illinois P, 2012, pp. 212–36.

Champlin, Charles. "Preminger's Assault on Hays Code." *Los Angeles Times*, 26 Apr. 1986, articles.latimes.com/1986-04-26/entertainment/ca-2444_1_production-code-seal. Accessed 24 Aug. 2018.

Courtney, Susan. *Hollywood Fantasies of Miscegenation: Spectacular Narratives of Gender and Race, 1903–1967*. Princeton UP, 2005.

Diawara, Manthia. "Black Spectatorship: Problems of Spectatorship and Resistance." *Film Theory and Criticism*, edited by Leo Braudy and Marshall Cohen, 7th ed., Oxford UP, 2009, pp. 767–76.

Doane, Mary Ann. *The Desire to Desire*. Palgrave MacMillan, 1987.

Dyer, Richard. "Coloured White, Not Coloured." *White: Essays on Race and Culture*, Routledge, 1997, pp. 41–81.

Eisner, Lotte H. *Fritz Lang*. 1977. Da Capo Press, 1986.

Elsaesser, Thomas. *European Cinema Face to Face with Hollywood*. Amsterdam UP, 2005.

Finger, Michael. "Banned in Memphis: The Dark Days of Lloyd T. Binford, Known from Coast to Coast as the Toughest Censor in America." *Memphis Flyer*, 8 May 2008, memphisflyer.com/memphis/banned-in-memphis/Content?oid=1144204. Accessed 24 Aug. 2018.

Friedman, Ryan Jay. "'Enough Force to Shatter the Tale to Fragments': Ethics and Textual Analysis in James Baldwin's Film Theory." *ELH*, vol. 77, no. 2, Summer 2010, pp. 385–412. doi: 10.1353/elh.0.0088.

Fujiwara, Chris. *The World and Its Double: The Life and Work of Otto Preminger*. Kindle ed., Farrar, Straus and Giroux, 2009.

Geltzer, Jeremy. *Dirty Words and Filthy Pictures: Film and the First Amendment*. U of Texas P, 2015.

Gunning, Tom. *The Films of Fritz Lang: Allegories of Vision and Modernity*. BFI, 2000.

Kapsis, Robert E. *Charles Burnett: Interviews*. UP of Mississippi, 2011.

Kenan, Randall, editor. *The Cross of Redemption: James Baldwin Uncollected Writings*. Pantheon, 2010.

Leeming, David. *James Baldwin: A Biography*. Arcade, 1994.

Melville, David. "Kissin' the Breeze Goodbye: Otto Preminger and *Carmen Jones*." *Senses of Cinema*, no. 66, 18 Feb. 2013, sensesofcinema.com/2013/cteq/kissin-the-breeze-goodbye-otto-preminger-and-carmen-jones/. Accessed 24 Aug. 2018.

Mulvey, Laura. "Visual Pleasure and Narrative Cinema." *Film Theory and Criticism*, edited by Leo Braudy and Marshall Cohen, 7th ed., Oxford UP, 2009, pp. 711–22.

Preminger, Otto. *Autobiographie*. Translated by André Charles Cohen. 1977. Jean Claude Lattès, 1981.

Renoir, Jean. *My Life and My Films*. Translated by Norman Denny, Da Capo, 1974.

Rosenbaum, Jonathan. "*Carmen Jones*, Review." *Letterboxd*, 4 Sept. 2016, letterboxd.com/jrosenbaum2002/film/carmen-jones/. Accessed 24 Aug. 2018.

Silverman, Kaja. *The Subject of Semiotics*. Oxford UP, 1983.

Small, Courtney. "Blind Spot: *Carmen Jones*." *Cinema Axis*, 31 Jan. 2017, cinemaaxis.com/2017/01/31/blind-spot-carmen-jones/. Accessed 24 Aug. 2018.

Smedley, Nick. *A Divided World: Hollywood Cinema and Émigré Directors in the Era of Roosevelt and Hitler, 1933–1948*. U of Chicago P, 2011.

Smith, Jeffrey Paul. "Black Faces, White Voices: The Politics of Dubbing in *Carmen Jones*." *The Velvet Light Trap*, no. 51, Spring 2003, pp. 29–42. doi: 10.1353/vlt.2003.0010.

Stallworth, Ron. *Black Klansman: Race, Hate and the Undercover Investigation of a Lifetime*. Flatiron Books, 2018.

Stewart, Jacqueline. "Negroes Laughing at Themselves? Black Spectatorship and the Performance of Urban Modernity." *Critical Inquiry*, vol. 29, no. 4, 2003, pp. 650–77. doi: 10.1086/377724.

Stokes, Melvyn. *D. W. Griffith's "The Birth of a Nation": A History of the Most Controversial Motion Picture of All Time*. Oxford UP, 2008.

Thompson, Kristin. "The Concept of Cinematic Excess." *Narrative, Apparatus, Ideology: A Film Theory Reader*, Columbia UP, 1986, pp. 130–42.

2

Picturing Jimmy, Picturing Self: James Baldwin, Beauford Delaney, and the Color of Light

James Smalls

Through his own writings and need to seek recognition from the public, James Baldwin (1924–87) encouraged the production of images of himself as a public figure represented in alternating circumstances of extroversion and introspection. Various forms of visual representation, including paintings, photographs, and graphic works, portray the writer as pensive, inspired, angry, or vulnerable, or as defiant activist and advocate for just causes. His visual representation by others became vital to an understanding of himself in relationship to the public (visible) world. Indeed, throughout the second half of the twentieth century, Baldwin's face had become so familiar to so many people that it was simply iconic. That iconicity started and was fueled by the African American artist Beauford Delaney (1901–79), who produced several intimate portraits of the writer.

It all started in 1941, when, at the age of sixteen, Baldwin arrived in New York City and posed nude for the painting *Dark Rapture*.[1] This would be the first of many visual representations of Baldwin by Delaney, although the only one of him in the nude. The image shows a dark-skinned youth seated cross-legged in an outdoor landscape setting and framed by a potted plant on one side with a tree located in the distance on the other. As with all subsequent portraits of the future writer, this one is thickly painted and luminous. Here, Delaney employs expressive gestural brushstrokes and a range of brilliant colors inspired by Matisse and Cézanne, and chosen for symbolic, emotional, and aesthetic effect.

The words "dark" and "rapture" of the portrait's title reveal a lot about the early relationship between the two men. The former term references racial distinction in an affirming and desirous way, whereas the latter connotes an affective feeling of intense spiritual pleasure or perhaps even carnal joy. *Dark Rapture* constitutes one of several visual and conceptual starting points for looking at Baldwin and Delaney as emotionally, historically, and artistically linked figures. The writer and painter shared biographical as well as emotional and artistic traits. From their very first meeting in the early 1940s, Delaney became Baldwin's confidant, his father figure, black and gay soul mate, his "navigator, his wing man, his source, his rock," his moral compass, his muse (Kelleher). Delaney viewed Baldwin as a spiritual son, and Baldwin later called Delaney his spiritual father and "principal witness" (*Price* 832). From the first time they met, the young Baldwin sensed a natural connection with Delaney. Each was a mirror reflection of the other—"father" and "son" in art. Both were black men, artists, gay, outsiders, and ministers' sons who would help one another through "crucial passages in life" (Leeming, *Baldwin* 33). When Baldwin wrote about his friend, he was essentially referencing himself, seeing the artist as "a later version" of the writer (Dempsey 70; Leeming, *Baldwin* 33). Likewise, and to a certain extent, all portraits produced by artists are self-reflexive in that they say as much about the intended subject of the image as they do about the creator. This is true with the portraits of Baldwin by Delaney, particularly given the extremely close relationship between the two men.

Both writer and painter validated so many aspects of each other's being and essence. Baldwin, through writing, and Delaney, by way of visual representation, attempted to come to grips with their shared concerns about matters of identity, exile, and belonging. In the pages that follow, I consider three portraits of Baldwin that Delaney produced in 1945, 1963, and 1965 and discern how Delaney saw Baldwin and what Baldwin saw in and learned from Delaney. Most significant for this chapter is that both men were creative individuals who left behind visual and verbal traces of their worldly and spiritual journeys (Dempsey 60). The portraits of Baldwin by Delaney discussed here constitute such traces for bridging the affective with the visual and visuality.

The word "visuality," first coined in 1841, refers to qualities related to making mental images of abstract or elusive ideas, such as heroism or love. In recent decades, the term has become a keyword in the field of postmodern visual culture studies and has taken on additional nuances of meaning. According to the art critic and art historian Hal Foster, there is a distinction between "vision" and "visuality." The first term calls attention to the biological functions of the eye and the human visual system, while the second references cultural practices and values that complexly engage the political, racial, sexual, and so on, as these relate to vision. In other words, "vision" alludes to "the physical processes of sight" and "visuality" to its "social fact" as a complex system of cultural codes operative within the history of art (Mirzoeff 54; Foster ix–xiv). Delaney's portraits of Baldwin exist at the interface between art and social life. That is, they reflect social realities as well as artistic conventions. As such, they exemplify a charged form of visuality.

Although "vision" and "visuality" interrelate, they should not be seen as binary opposites. In this context, Delaney's portraits of Baldwin can be taken as visual representations that analyze the formal dimensions of vision (sight) through such stylistic elements as color, light, line, and form, while simultaneously setting in motion a complex system of cultural codes that engage social, racial, and ideological matters within and beyond the domain of the visual. For Baldwin, Delaney's paintings are more about visuality than they are about vision in that they engage seeing as socially formative and socially productive. Delaney's portraits as well as his visually manifested psychological and spiritual insights into Baldwin, and Baldwin's lucid responses to the artist's images of him, allow for an analysis of the social construction of the visual and the visual construction of the social by way of representation. As portraits, these works manifest visual forms of both individual and collective identities.

Baldwin maintained a complex relationship to collaboration, visuality, and representation. Delaney's portraits of him constitute visual records that provide a sense of how the painter viewed and interpreted the inner character of the writer. Likewise, Baldwin commented on how he learned from Delaney and his art through the written word primarily in his notes and essays. Throughout his career, Baldwin produced many eloquent characterizations of Delaney's paintings, calling attention to the artist's uncanny power of light. Consider this passage:

> And this window was a kind of universe, moaning and wailing when it rained, bitter with the thunder, hesitant & delicate with the first light of the morning & as blue as the blues when the last light of the sun departed. Well, that life, that light, that miracle are what I began to see in Beauford's paintings, and this light began to stretch back for me over all the time we had known each other, over much more time than that, with the power to illuminate. (qtd. in Valentine)[2]

Contained in this characterization of Delaney's art is a reverential, nearly sacred tone. Baldwin views Delaney's works as beacons or icons of spirituality through their use of light and color, describing them as windows onto life and light.

From 1941 through the 1960s, Delaney produced portraits of Baldwin that depict much more than the writer's likeness. They express Baldwin's "life essence," his "inner light" as Delaney saw it at various stages of the writer's life and career. They also represent profound expressions of Delaney's fondness for Baldwin. In these portraits, Delaney engaged in two types of vision, one of the reading of external phenomena and the other of seeing on a deeper and intangible plane of meaning what one might call spiritual or transcendent. As evidenced by the selected portraits discussed here, Delaney saw the world and Baldwin through a "cosmic" lens, a point of view that reflects, in part, the significance of Delaney's combination of realism and abstraction. Already, by the time he had arrived in New York City in 1929, Delaney's style had begun to vacillate between figurative representation and expressive abstraction—a wavering that becomes significant to the function and meaning of the portraits under consideration.

The vacillation between figurative and abstract representation parallels the Baldwin–Delaney relationship as one in which the verbal and the visual complement one another. Within such a dynamic, the portrait alone becomes a challenging means of describing the inner life of the painted subject, especially when the achievement of a descriptive likeness is presumed to define a sitter's personality or character, both of which are socially and culturally determined. It is here that the portrait as a conveyor of representative "truth" fails. It succeeds, however, if we consider portraits in general as "approximation[s] of a relational model between artist and sitter rather than as a faithful construction" (Brilliant 38–39). In this regard, the only true subject of Delaney's portraits of Baldwin are "the accretions of the self that constitute 'a life'—a person's role in society, his character, his appearance, his reputation and reception, his fate and his fame" (Brilliant 46).

Portrait of James Baldwin (1945)

Delaney's 1945 *Portrait of James Baldwin* (Philadelphia Museum of Art)[3] is an early depiction of the writer, painted a few years after the men first met in New York City. It is a personal tribute to the early yet vital relationship between the writer and the artist. Here, Baldwin is twenty-one years old. Closely cropped and vibrantly executed, the writer's face occupies the greatest portion of the painted surface, causing Baldwin's countenance to jump out from the canvas with a near-sculptural insistence in occupying our place. The immediacy between viewer and subject becomes palpable, created by strong and dark outlines that define specific features of the face, such as eyes, nose, lips, and shape of the head and neck. Delaney renders Baldwin's eyes in slightly different sizes and with varied treatment, a pictorial device detected in many of Delaney's self-portraits as well as in Pablo Picasso's paintings, of which Delaney was familiar.

Delaney's attention to the shape and intensity of the eyes relates to the artist's interest in the notion of seeing (vision) and insight (visuality) into people, places, and experiences. Baldwin spoke often of Delaney's inner (psychological/emotional) and outer (sociological/historical) eye as "a new confrontation with reality" (Katoch) that resulted in his triumph in "transcend[ing] both the inner and outer darkness" (Baldwin, "On the Painter" 45). Baldwin describes how Delaney taught him to respond to life as an artist: "to look for truth and reality where others could not see it" (Katoch). The writer remarked how, despite Delaney's poverty and unstable mental state, "he is *seeing* all the time" (Baldwin, "On the Painter" 45). Baldwin's experience of revelation was one about perceptive vision that leads, "directly and inexorably, to a new confrontation with truth and reality—the ability to *see*" (Katoch). The palpable and the conceptual nuances of seeing, of revelation, of seeing the light, were as important for the writer as they were for the painter. Baldwin also admitted that it was not Delaney's painting that at first caused him (Baldwin) to begin to see but, rather, a shared New York City urban encounter and experience. This would be one of a series of revelations stirred by Delaney's example:

> I remember once walking in the Village with the black painter Beauford Delaney. We were stopped at a street corner waiting for the traffic light to change, and Beauford pointed down and said, "Look," I looked and all I saw was water. But he insisted: "Look again." Which I did, and I saw oil in the water and the city reflected in the puddle. For me this was a revelation, which cannot be explained. He [Beauford] taught me to see, and to trust what I saw. Often it is painters who show writers how to see. And once you've had this experience, you see in a different mode. (Leeming, *Baldwin* 33)

Although dating to the early years of the Baldwin–Delaney relationship, of the many future portraits that Delaney would produce of Baldwin, this one is considered to be among his most direct and expressive. Given the scrutiny placed on physiognomic details, the portrait was most likely painted from life rather than from memory. The intensity of the facial expression and the color palette recall portraits rendered by Vincent Van Gogh. The piercing eyes, the strongly defined nose and lips, and the trunk-like neck all give Baldwin an unforgettable iconic presence, as does the frontal and close-up viewpoint. The passages of brilliant color are daringly juxtaposed and radiate with an energy that is indicative of the intellect and personality ascribed to the future author of so many insightful essays and novels.

As Baldwin's "principal witness," as a person who became intimately familiar with the writer and his development as a human being, a writer, and a celebrity over the years, Delaney's portrait not only powerfully affirms the artist's powers of a penetrating kind of visuality into the historical and spiritual dimensions of Baldwin himself, but in doing so demonstrates the artist's own distinguished contribution to American modernism by way of his almost magical use of rippling color in order to create a shifting surface across the skin that becomes suggestive of the movement of light and the passing of time (Tempkin 109; Wallace).

Baldwin served as a witness to Delaney's changing vision and took note of how his paintings "underwent a most striking metamorphosis into freedom" (Baldwin, "On the Painter" 45). Freedom for Baldwin was not an abstract notion. It meant "the end of innocence," that one has "finally entered the picture," that is, that one has accessed "life" (truth) (Leeming, "Interview" 54). Paralleling his ideas against and through the symbolic language of prophecy engaged by the late eighteenth-century writings of William Blake on innocence and experience, the state of innocence for Baldwin was equivalent to enslavement—that is, to a failure to see.[4] It is with this notion that he made the conceptual connection with Delaney's paintings. That liberation was predicated on light, what Baldwin called "that life, that miracle" (qtd. in Valentine). In front of a Delaney painting, Baldwin confessed, "we stand in the light … which is both loving and merciless" (Baldwin, *Collected Essays* 721). Baldwin's revelation at seeing Delaney's works was not one associated with sudden enlightenment but rather resulted from "a breathing cycle that serves as a revelation that keeps on revealing" (Darton). Baldwin's use of the term "breathing cycle" is, in this instance, employed figuratively rather than literally. Here, I believe Baldwin was referring to the process of taking time with the work, as one does by the process of inhaling and exhaling to meditate and embark on a spiritual journey inward. That "breathing cycle" can be seen in two portraits of Baldwin by Delaney, one dating from 1963 and the other from 1965.

Portraits of James Baldwin (1963 and 1965)

Soon after Delaney moved to Paris in 1953, he began suffering from bouts of depression. He also started hearing voices and commenced drinking heavily. Painting served as a therapeutic means to calm the voices in his head. It was also at this time that his painting style began to change, becoming more abstract as his use of color and light intensified. Although his more purely abstract compositions increasingly gained attention from art critics and the public, he continued to produce figurative paintings, most notably portraits, oftentimes combined with strong abstract elements. Delaney's portraits of Baldwin from 1963 on must be considered in this context of stylistic and psychological change. As the subject of these portraits, Baldwin provided

Delaney a space of psychological and emotional comfort. As such, they constitute acts of both friendship and love that both men shared, if not craved (Kelleher).

Delaney's *Portrait of James Baldwin* from 1963[5] has been described as "heated and confrontational, its harsh colors roughly applied" and glowing with the vibrant, Van Gogh-inspired yellow the artist often used after he moved to Paris in the early 1950s (*Les Amis*). In the work, Delaney joins "a sense of intimacy with elements of abstraction" (Morse). He exaggerates Baldwin's facial features, focusing on his large eyes, oval head, and slender neck and shoulders. Here, the artist "plays with color by using a vibrant array of pastels and stylized forms" (Morse).

Unlike the 1945 portrait, which was a result of several sittings by Baldwin, this portrait and the one dating to a couple of years later were produced from memory and were coupled with Delaney's interest in the study of light. These works are not, however, about nostalgic affection. Rather, their roughly applied paint and increasingly bold colors hint at the inner anxieties and Delaney's search for "truth," albeit elusive, about Baldwin. Delaney's 1963 pastel portrait is "chromatically complex" with its predominant yellows "darkened by harsh greens, violets, and reds" (Exhibition label). The portrait serves as a medium for capturing the emotional intensity of Baldwin and Delaney's long friendship. It successfully manages to conflate "the slender youth with the mature man, expressing the artist's memories, anxiety, pain, and devotion over time" (Exhibition label).

These portraits of Baldwin provide visual evidence that the artist maintained a long-term involvement with color and light. His 1963 portrait is more about the concreteness of the former rather than any attempt at capturing the sitter's likeness. As a modernist, Delaney's focus is on the materiality of the medium (pastel) with little tonal difference. David Leeming, biographer of both Delaney and Baldwin, acknowledges Delaney's celebration of the color yellow as the substance of light in relation to paint, light, and spirituality. Delaney's concern with the play of light and its rather specific qualities renders his painted surfaces a place of spiritual significance. The importance of color and light in Delaney's art was recognized and rendered aesthetically and philosophically significant by Baldwin, who considered the combination of both as a way to enter into and appreciate the life lessons revealed to him by the artist.

As seen in both the 1963 and 1965 portraits, Delaney took comfort in the warmth and healing quality of a particular shade of yellow, rendered as extremely radiant and frantic, with a vibrancy that nearly blinds the spectator (Snyder). Yellow, when considered in tandem with aspects of Delaney's biography, immediately calls to mind the life and torment of the artist Vincent Van Gogh, who also fixated on that color and "poured the torture of mental illness into his art" (Capozzola 12). Delaney revered Van Gogh and often wrote notes to remind himself of "the sculpture and structure of color" as Van Gogh had done (Cohen 227). But Delaney's obsession with yellow was of emotional and psychological significance, for while he was painting portraits of Baldwin throughout the 1960s, Delaney suffered increasingly from episodes of depression and alcohol consumption. These burdens have a lot to do with his psychological and emotional journey inward and their effects became outwardly visible through his paintings, including the portraits. By 1961, alcoholism and schizophrenia eventually took over his life and were to be the causes of repeated hospitalizations and of his eventual death in March 1979.

Delaney's canvases are not unmediated illustrations of his mental state. When he was engaged in the act of painting, the artist felt in control of the voices in his head. It was by way of putting paint on the surface and moving it around that he was able to confront the belief that, as Baldwin had written in 1955, "the only real concern of the artist [should be] to recreate out of the disorder of life that order which is his art" (qtd. in Capozzola 12). As had been the case with Van Gogh, painting for Delaney was an act of faith and internal healing, a move that required both physical presence in front of the subject and spiritual transcendence beyond the subject. The finite limits of painting as a medium allowed Delaney to open up to an abstract language that was based in a combination of vision (outward forms) and intuition (inward journey). His painted surfaces, as seen in the 1963 portrait, transform different sensations of light and color on the canvas while also creating the illusion of inwardly expanding space. His concern with the play of light makes his painted surfaces a place of spiritual significance. However, his use of light is inseparable from his focus on the color yellow, which, again, became his psychological and spiritual obsession and solace. With the artist, bright yellow and the intensity of light are symbolic of revelation, regeneration, and redemption—themes that are also prevalent in many of Baldwin's writings (Morse).

At the time the portrait was created, Baldwin was at the height of his literary powers, and themes of light, healing, and redemption abounded in his controversial novel *Another Country* (1962), which had become a bestseller, and his recently published *The Fire Next Time* (1963). This is one of several portraits of Baldwin that Delaney conjured, again not from the live model but rather from a combination of memory and the careful study of light. In turn, it was Baldwin who recognized, understood, and best articulated, through words, Delaney's journey inward (the "inner light") as a means of revelation. Light for both Delaney and Baldwin was metaphorical, signifying a search for truth and reality where others could not see it. That is, through symbolic reference to luminosity via words and images, both men sought that middle ground between vision and visuality. In his writings, Baldwin, taking Delaney as his artistic and spiritual muse, was often preoccupied with the concept of seeing and not seeing the light—a perception also related to exile. Both Baldwin and Delaney felt compelled to transplant themselves to France as a gesture toward seeing more clearly. Exile offered both men "the space to work through [their] sense of being different; it also gave [them] somewhere to hide from that difference" (Capozzola 10). For both, exile was an experience considered as both spiritual and physical.

Several of Baldwin's essays published in *Notes of a Native Son* (1955) dealt with the condition of the exile as a result of difference. Throughout those texts, Baldwin chose his words carefully, insisting that he was not an expatriate but an exile, someone who had been rejected by America. Delaney implicitly agreed in noting there was a marked difference between the expatriate and the exile: "One must belong before one may not then belong. I belong here in Paris. I am able to realize myself here. I am no expatriate" (Stovall 181). For Delaney, to belong meant to be accepted. Delaney's portraits of Baldwin grapple with the dichotomy between the expatriate and the exile, that between the physical and the spiritual by way of form, color, and light on a two-dimensional surface. The portraits are visual attempts by Delaney to find a consoling space somewhere in between the spiritual and physical realms, in between the inward journey and the outward hardships of existence.

A related point in association with exile is that Baldwin and Delaney shared existential unease about defining the "self" and carried anxieties over identity and alienation. According to Douglas Field, these sentiments permeated much of post–Second World War culture and fed into an attraction to exile and expatriation for large numbers of American writers, artists, and filmmakers (178). This was especially true for African Americans whose status as racial pariahs in the United States contributed to urgencies around these concerns. In many of his novels, Baldwin created protagonists who, much like himself, "are frequent travelers in search of a sense of home, characters who confuse the physical displacement of exile with an interiority of belonging" (Field 188). The notions of alienation, physical displacement, and search for interiority are visually manifested through Delaney's probing portraits of Baldwin. In order to better understand this dynamic, it is important to mention the significant role that portraiture has played in the connection between African American art and identity formation, re-formation, and de-formation. The African American portrait is, in its literal and figurative operations, a method of social and psychological negotiation, adjustment, and intervention. Such is the case with many of the painted and drawn portraits of Baldwin by Delaney.

As a genre, portraiture has been central and critical to aspirations of identity and confirmation in African American visual representation. In the United States, African Americans have felt the pressing need to reconstruct their image ever since their arrival in the Americas. This desire was accelerated during the Harlem Renaissance and New Negro

Movement, a time period and cultural events that exemplified the power and necessity of refashioning and (re)naming the self. In the art-historical literature, Delaney's portraits of Baldwin are typically described as creative attempts by the artist to plunge deeper into the "inner soul" of the writer, that part of the self or character that is elusive. However, the very nature of portraiture thwarts the endeavor and enforces limits, for it is the superficiality of the outward appearance of the subject of the portrait and the attempt at rendering a likeness that frustrate the desire to know the subject's interiority.

Although Delaney's portraits of Baldwin often show brilliant light and vibrant colors, there is a formal stillness about them. That is to say, there exists "a heightened degree of self-composure that responds to the formality of the portrait-making situation" (Brilliant 8). The solemn quietude of Delaney's 1945 and 1963 portraits of Baldwin indicates the seriousness of the endeavor and the timelessness of the portrait image as a statement intended to sum up a life. In an attempt to describe Baldwin's "inner life" through an image of likeness, the portraits themselves become private displays rendered public due to Baldwin's growing reputation and notoriety as a literary celebrity and cultural icon. As self-conscious exercises into probing the interior life of the sitter as well as himself, Delaney's portraits of Baldwin escape from the boundaries of privacy into the public realm, thereby confusing and troubling the line between the two.

Delaney's 1965 *Portrait of James Baldwin*,[6] now located at the Chrysler Museum, was painted while the two men were in Paris but also when Baldwin was an active participant in the civil rights movement. Typical of Delaney, the portrait contains many vibrant colors that release a nearly palpable "psychological energy" (Snyder). The artist's close relationship with Baldwin had much to do with the intense intimacy of the portrait. Behind the face is a chromatically charged lemon-yellow backdrop that brings the face of the subject into sharp focus. Both the background and Baldwin's face are impressionistic, employing highly textured strokes of mustard-colored paint to highlight prominent features, such as Baldwin's forehead, brow, nose, and chin. Pastel blues, warm pinks, burnt reds, and flecks of lavender add dimension to the darker, receding parts of the face. In his written reflection on this portrait, Baldwin fixated on the philosophical phenomenon of alternating vision—of seeing and not seeing, of revelation and ignorance. Baldwin wrote that "Beauford's work leads the inner and the outer eye, directly and inexorably, to a new confrontation with reality" (Baldwin, "On the Painter" 45).

Both the 1963 and 1965 portraits of Baldwin are charged with a combined human presence and spirituality through the use of color and light, and the materiality of the medium. In each, the lone figure of Baldwin is placed in "the special intersection of the world of light and the subjective consciousness" that Delaney attempted to bring to his portraits (*Les*

Amis). Both images are also expressive, most notably in the rendering of the eyes, bringing to life the expression that "the eyes are the mirror of the soul and reflect everything that seems to be hidden; and like a mirror, they also reflect the person looking into them" (*Les Amis*). As the most intimate and expressive feature of the face, the eyes draw us close to the mind, soul, emotions—the "inner life" of Baldwin who "finds his place in history through his literature" as well as through the unique visual language of Delaney (*Les Amis*).

Conclusion

Over the decades since his death in 1987, James Baldwin's image has proliferated in various visual forms that include, in addition to paintings and photographs, pencil drawings, caricatures, graphic media, cinema, murals, and watercolors. The sheer number of these in existence today attests to Baldwin's visual ubiquity. He is perhaps one of the most, if not *the* most, visually represented writer of the twentieth century. Through these forms of visual representation, we get a sense of his temperament and changing moods that hint at an internal life at specific historical moments. Through various mediums, he has been portrayed as pensive, inspired, coy, playful, vulnerable, and angry in his assorted roles as writer, orator, civil rights leader, and advocate.

Baldwin gradually came to understand that living a public life meant posing for pictures, constantly negotiating between the public and the private, the exterior and the interior, agency and inward reflection. For Baldwin, the search to attain a sense of self that was both coherent and compassionate became a motif in his life, in his writing, and in his visualization by others. Delaney's portraits of Baldwin set out to expose the tensions of the public (outer/physical/objective) and private (inner/psychological/emotional) self. Similarly, Baldwin's writings and commentaries about Delaney focus on the artist's public struggles as a black artist in a white-dominated society and his tumultuous inner visions tormented by mental illness, poverty, and the tortuous process of coming to terms with his homosexuality.

Delaney's paintings in general, and his portraits of Baldwin in particular, are less about aesthetic appreciation of what is seen or recorded and more about attempts at revelation of things not seen by way of the visual. It was Baldwin, the subject of these and many other portraits by Delaney, who perhaps had the profoundest understanding of the artist's external and internal worlds along with insight into his own inner vision. Baldwin is at his most eloquent when he makes observations about the visual by way of Delaney's art. Baldwin noted, for example, that Delaney clearly "practiced seeing first, then painting" (Baldwin, "On the Painter" 45). His aim, Baldwin insisted, was

> not to produce fine art for us to look at from a distance, but rather, to see things we do not want to see; to see our world and to love even that which is considered the least of it. He transformed darkness into beauty—a beauty that seemed to have mattered most to him ... We can only comprehend Delaney as an artist after we have learned the practice of seeing the world—not merely its colors or its dimensions, but the spirit of the light shaping it in our eyes and minds. (Baldwin, "On the Painter" 45)

Baldwin's words not only conjure a powerful philosophical statement in and of itself but also reveal the depths of the writer's penetration into Delaney's mode of seeing beyond the visual. Writer and painter were truly spiritual father and son, for it is Delaney's portraits of Baldwin that reveal the deepest insights into the writer, and reciprocally, it is Baldwin's words here and elsewhere that reflect the author's profoundest respect for and awareness of Delaney's inward journey.

Notes

1 An image of this painting can be accessed at lesamisdebeauforddelaney. blogspot.com/2011/08/beaufords-portraits-of-james-baldwin.html.

2 This quote is based on notes taken from an essay written by Baldwin and now located in the Schomburg Center for Research in Black Culture as part of a restricted archive that was recently acquired by the center.

3 An image of this painting can be accessed at philamuseum.org/collections/ permanent/92320.html.

4 In recent years, scholars have noted parallels in terms of style and content between some of Baldwin's writings and those of William Blake. See Shulman 151–70.

5 An image of this painting can be accessed at npg.si.edu/object/npg_NPG.98.25.

6 An image of this painting can be accessed at antiquesandthearts.com/chrysler-museum-enhances-collectionwith-beauford-delaney-portrait-of-james-baldwin/.

Works Cited

Baldwin, James. *Collected Essays*. Library Classics of the United States, 1998.
Baldwin, James. *Notes of a Native Son*. Beacon Press, 1955.
Baldwin, James. "On the Painter Beauford Delaney." *Transition*, no. 18, 1965, p. 45.

Baldwin, James. *The Price of the Ticket*. St. Martin's Press, 1985.

Brilliant, Richard. *Portraiture*. Harvard UP, 1991.

Capozzola, Christopher. "Beauford Delaney and the Art of Exile." *Gay & Lesbian Review*, vol. 10, no. 5, Sept.–Oct. 2003, pp. 10–12.

Cohen, Rachel. *A Chance Meeting: Intertwined Lives of American Writers and Artists, 1854–1967*. Random House, 2004.

Darton, Eric. "The Unusual Door: Preliminary Notes on James Baldwin and Pedagogy." *Tupelo Quarterly*, vol. 1, no. 4, 14 July 2014, tupeloquarterly.com/the-unusual-door-by-eric-darton. Accessed 24 Aug. 2018.

Delaney, Beauford. *Dark Rapture*. 1941, private collection.

Delaney, Beauford. *Portrait of James Baldwin*. 1945, Philadelphia Museum of Art. "Collections: *Portrait of James Baldwin*," *Philadelphia Museum of Art*, 2018, philamuseum.org/collections/permanent/92320.html. Accessed 25 Aug. 2018.

Delaney, Beauford. *Portrait of James Baldwin*. 1963, Smithsonian National Portrait Gallery. "James Baldwin," *Smithsonian National Portrait Gallery*, npg.si.edu/object/npg_NPG.98.25. Accessed 25 Aug. 2018.

Delaney, Beauford. *Portrait of James Baldwin*. 1965, Chrysler Museum of Art. "Portrait of James Baldwin," *Chrysler Museum of Art*, chrysler.emuseum.com/objects/64333/portrait-of-james-baldwin?ctx=4fbee5c7-cf0a-4cf6-8867-3ab41def51f3&idx=0. Accessed 25 Aug. 2018.

Dempsey, Joan. "Waiting for You: Beauford Delaney as James Baldwin's Inspiration for the Character Creole in 'Sonny's Blues.'" *Obsidian: Literature in the African Diaspora*, vol. 12, no. 1, 2011, pp. 60–78. JSTOR, jstor.org/stable/44489341. Accessed 24 Aug. 2018.

Exhibition label for *James Baldwin*, by Beauford Delaney. "James Baldwin," *Smithsonian National Portrait Gallery*, npg.si.edu/object/npg_NPG.98.25. Accessed 18 Dec. 2017.

Field, Douglas. "'One Is Mysteriously Shipwrecked Forever, in The Great New World': James Baldwin from New York to Paris." *Paris, Capital of the Black Atlantic: Literature, Modernity, and Diaspora*, edited by Jeremy Braddock and Jonathan P. Eburne, Johns Hopkins UP, 2013, pp. 175–99.

Foster, Hal, editor. *Vision and Visuality*. Bay Press, 1988.

Katoch, Rudy. "James Baldwin, Art and Queer Culture." 2 Dec. 2014, rudykatoch.com/james-baldwin-art-queer-culture/. Accessed 17 July 2016.

Kelleher, Maureen. "Art Essay: Ba'lls to the Wa'll, Ya'll." *Art Times Journal*, July 2014, arttimesjournal.com/art/Art_Essays/july-14-maureen-kelleher/beauford-delaney.html. Accessed 24 Aug. 2018.

Leeming, David. "An Interview with James Baldwin on Henry James." *The Henry James Review*, vol. 8, no. 1, Fall 1986, pp. 47–56. doi: 10.1353/hjr.2010.0001.

Leeming, David. *James Baldwin: A Biography*. Alfred A. Knopf, 1994.

Les Amis de Beauford Delaney. "Beauford's Portraits of James Baldwin—Part 2." 20 Aug. 2011, lesamisdebeauforddelaney.blogspot.com/2011/08/beaufords-portraits-of-james-baldwin_20.html. Accessed 24 Aug. 2018.

Mirzoeff, Nicholas. "On Visuality." *Journal of Visual Culture*, vol. 5, no. 1, 2006, pp. 53–79.

Morse, Eleanor. "James Baldwin: Beyond Black and White." *Face-to-Face*, National Portrait Gallery, Smithsonian Institution, 4 Nov. 2014, npg.si.edu/blog/james-baldwin-beyond-black-and-white.

Shulman, George. "Baldwin, Prophecy, and Politics." *A Political Companion to James Baldwin*, edited by Susan J. McWilliams, UP of Kentucky, 2017, pp. 151–70.

Snyder, Megan. "Delaney's 'Portrait of James Baldwin' Placed at Chrysler Museum." *Mace & Crown*, 2016, maceandcrown.com/2016/03/05/james-baldwin-chrysler-museum. Accessed 18 Dec. 2017.

Stovall, Tyler. *Paris Noir: African Americans in the City of Light*. Houghton Mifflin, 1996.

Tempkin, Ann. "Additional Information on *Portrait of James Baldwin*, by Beauford Delaney." *Philadelphia Museum of Art*, philamuseum.org/collections/permanent/92320.html. Accessed 24 Aug. 2018. Originally published in *Gifts in Honor of the 125th Anniversary of the Philadelphia Museum of Art*, Philadelphia Museum of Art, 2002, p. 109.

Valentine, Victoria L. "Schomburg Acquires James Baldwin Archive, Including Letters to Beauford Delaney Who Painted Many Portraits of the Writer." *Culture Type*, 15 Apr. 2017, culturetype.com/2017/04/15/schomburg-acquires-james-baldwin-archive-including-letters-to-beauford-delaney-who-painted-many-portraits-of-the-writer. Accessed 24 Aug. 2018.

Wallace, Caroline. "Beauford Delaney: Portrait of James Baldwin." *Haus der Kunst*, postwar.hausderkunst.de/en/artworks-artists/artworks/portrait-of-james-baldwin-portraet-james-baldwins. Accessed 24 Aug. 2018.

3

Lessons in Light: Beauford Delaney's and James Baldwin's "Unnameable Objects"

Tyler T. Schmidt

I encountered it again this summer at The Studio Museum in Harlem: Max Petrus's photograph *Beauford Delaney and James Baldwin, Paris, France, 1976*. In the image, the two hold hands as they walk down the street; but Baldwin, looking away from the camera at something outside the frame, walks ahead as if leading Delaney.[1] In his last years, Delaney looks, with his high halo of white hair and bushy beard, saintly. Beatific if not exactly beaming in the way poet Edward Field remembered his own first meeting with the painter: "While Beauford sketched me shortly after I met him, he gave me my first marijuana cigarette, and I promptly fell asleep, only to awaken hours later to find him beaming at me from his easel—Beauford always beamed in a particularly embracing way" (11). Field's snapshot of Delaney in prose, one in which marijuana is cited as a kind of fuel for the imagination, functions as a record of the painter's own creation of a portrait in paint; the moment underscores the unsteady relationship between seeing, painting, and writing as well as the murky layers of historical remembrance that this chapter, shuttling similarly between word and images, explores.[2]

Petrus's image of Delaney and Baldwin always surfaces first when I think of the pair, the sort of queer coupling that shapes so many of us in the tribe of "sexually different" looking for ancestry. Civil rights celebrity leads his teacher, roles inverted. It is an image that leads us to contemplate the ways the radical imagination shuttles between and is fostered within these bonds across age, region, sex, and genre. The images collected in one's mind of symbolic brotherhood, the queer kinship formed through visual and textual associations, could be seen as acts of the radical imagination and it is one of the forms that this essay examines or perhaps (risking irritation) enacts. In positioning Baldwin and Delaney as collaborators, as kindred commentators of the civil rights movement, I am particularly interested in portraiture, including both men's negotiations of its limits, as a site where the radical imagination is expressed. The radical imagination of Baldwin and Delaney (though in his case its use is more opaque) is predictably characterized as an expression of political consciousness that challenges systems of oppression and equally pervasive, corrosive racial representations. My inquiry into Baldwin and Delaney as artistic interlocutors interested in new narratives about the civil rights movements defines the radical imagination more broadly to encompass what Janice Radway describes as an "attentiveness to the affective, the cultural, and the experiential" (xii). It is an approach to history and its icons informed by an "abnormal sensitivity," a concept I examine more fully below.

Baldwin paid homage to Delaney as mentor, muse, brother, guide, and broken prophet in so many ways. "He became, for me, an example of courage and integrity, humility and passion. An absolute integrity: I saw him shaken many times and I lived to see him broken but I never saw him bow," he writes in "The Price of the Ticket" (1985), a couple of years before his own death (832). Petrus's photo of the pair is an image of first recall, too, because it is a moment of care. Delaney appears a bit disoriented. I remember this because I recognize the brokenness.

It is almost impossible to write about the relationship between Delaney and Baldwin and not slip into the syrupy language of brotherhood and muse that I just used. Baldwin did much to craft these romantic notions when he baldly spoke of his artistic debts to Delaney: "His example operated as an enormous protection" against a racially monolithic art scene in the West Village, showing Baldwin "that a black man could be an artist" ("Price" 832). Baldwin's attention to his guide's "absolute integrity" is also a helpful description of Delaney's approach to portraiture, particularly the figures of racial activism and aesthetic conundrums discussed in this chapter.

The importance of Delaney to Baldwin as spiritual and artistic mentor is often cited but the imprint of Baldwin's writings about America's racial struggles in the 1960s, particularly "Letter from a Region in My Mind," on Delaney's civil rights portraits, including his Rosa Parks series, deserves fuller attention for what we might learn about portraiture as a site of the radical imagination and as an underappreciated genre in civil rights movement art. Furthermore, the intellectual/aesthetic exchanges between Baldwin and Delaney invite us to think more expansively about how certain kinds of coexistences redefine activism. In this chapter I consider a divergent collection of artifacts—paintings, poems, prose portraits, film—as particular engagements within the civil rights movement in order to better understand the ongoing, largely improvisational collaboration between Delaney and Baldwin. Looking at several of Delaney's paintings that engage both abstraction and social commentary, I discuss these images as crucial forms of activism and connect them to Baldwin's own expansive aesthetic instruction, key moments of which he documented in his essays.

A formative text that inspired Delaney to comment visually and more overtly on the civil rights movement was Baldwin's "Letter from a Region in My Mind," published in the November 17, 1962 issue of *The New Yorker*, an essay that gained widespread attention. The letter's candor about the damages of racism, most devastating for black Americans but also for white people, resonated with Delaney. He praised Baldwin for how the essay articulated "so much that we feel but cannot put into words," and tellingly, given the financial and psychological hardships that marked this period of Delaney's life, his admiration extended to Baldwin's ability to navigate as an artist, "to keep your life moving and of one piece" (Leeming 159). Delaney's shattered self found reflection in Baldwin's missive: "One did not have to be very bright to realize how little one could do to change one's situation; one did not have to be abnormally sensitive to be worn down to a cutting edge by the incessant and gratuitous humiliation and danger one encountered every working day, all day long" ("Down" 298). Reading Delaney's art as an overlooked form of civil rights discourse asks us to be, indeed requires us to be, abnormally sensitive to the aesthetic choices and political projects of both Delaney and Baldwin, particularly their collaborative interchange of creativity and political principles. In reseeing this work we might come to the conclusion that the radical imagination is concerned as much with embracing this abnormal sensitivity as a necessary and valuable political stance as it is with leveling more overt forms of political critique. Given the ways that queers were historically thought of as being overly sensitive, fragile, and dramatic, just "too too," this charge to embrace an abnormal sensitivity is particularly compelling to those in our current cultural moment who see racial and sexual injustices as well as our actions to remedy them as often interdependent. As the textual readings that follow illustrate, Baldwin directs us to think about Delaney's portraits as a practice of sensitivity to the painted subject and to us as viewers returning to see these paintings anew.

As preface to our inquiry into these sensitive portraits, briefly consider two realist images of Delaney by Georgia O'Keefe as well as Delaney's 1962 self-portrait in radiant yellow. In a charcoal drawing of Delaney from 1943, O'Keefe renders him disembodied, hovering in white space, looking wide-eyed at the viewer and warmly smiling. While O'Keefe may have not intended her pastel of Delaney from the same year, a wartime portrait, as a civil rights statement, this visual artifact integrates him into a circle of American modernism that bears the heavy imprint of O'Keefe's curation and aesthetics. Delaney's biographer David Leeming notes that the painter's journals commented on modernist photographers including Stieglitz and Steichen and were full of reflections on light and composition. Leeming writes that Beauford "found a concern for light and the possibility of using light and color abstractly to express the true 'reality' of a subject" (63).

In exploring the potential of portraiture as a form of tribute or icon creation, Delaney, in sharp contrast to O'Keefe's renderings of him, embraced abstraction as an approach that could better reveal the complexities of a sitter's interior selves. This desire to do something different with the form is evident in his 1962 *Self Portrait*, which Amy M. Mooney claims "functions as an assertion of independence" (qtd. in Mercer 37). While this independence has largely been understood as aesthetic, a repeated investigation into what Eloise Johnson has described as "fauvist-infused abstraction," we might understand it, through Baldwin's discussion of artists' roles in social change, as an assertion of social freedom (46). In this self-portrait, Delaney's ochre face and bulky sweater, thick with paint, share a chromatic affinity with his portrait of Marian Anderson and the first of his Rosa Parks paintings, images that can be more convincingly located within the context of the civil rights movement.[3]

Delaney's "enormous painting" of Marian Anderson (1965) is one of the most direct examples of the intellectual/aesthetic interplay between Baldwin and the painter. It memorialized the concert, "fixed it in time" as Baldwin phrased it, that he attended as Delaney's guest, an event that Baldwin named as pivotal to his understanding of art and activism ("Price" 832). In Delaney's portrait, Anderson radiates dignity and grace in a field of his signature yolky yellows.[4] In "The Price of the Ticket," decades later, Baldwin gives us a fuller—vibrant with affect—context for reading the portrait: "I still remember Miss Anderson, at the end of that concert, in a kind of smoky yellow gown, her skin copper and tan, roses in the air about her, roses at her feet." Baldwin names the memory that has traveled with him through the years, retrieves it and tries to paint the image through words, a paired portrait that competes and complements Delaney's own painting, which Baldwin stresses "he painted it, he said, for me" (832).

Positioned in contrast and salve to the indignities of Baldwin's job in the army, Delaney and Anderson (coupled in Baldwin's literary imaginary) instill in young Baldwin new forms of racial consciousness and aesthetic education.[5] Working as a railroad hand in Bell Mead, New Jersey, where the army was building a depot, Baldwin, who had to defer college and his writing aspirations to help support his family, resented the backbreaking labor and the racial animosities at the plant as well as the daily indignities and confrontations of living in a segregated, provincial town (Campbell 23–26). Delaney and Anderson, writes Baldwin, "were on hand to inform me that I had no right to permit myself to be defined by so pitiful a people" ("Price" 831). Offering models of the creative life, crucially as artists intent on challenging Jim Crow constrictions, Delaney and Anderson are positioned as an earlier generation of civil rights activists from which Baldwin as a black artist has benefited. He explains grandly: "If Beauford and Miss Anderson were a part of my inheritance, I was a part of their hope" (831).[6] Baldwin explicitly names Anderson's role as a civil rights activist, mentioning her navigation of segregated concert halls and her infamous exclusion by the Daughters of the American Revolution.[7] Delaney and Anderson, coupled in Baldwin's essay, become queer conduits to a storehouse of unconventional civil rights images and narratives.

In 1965, the year Delaney painted Marian Anderson, Baldwin penned his now well-known poetic tribute to the painter in *Transition,* "On the Painter Beauford Delaney." In it, he suggests the ways Delaney's paintings were a source for his aesthetic education with the oft-quoted statement "his seeing caused me to begin to see." Beauford's relentless reseeing and lessons on light were instructive for Baldwin, but when he states that "memory is a traitor and that life does not contain the past tense," referencing Delaney's propulsion to reject previous encounters with an object or person in order to see them anew, Baldwin cues us into his approach to history, specifically America's persistent oppressions and racial violence. Delaney's abstractions always seem to radiate in the now and Baldwin, as critic, reoriented himself to history through Delaney's example. He had to encounter the nation's racial conundrums, to "be prepared to see them every day," with an equally new gaze ("On the Painter" 720). Here might be the truly radical aspect of Delaney's lesson to Baldwin in seeing, the wrangling of the artist's attention away from the past. For a writer so urgently rooted in the historical, in a politics that insists his readers develop a similar historical consciousness, Delaney's call to see "anew," to narrate a history that is always girded in an unfolding "now," unsettled Baldwin's writing practices.

It is notable that Baldwin continues his meditation on seeing in his underappreciated essay "The White Man's Guilt," published in *Ebony* in August 1965, a few months after his essay on Delaney. He begins by naming white Americans' paradoxical vision: their refusal to see what they see. Here Baldwin's comments on color, unlike in his tribute to Delaney, are explicitly political. The "color of my skin," he writes, "seems to operate as a most disagreeable mirror," reflecting for white people their role in "an appallingly oppressive and bloody history." He notes that white people also see in his black presence a "disastrous, continuing, present condition which menaces them, and for which they bear an inescapable responsibility" (722). Complicating his earlier claim that "life does not contain a past tense," Baldwin instructs white Americans to reorient themselves to the past, to realize that "the great force of history comes from the fact that we carry it within us" (723). The persistence of history, as something shaping our present interiority, is an idea we see enacted in Delaney's pictorial response to the civil rights movement. Color as a disagreeable mirror for the white viewer might then, when extended to aesthetics and to what I have come to see as unexpected visual forms of civil rights activism, offer a useful theory for reading Delaney's politically slippery portraits of the 1960s. White Americans can no longer hide "behind the color curtain" (726); they are rousted by Baldwin, in this essay indebted to the visual rhetoric of painters, to account for a history that has "led them to a fearful, baffling place" (724).

The positioning of "The White Man's Guilt" is a complex one. Baldwin invites *Ebony*'s largely black readership to contemplate white people's historical avoidances as well as his proposals for getting Americans beyond this impasse; but he also directly hails, with echoes of Wright, white readers: "White man, hear me!" (722). Magdalena Zaborowska places the text within a body of "antiviolence literature" that "combined literary aesthetics with Baldwin's public activism by bringing together oral histories, political commentary and autobiography" (206). Baldwin's commitment to the literary imaginary at the end of the essay, specifically the image of the New England factory from Henry James's *The Ambassadors*, is what initially led me to the essay, curious to see James's utility in thinking about white guilt. Baldwin points out that James left us a kind of riddle: "We never know what this factory produces, for James never tells us" ("White Man's Guilt" 727). Again we arrive at a visual paradox: to imagine what we can't see, to see what isn't named. The factory's "unnameable objects" manufactured "at an unbelievable human expense" is employed by Baldwin in an attempt to see an abstraction—white supremacy—whose impact and reach are palpable, visible, and concrete.

Alongside the image of white people, "barricaded inside their history," who "remain trapped in that factory," Baldwin pays tribute to the "old men and women of Montgomery—those who waved and sang and wept and could not join the marching, but had brought so many of us to the place where we could march" ("White Man's Guilt" 727). This conclusion illustrates Baldwin's indebtedness to a visual discourse to both honor civil rights activism, including its invisible ancestry, and to formulate his own critique of white Americans' complacency. His acknowledgement of the ancestors watching from the margins, how present-day activism is indebted to the subtleties of history, provides a fitting frame for revisiting Delaney's own tribute to one of those marchers, Rosa Parks.

"She ain't getting up"

Beauford Delaney completed the first of three unconventional portraits of Rosa Parks in 1967, a time when he was closely following the protests by both antiwar demonstrators and disenfranchised African Americans in cities across the United States. It was the year, too, when Delaney took a course on modern art at the Musée d'Art Moderne, Paris, and told Henry Miller of his renewed commitment to portraits of black Americans rendered "in my fashion" (Leeming 172). The few critics who have mentioned Delaney's Rosa Parks series, noting that his exchanges with Baldwin in 1963 on America's ever-evolving civil rights struggles prompted early sketches for his Parks paintings, have not interpreted them as the activist, aesthetic experiments that they clearly are intended to be (Leeming 158–60; Wells). While a bit mysterious and incongruous as a series, they are important examples of Delaney's refusal to bifurcate his abstract paintings from his portraits, his refusal to "maintain stylistic consistency to which most Abstract Expressionists adhered" (Gibson 106).[8]

A radical imagination demands a reseeing, a re-visioning that is, of course, always a reckoning with competing and silent histories. We reckon with Rosa Parks, civil rights icon, differently when we return to Delaney's unexpected portraits of her precisely because it is her iconicity that is stripped away in the emotional intimacy, odd coupling, and impenetrable postures. In *Rosa Parks* (aka *Woman Seated on Bench*), from 1967, she sits in swirls of yellow; indeed, Parks is nearly levitating if we surrender to this plane of abstraction.[9] And of course we do. Delaney's yellows are always welcome.[10] We dally in the sunlight with the ever-hatted Ms. Parks. The rough swirls of her dress match the same-hued textures of the background. In a style described by Eloise Johnson as "fauvist-infused abstraction," the stature of Parks is rendered, through broad lines and thick paint, more monumental and nuanced than her undecipherable expressions (46). Her arms are crossed at the chest. Self-protection. Pointed refusal. Gestural defiance. What? It holds a bit of the "nah" printed on the Rosa Parks T-shirts that circulate in our current moment. We honor our outlaws differently now.

In the second untitled painting in the series, known as *Two Women Sitting on a Park Bench (Rosa Parks)* (from around 1970), we see Parks again enclosed, face unreadable to us, in a scene painted with sharper lines and details.[11] The pale expanse of sky and the watery yellow-green of land are pure planes of color. Parks is dressed in a bold red, from hat to dress to stockings. She is a vibrant figure among the pale hues. Richard Powell describes these moments, drawing from Henry Miller's insights into his work, as "chromatic excesses" (16). She sits on a bench with a white woman. In communion albeit a cold one, their relationship is unclear. The abstracted faces and averted gazes remind us that Delaney's Marian Anderson looks steadily ahead. The optimistic reader might view the painting as an integrationist statement or as one of feminist solidarity. Yet the white woman clutches her child in an almost possessive pose. Parks's hand rests at her neck. Though a public space, the moment feels undeniably private. A sense of turning in—a queer choice for a tribute to a public activist—permeates all the paintings in this series. Delaney turns back in the late 1960s to a revered activist made famous by protests of the 1950s and sees an intimate Parks, solitary and tentatively tethered.

Delaney's paintings of Parks reveal his unconventional approach to portraiture. The latter two paintings in the series blur the line between landscape and portrait. And all are distinct from Delaney's other portraits, such as those of Marian Anderson, Ahmed Bioud, or Stanislas Rodanski, in that abstraction dominates the canvas. His painting of Howard Swanson in 1967 comes closest to the style and mysteries of his first Parks painting completed the same year. Richard Powell argues that portraiture for Delaney was a "vehicle for sorting out an array of primarily visual issues: concerns of color and form that could easily be coupled with his painting a friend's likeness or an esteemed individual's spirit" (21). But portraiture for Delaney provided more than a space of aesthetic experimentation; it was a vehicle for thinking through new ways to express civic engagement, specifically a genre to tell different civil rights stories, a space to reimagine heroes.

In his textual tribute to Lorraine Hansberry, "Sweet Lorraine" (1969), as well as his rendering of Huey Newton discussed later, Baldwin also experiments with the portrait, focusing more on Hansberry's interiority than physicality. He describes her as a "small, shy, determined person, with that strength dictated by absolutely impersonal ambition" (757–58). Baldwin understood the artist as activist; Delaney's Parks paintings urge us to think of the activist as artist. The Parks series circumvents the patriotic impulses that portrait painting too often indulges, but Delaney doesn't elide the political. The paintings, while not precisely activist art, pay tribute to activism. In linking these portraits of Parks, the activist, to Marian Anderson, the artist, viewers can consider the symbiotic relationship of art and social change.

In turning to Delaney's third painting of Parks, from 1970, one is struck again by a pronounced shift in palette. In She Ain't Getting Up, Mrs. Parks, the wash of winter feels more mournful.[12] Its Parisian grays transport her and then us as viewers to this wintery space. A shadowy figure in the background steals her solitude. The black tree branches fracture the cloudy canvas. Only in this third painting does Parks look out to the viewer, her hands crossed at her lap. It would not be wrong to see bits of Delaney in her face as portraits inevitably contain snippets of their maker. Delaney's yellows are distilled now to dress and hat. She provides the only color to this wintery palette: Baldwin's disagreeable mirror held up in this fog of whiteness. The painting captures an activist in a solitary moment, in the middle of a different, more private, practice of freedom. In her reading of his 1962 self-portrait, Ann M. Mooney notes that Delaney's "deep saturation of yellow ... has a lasting afterimage" (qtd. in Mercer 87), and though the yellow here is paler, it similarly lingers in one's memory. The series as a whole might be thought of as an exploration of the afterlife of Rosa Parks. Not because she was gone or irrelevant in the late 1960s and 1970s when they were created, but because through experiments with color, line, and abstracted figuration, Delaney renders a woman in realms not quite here.

Part of the mystery of the series is temporal. Why does Delaney return to Parks in the late 1960s, over a decade after her acts of resistance, which by then had already been calcified into legend? The "delay" of Delaney's tribute is a queer choice, one that suggests he wanted to intervene in that mythmaking, to show us someone different. Heather Love's ever-insightful work on queer artists who "turn backward" highlights the "temporal splitting at the heart of all modernism" (6). Delaney possesses such a "temporal ambivalence," looking back in order to forward new understandings of paint and portraiture (8). Expressing his own skepticism of lineage, Delaney declared: "I don't want to know whom people descend from. I want to know what they are ascending to" (Powell 22). In unmooring her from the visual contexts (photographic, collective) from which she is typically read, Delaney places Parks within that ascendant vision, transporting her in a sense through the mysteries of abstraction (or at least an antirealism) to us today. Similarly, Baldwin cycles back in 1985 to the Marian Anderson concert of the early 1940s through Delaney's portrait of her from 1965. Baldwin's return occasions a new understanding of the Anderson painting as a tribute to Baldwin and Delaney's shared love of music and as a memento of the concert, a site of reevaluation of both race and art. For both artists, the radical imagination toys with, restructures, both temporality and affect. This is one of the moments of queer kinship mentioned in the opening of this chapter that I believe defines such an imagination. Delaney and Baldwin should be read as kindred artists interested in telling, in word and images, the histories contained in our now.

Delaney's rendering of Parks in 1967 repositions her away from the iconic status as citizen objector. In wresting her (letting her rest) from the photograph, the dominant medium for representing her and the civil rights movement more broadly, Delaney deviates also from more traditional forms of portraiture to experiment with a different mode of storytelling. In her nuanced analysis of its importance as both documentation and a form of activism in the civil rights movement of the 1960s, particularly in the organizing efforts of the Student Nonviolent Coordinating Committee (SNCC), Leigh Raiford notes that photography "proved a more accessible, contemplative, and democratic medium" (1132). To assert the painted portrait as both an underused and under-recognized mode of civil rights art, the history of portraiture as an often rarefied genre for the elite must be confronted. It is a tradition most often used to record the lives of wealthy patrons and a society's most famous figures. Portrait paintings, unlike the photographs of the movement that were circulated on posters and in newspaper articles, are often housed in private collections and museum holdings, limiting their reach and perhaps compromising their activist potential. In addition to the assumed elitism of portraiture, Delaney's experimentation, his incorporation of abstractionist and expressionist qualities, in his paintings of Rosa Parks risks further inaccessibility. Yet it is their distinctiveness as ill-fitting forms of activist art that merit their analysis in contrast to the "social movement photography" we so rightly revere (Raiford 1132).

In refusing the documentary mode found in much of the (or at least the best known) art of the civil rights movement, Delaney offers another way of seeing Parks. Baldwin arguably learned how to tell a different story, or to tell a story differently, from studying Delaney's portraits. In her analysis of iconic photographs of Rosa Parks, Nicole R. Fleetwood argues that the staged imagery of civil disobedience reduced her to a symbol of social change within a "decontexualized past" (34). Recognizing the power and necessity of art "to actualize black freedom struggles" as "part of what we might call the theater of social protest" (36), Fleetwood helps us see a different theatrical impulse in Delaney's staging of Parks in these mercurial portraits of protest. Given the increasingly institutionalized memories of the civil rights movement, paintings like Delaney's that reject social realist modes for representing heroism by embracing abstraction and illuminating interiority hold a growing importance in how we reimagine a more textured history of racial change (and the memories that accompany it) in America.

Baldwin's difficulty in representing Huey Newton, another looming figure of the Movement, is an interesting counterpoint. Mischievously describing Newton as "everybody's favorite baby-sitter" for his "most scrubbed" good looks, Baldwin balks at the same sort of domestication to which Parks was subjected. The "moment one tries to place him in any ordinary, respectable setting something goes wrong with the picture, leaving a space where one had thought to place Huey" ("To Be Baptized" 460). Even as Baldwin attempts to paint a picture of Newton, his physical appearance and scrutinizing mind, he names his failure to do so. The complexity of Huey's humanity disrupts representation—"something goes wrong with the picture." Baldwin's description of the impossibility to capture his subject as "leaving a space" gestures to abstraction, including the empty spaces in Delaney's portraits of Parks, an approach he embraced to convey the complexities and illegibility of his subject (460).

More recent scholarly efforts to radicalize Parks (or at least challenge her "domestication") provide a productive tension to Delaney's unexpected imagining of her, at least in part, in genteel, depoliticized, highly aestheticized ways. Jeanne Theoharis in her illuminating *The Rebellious Life of Mrs. Rosa Parks* writes to restore Parks to her complexity beyond one-dimensional icon, co-opted in a narrative of whitewashed American patriotism. Her historical redress provides insights for better appreciating the affective registers of Delaney's Parks paintings. Parks, for example, laments in letters the cultivated distance necessary for the civil rights protester, the sense of outsiderness that those who rebelled against segregationist customs no doubt felt: "We soothe ourselves with the salve of attempted indifference" (qtd. in Theoharis x). The alienation in Delaney's paintings of Parks, or certainly the turning in or reticence toward the viewer one feels, corresponds powerfully with Parks's own writing about loneliness. "I am nothing. I belong nowhere … There is just so much hurt, disappointment and oppression one can take" (qtd. in Theoharis xii). Delaney's approach to portraiture conveys this emotional weight of activism, perhaps invoking both the alienation and sense of unbelonging that marked his own struggles with depression. It would not be overdramatic to claim that Delaney recognized Parks's hurt and loneliness and rendered it as part of her heroism.

Theoharis also rightly questions acts of memorializing Parks that problematically simplify and sanitize her history as an activist. She argues that the recent dedication of a statue of Parks in the US Capitol "was treated as an act of racial justice in itself, the ceremony a stand-in for more concrete action" (vii). Danielle McGuire's interest in the early activism that shaped Parks's racial consciousness speaks to the often overlooked gendered dimensions of the civil rights movement. Parks was "deeply affected by the injustice in the Scottsboro case" and quickly became committed to documenting black women's often futile attempts to seek justice in "interracial rape cases" (15).[13] These scholarly revisions to the dominant narratives of Parks as an activist provide a context for reading Delaney's Parks paintings from a feminist perspective. I am interested, too, in Delaney's use of notation, a subscript invisible to viewers, to return these rather intimate portraits to statements of civil disobedience. Voicing Parks, Delaney wrote, "I will not be moved" and "She ain't getting up, Mrs. Parks" alongside sketches and on the backs of paintings. These inscriptions add another layer of vocality to these obliquely narrative paintings.

This voicing of Parks might be productively read alongside Rita Dove's examination of this historical moment in the poem sequence, *On the Bus with Rosa Park* (1999), which situates Parks's activism alongside lesser-known women of the civil rights movement, including Claudette Colvin and Mary Smith Ware, whose acts of civil disobedience predated Parks's. In doing so, Dove chips away at the mythology (one that still circulates today) of the lone heroine whose fatigue prompted a spontaneous refusal. The section also interrogates the limits of historical "recovery," the impossibility of adequately rendering Parks's role in "the history she made for us sitting there" (Dove 87). Both Delaney and Dove attempt through a modernist approach, blurred and fragmented, to capture Parks's dignity but also to convey her inscrutability. Dove's declaration that "Doing nothing was the doing" (83) provides a satisfying echo to the recurring image by Delaney of Parks at rest on a park bench.

The art of Delaney and Dove challenge, revise, but also retell civil rights history and grapple with the era's mythologies. Dove's poems underscore the often vexed relationship between our present memorializing and past activism. Decades earlier, Delaney was already looking back to an earlier public Parks and replacing her (by which I mean resituating her but also providing a substitute iconography of her) with more private, almost opaque portraits that need to be read in conversation with American folk painting, abstract expressionism, and postwar portraiture invested in racial and painterly intimacies. Baldwin, in conversation with Delaney, underscores that *how* we remember, the shape of our historical memory, are often crucial layers in the creative and critical investigations of African American artists.

The monumental fact of their presence

Because Delaney is overlooked as a cultural worker in relation to his era's civil rights movements—in the United States and his adopted France—I'd like to consider one more example of what I consider his visual activism. Delaney's under-loved *The Street Sweeper/Le Balayeur* (1968) should be situated within the trajectory of portraits of famous black Americans including Marian Anderson and Rosa Parks, works which Delaney explicitly named as responses to (or better named, I think, as contributions to) the civil rights movement. But the portrait is arguably even less understood as a contribution to the vibrant postcolonial critiques emerging in Paris and London in the 1950s and 1960s by African and Caribbean writers. The year of its creation, after all, was 1968, when student marches and worker strikes in Paris left Delaney rattled. *Le Balayeur* reminds us that we must return to Delaney's aesthetics and politics in order to position them in more transnational and trans-genre contexts.

Before considering *Le Balayeur*'s muted citations of these converging histories (anti-colonial movements, union organizing, America's urban unrest and civil rights protests), we should be sensitive to its visual radiance: its palette of watery yellows, muted lilac, an underwash of green.[14] His broom, the tool of his trade (and to some eyes the emblem of his subjection), disappears like the streetlamp into the blizzard of Delaney's famous lemony yellow, here more muted. The geometry of his legs is reminiscent of paintings by Bill Traylor, another modernist wonder. The remarkable portrait painter Kerry James Marshall has argued that artists like Bill Traylor and William Edmondson, who created outside segregated, exclusionary art institutions, have been resituated "from 'folk' to 'modern' artist" by an elitist, racially oblivious art world, an act which "underscores the capacity of reigning authorities to assess and confer ultimate value—a vital function of any supremacist franchise" (232). This "promotion" from folk hero to postwar urban subject names the liminal status, the ambiguous figuration of Delaney's street sweeper in postwar France. Marshall's comments about the problematic racial protocols of the art world intersect with the artistic representations of black workers discussed below, including the "prevailing equation of black art with manual labor" within the art world (Ott 109).

The street sweeper was a figure repeatedly cited to represent both the dignified resilience and economic struggles of the (post)colonial subject. Michel Tournier's 1986 *La Goutte d'or* (*Golden Drop*), for example, centers on an Algerian immigrant working as a street sweeper. In the 1968 film version (*Mandabi*) of Senegalese writer Ousmane Sembène's novel *Le Mandat* (*The Money Order*), published just two years before Delaney's painting, a nephew in Paris works as a street sweeper and sends money to family in Senegal. A scene in the film begins with a shot of the Eiffel Tower panning down to a twig-bound broom being dragged across the pavement. After observing the nephew, Abdou, mailing a letter home, broom in hand, we find him swirling water to clean the gutters with the Arc de Triomphe in the background. The juxtaposition of monuments to French nationalism and the immigrant labor that undergirds it could not be more overt. Interestingly, the nephew's work in Paris isn't named in the novel. There is only mention in Abdou's letter that "I have not come to France to play the beggar or the bandit, but to find work and earn a little money and, God willing, to learn a good trade. There is no work in Dakar" (Sembène 86). Sembène's decision to imagine him as a street sweeper, a job that belies the fantasies of rapid upward mobility held by his family back home, underscores both the marginalization and centrality of African immigrants to France's economy and indirectly critiques the barriers faced by these laborers attempting to integrate the country's trade unions.

Historian Pascal Blanchard, a chronicler of "Black France," in forwarding a narrative that in his words "is not just a history of victimization" cites "the exploited black street-sweeper" as one of the problematic symbols on which a reductive history might fixate (qtd. in Barbier). But Delaney's portrait urges us not to bypass this urban worker whose labor concretely cleans the city so quickly in a desire to find more attractive symbols of dignity and rebellion. His rendering of the street sweeper offers an aesthetic and social space that circumvents the victim/hero binary that too often dominates in images and narratives about immigrants. I would argue that in departing from a documentary, social realist style (popular not only in civil rights photography but in proletarian art of the early to mid-twentieth century), Delaney finds abstraction a practice that troubles the fixity of both racial identity and our historical accounts of it. This, too, is the intellectual labor of the radical imagination.

John Ott's thoughtful analysis of Palmer Hayden's *The Janitor Who Paints* (ca. 1937, 1940) as an invocation and reworking of the janitor as a proletarian hero is helpful for considering the pitfalls and promises of Delaney's representation of the street sweeper, another manual laborer burdened with symbolic sentimentality. Both Hayden and Delaney appeared in the Harmon Foundation's film *A Study of Negro Artists* (ca. 1937), which Ott analyzes in his excellent critique of the art world's fetishization of black labor and the problematic narratives it cultivates of black artists as "working-class amateurs" (Ott 107). Hayden's claim that *The Janitor Who Paints* was intended as a "protest painting" (Ott 102) offers a way of thinking about the overlaps and tensions between black laborers and black art, as well as African American artists' identification with and, for many, own employment as manual laborers in the early years of their careers. These conundrums and complexities are invisible in a surface reading of Delaney's portrait, but in aligning him with Hayden's janitor and Sembène's street sweeper, broader cultural critiques emerge.

In the tour de force "Take Me to the Water" (1972), in a collection dedicated, in part, to Delaney, Baldwin invokes a diasporic proletariat that helps to texture my reading of *Le Balayeur* as a postcolonial portrait aligned with the painter's investment in civil rights struggles throughout the world. With his characteristic preacher's rhetorical sweep, Baldwin writes:

> The South African coal miner, or the African digging for roots in the bush, or the Algerian mason working in Paris, not only have no reason to bow to Shakespeare, or Descartes, or Westminster Abbey, or the cathedral at Chartres: they have, once these monuments intrude on their attention, no honorable access to them. Their apprehension of this history cannot fail to reveal to them that they have been robbed, maligned, rejected: to bow down before that history is to accept that history's arrogant and unjust judgment. (381)

Baldwin's mention of intrusive monuments (many built by the exploited or enslaved black masons he names) is an uncanny echo of our present moment of contested Confederate statuary (and a reminder of art's role in the promulgation of our national myths). Baldwin has an uncanny way of doing that: leading us to our present moment. He was a prescient intellectual but his irritation with false monuments is further evidence that racial dispossession is America's changing same. Yet Baldwin wants us to consider black Americans' unequivocal rejection of this white-authored history: "It is not so easy to see that, for millions of people, life itself depends on the speediest possible demolition of this history, even if this means the leveling, or the destruction of its heirs" (381). In order to emerge from a painful history, Baldwin writes that subjugated people (to call them citizens would be a lie) must be able to "add to history the monumental fact of their presence" (381). Not leaving Baldwin's invocation of a geographically vague Africanness unremarked, the image of a diasporic proletarian that he crafts, idealized and invisibly gendered as it may be, provides an almost perfect lens for reseeing Delaney's *The Street Sweeper*. Like Baldwin, Delaney is reconceiving the idea of the "monument," not one built of stone or marble, rather one defined by bodily presence and unrecognized toil. By classifying Baldwin's "Take Me to the Water" and Delaney's portrait as textual and visual monuments that intervene in Eurocentric histories, we can better understand them as political projects that refigure the dispossessed and subjugated as crucial participants in global civil rights struggles. In Delaney's vision, the seamstress activist and the postcolonial street sweeper "have no reason to bow" to a history that has unwritten them (381).

Critic John Berger's term "heroic potentiality" can be usefully applied to the Parks paintings and *The Street Sweeper*, naming these figures' possible resonances for black viewers in both France and the United States in the late 1960s. Berger writes, "The function of the hero in art is to inspire the reader or spectator to continue in the same spirit from where he, the hero, leaves off." And then goes on: "The hero must be typical of the characters and class who at that time only need to be made aware of their heroic potentiality in order to be able to make their society juster and nobler" (211). The viewer, then, is prompted to take up the work of social justice, of racial equity, of anti-colonialism, finding her potentiality in the swirls of abstraction. We should, of course, be leery of cultural heroes, even those poised within the aesthetically innovative. Baldwin was rightly suspicious of mythmaking, witnessing personally and socially how these mythologies undergirded white supremacy. In "A Talk to Teachers" (1963), he notes, "What passes for identity in America is a series of myths about one's heroic ancestors" (683). The now-sanitized histories of Rosa Parks remind us that heroism is always subject to revisionist erasures. As Jeanne Theoharis notes, "We have grown comfortable with the Parks who is often seen but rarely heard," with an "image of Parks ... stripped of her political substance" ("How History"). Delaney's repeated attempts to capture Parks and Baldwin's struggles to represent Newton speak to the artistic challenges of figuring a person's inevitable mysteries and political intensities.

Delaney, in his journal, writes, "Keep balance between social forces and the individual," providing us a guide for reading the interplay between abstraction and portrait in these works, specifically how abstraction might be understood as a representation or better yet an invocation of those social forces imprinting the individual (Leeming 63). In this way, the street sweeper is also a figure of abjection; the social conditions that surround him—the indignities of segregation, the effects of white supremacy, postcolonial migration, labor exploitation—are not directly cited but they need not be opaque to us as viewers. The attention, however small, given to the interchanges between Delaney's portraits and his study of the events and writings about the civil rights movement in America highlights that critics have failed to consider the role that anti-colonialist writing and organizing in Europe may have played in Delaney's paintings, including *Street Sweeper* and *Café Scene* (1966). Baldwin's hailing of the black laborers across the African diaspora, the monumentless tribe, in "Take Me to the Water" is also a part of the postcolonial context that shaped Delaney's creative practice.

"Great art can only be created out of love," writes Baldwin in his essay on Delaney ("On the Painter" 721). The loving gaze that Delaney casts on the street sweeper, an identification with his blackness, still marked as foreign to the Parisian cityscape of 1968 (and in many ways alienated again now), informs his approach to portraiture more broadly. The image is one of his most instructive contributions to the US civil rights movement, implicitly linking his nation's quotidian heroism to the era's anti-colonial movements and insisting that a loving gaze (and inviting the white viewer to do the same) is its own act of heroic potentiality, that the affective layers of creativity and collaboration house their own activism. Painter Kerry James Marshall speaks persuasively on the necessity of a younger generation to confront "broader representations of human ideals than the post-imperial models" that populated his own training as an artist. Like Marshall's depiction of "heroic black figures who literally embody the artist's faith in the power of representation," Delaney celebrates the beauty of the black figure (Roelstraete 49). Given my interest in this chapter in the production of historical memory, how it changes and how it can be dangerously simplified, Baldwin's attention to the racialized mythologies churned out in America's imagination "factories" of white supremacy and his call to a diaspora of black laborers to memorialize their own existence, as I have demonstrated, can be profitably placed in conversation with Delaney's portraits as intimate monuments to the resilience and beauty of black people.

We often turn to images of enclosures for our feelings, containers that hold them, but Delaney's planes of abstraction can also be affective plains where depression and postcolonial disenfranchisement suitably sprawl. Delaney battled with what he called "periods of depression and negation" and relapses into alcoholism during this period (Leeming 159). But in these planes of luminosity, lessons in seeing, liberating acts of self-creation also swirl. In departing from a rigid realism in his depiction of Parks and the unnamed street sweeper, Delaney permits these figures to possess mystery. Explaining his affinity to abstraction, Delaney notes, "A form if it breathes some, if it has some enigma to it, [then] it is also the enigma that is abstract" (Gibson 106). As an antidote to white people's refusal to see their history, Baldwin admires black people's (and perhaps "enlightened" white people's) "attempts to re-create oneself according to a principle more humane and more liberating ... the attempt to achieve a level of personal maturity and freedom" ("White Man's Guilt" 723). Through this lens, Delaney's reimagining of civil rights activism (in subject matter and style), the merging of the figurative and the abstract, the union of the black American civil rights activist and the black French migrant worker, become crucial acts of self re-creation, part of the process for Delaney of crafting his own personal and aesthetic freedom. These paintings in their refusal to adhere to the trends and mandates of the art world and in their documentation of black people laboring toward liberation are activist art. Baldwin read Delaney's increasing moves towards pure abstraction, his color experiments, as "a most striking metamorphosis into freedom"

("On the Painter" 721). This was their shared project, a new vision of activism, the artist who claimed but also enacted on the page and canvas, not only the difficulties of representation but the practices, barriers, and feelings of freedom. Their collaborative examination of color and portrait, though underappreciated, is deeply entwined with the activism and art of the civil rights movement.

Light holds promise. Baldwin said it sparked a "new confrontation with reality" ("On the Painter" 721). It also illuminates the "great pain and terror" of our collective racial histories, including the unnameable objects produced in today's race factories ("White Man's Guilt" 723). Delaney's blizzard of color also cloaked the unnameable: his own racial pain, years of mental fragility, the cold winters of Clamart. Delaney was asked in 1969 if he was compelled to return to the United States "where the action is"; his response was "I can't go home because I never really left ... the body goes somewhere, that's all" (Leeming 175). Delaney's *Street Sweeper* reminds us that the "action" of political protest was occurring in Paris, too, in student protests, workers' strikes, anti-colonial intellectual work, and the ephemeral labor of city workers. The placement of his very personal sense of civil rights icons within abstraction asks us to ponder "where do bodies go?" and to conclude, at least visually, at least imaginatively, wherever they'd like.

Notes

1 This is one of a series of images taken by Max Petrus (a friend of Baldwin's) during Delaney's stay at St. Anne's Hospital for the Insane in Paris, to which he was admitted in the spring of 1975 and where he died, after several attempts to live independently, in March 1979.

2 I would like to thank Jessica Yood for her gentle and generous feedback during the composing of this chapter. Her guidance through my own enigmatic abstractions was crucial to its revisions.

3 An image of Delaney's 1962 self-portrait is available at the Detroit Institute of Arts website at dia.org/art/collection/object/self-portrait-42327. For links to color images of many of the paintings discussed in this chapter, please refer to the endnote corresponding to the mention of the painting in the text.

4 An image of the portrait of Anderson can be accessed at vmfa.museum/piction/6027262-7989392/.

5 Ralph Ellison in his essay "The Little Man at Chehaw Station" (1978) reminds us that these two, ideological transformation and aesthetic innovation, often occur in tandem.

6 Matt Brim argues that Baldwin's inheritance included a "sense of responsibility to defy the terms used by others to define his existence: 'black,' 'gay,' 'male,' 'writer'—terms of contestation, not connection" (41–42).

7 For a fuller discussion of the importance of Marian Anderson to Delaney, see Powell 23–25.

8 For a discussion of artists, including Delaney, whose work defied the edict of "pure" abstraction, see Gibson 88–113.

9 An image of *Rosa Parks* (aka *Woman Seated on Bench*) can be found at lesamisdebeauforddelaney.blogspot.fr/2010/04/beauford-and-civil-rights-movement.html.

10 The Rosa Parks paintings are curiously missing from Richard Powell's insightful analysis of Delaney's lifelong exploration of the color yellow as well as his aesthetic complexities and layered approaches to portraiture.

11 An image of *Untitled (Two Women on a Bench)* (ca. 1970) can be found at: lesamisdebeauforddelaney.blogspot.com/2014/05/rachel-cohens-tribute-to-beauford.html.

12 Beauford Delaney, *She Ain't Getting Up, Mrs. Parks* (1970). Private collection; courtesy of Michael Rosenfeld Gallery LLC, New York, NY.

13 Rosa Parks's role as an NAACP investigator of Recy Taylor's horrific rape in 1944 is slowly coming to broader public consciousness. The recent documentary *The Rape of Recy Taylor* (2017) explores Taylor's little-known role in the history of the civil rights movement. Taylor died recently on December 28, 2017, at 97 (Chan).

14 An image of *Le Balayeur* can be found at lesamisdebeauforddelaney.blogspot.com/2016/06/beauford-at-international-james-baldwin.html.

Works Cited

Baldwin, James. *Collected Essays*. Library of America, 1998.

Baldwin, James. "Color." Baldwin, *Collected Essays*, pp. 673–77.

Baldwin, James. "Down at the Cross: Letter from a Region in My Mind." Baldwin, *Collected Essays*, pp. 296–347.

Baldwin, James. "On the Painter Beauford Delaney." Baldwin, *Collected Essays*, pp. 720–21.

Baldwin, James. "The Price of the Ticket." Baldwin, *Collected Essays*, pp. 830–42.

Baldwin, James. "Sweet Lorraine." Baldwin, *Collected Essays*, pp. 757–61.

Baldwin, James. "Take Me to the Water." Baldwin, *Collected Essays*, pp. 353–403.

Baldwin, James. "A Talk to Teachers." Baldwin, *Collected Essays*, pp. 678–86.

Baldwin, James. "To Be Baptized." Baldwin, *Collected Essays*, pp. 404–74.

Baldwin, James. "The White Man's Guilt." Baldwin, *Collected Essays*, pp. 722–27.

Barbier, Marie. "'Blacks Are Not Regular Victims,' French Historian Says." *L'Humanité*, 9 Nov. 2011, humaniteinenglish.com/spip.php?article1928.

Berger, John. "A Few Useful Definitions." *Permanent Red: Essays in Seeing*. Writers and Readers, 1979.

Brim, Matt. *James Baldwin and the Queer Imagination*. U of Michigan P, 2014.

Campbell, James. *Talking at the Gates: A Life of James Baldwin*. Viking, 1991.

Chan, Sewell. "Recy Taylor, Who Fought for Justice after a 1944 Rape, Dies at 97." *The New York Times*, 29 Dec. 2017, nytimes.com/2017/12/29/obituaries/recy-taylor-alabama-rape-victim-dead.html?smid=pl-share. Accessed 24 Aug. 2018.

Delaney, Beauford. *Café Scene*. 1966, private collection. "Café Scene, 1966: The Beautiful in the Mundane," Hanna Gressler, *Les Amis de Beauford Delaney*, 15 July 2017, lesamisdebeauforddelaney.blogspot.com/2017/07/cafe-scene-1966-beautiful-in-mundane.html. Accessed 25 Aug. 2018.

Delaney, Beauford. *Marian Anderson*. 1965, Virginia Museum of Fine Arts. "Marian Anderson (Primary Title)," *VMFA*, vmfa.museum/piction/6027262-7989392/. Accessed 25 Aug. 2018.

Delaney, Beauford. *Rosa Parks* (aka *Woman Seated on Bench*). 1967, Michael Rosenfeld Gallery. "Beauford and the Civil Rights Movement," Monique Y. Wells, *Les Amis de Beauford Delaney*, 23 Apr. 2010, lesamisdebeauforddelaney.blogspot.fr/2010/04/beauford-and-civil-rights-movement.html. Accessed 25 Aug. 2018.

Delaney, Beauford. *Self Portrait*. 1962, Detroit Institute of Arts. "Beauford Delaney: Self Portrait, 1962," *Detroit Institute of Arts*, 2018, dia.org/art/collection/object/self-portrait-42327. Accessed 25 Aug. 2018.

Delaney, Beauford. *She Ain't Getting Up, Mrs. Parks*. 1970, private collection.

Delaney, Beauford. *Street Sweeper/Le Balayeur*. 1968, private collection. "Beauford at the International James Baldwin Conference in Paris," Monique Y. Wells, *Les Amis de Beauford Delaney*, 4 June 2016, lesamisdebeauforddelaney.blogspot.com/2016/06/beauford-at-international-james-baldwin.html. Accessed 25 Aug. 2018.

Delaney, Beauford. *Untitled (Two Women on a Bench)*. ca. 1970, private collection. "Rachel Cohen's Tribute to Beauford," Monique Y. Wells, *Les Amis de Beauford Delaney*, 10 May 2014, lesamisdebeauforddelaney.blogspot.com/2014/05/rachel-cohens-tribute-to-beauford.html. Accessed 25 Aug. 2018.

Dove, Rita. *On the Bus with Rosa Parks*. W. W. Norton, 1999.

Ellison, Ralph. "The Little Man at Chehaw Station." *The Collected Essays of Ralph Ellison*, Modern Library, 2003, pp. 493–523.

Field, Edward. *The Man Who Would Marry Susan Sontag: And Other Intimate Literary Portraits of the Bohemian Era*. U of Wisconsin P, 2007.

Fleetwood, Nicole R. *Troubling Vision: Performance, Visuality, and Blackness*. U of Chicago P, 2011.

Gibson, Ann Eden. *Abstract Expressionism: Other Politics*. Yale UP, 1997.

Hayden, Palmer. *The Janitor Who Paints*. ca. 1930, Smithsonian American Art Museum. "The Janitor Who Paints," *Smithsonian American Art Museum*, americanart.si.edu/artwork/janitor-who-paints-10126. Accessed 25 Aug. 2018.

Johnson, Eloise. "Out of the Ashes: Cultural Identity and Marginalization in the Art of Beauford Delaney." *Notes in the History of Art*, vol. 24, no. 4, 2005, pp. 46–55. doi: 10.1086/sou.24.4.23207949.

Leeming, David. *Amazing Grace: A Life of Beauford Delaney*. Oxford UP, 1998.

Love, Heather. *Feeling Backward: Loss and the Politics of Queer History*. Harvard UP, 2007.

Mandabi. Directed by Ousmane Sembène. Grove Press, 1968.

Marshall, Kerry James. "Sticks and Stones …, but Names … " *Kerry James Marshall: Mastry*, edited by Helen Molesworth, Rizzoli, 2016, pp. 231–35.

McGuire, Danielle. *At the Dark End of the Street: Black Women, Rape, and Resistance—A New History of the Civil Rights Movement from Rosa Parks to the Rise of Black Power*. Vintage, 2011.

Mercer, Valerie J., et al. "New Art for a New Self-Awareness." *Bulletin of the Detroit Institute of Arts*, vol. 86, no. 1/4, 2012, pp. 18–41. *JSTOR*, jstor.org/stable/43492324. Accessed 24 Aug. 2018.

Ott, John. "Labored Stereotypes: Palmer Hayden's *The Janitor Who Paints*." *American Art*, vol. 22, no. 1, Spring 2008, pp. 102–15. doi: 10.1086/587918.

Powell, Richard. *Beauford Delaney: The Color Yellow*. High Museum of Art, Atlanta, 2001.

Radway, Janice. Foreword. *Ghostly Matters: Haunting and the Sociological Imagination*, by Avery F. Gordon, U of Minnesota P, 2008, pp. vii–xiii.

Raiford, Leigh. "'Come Let Us Build a New World Together': SNCC and Photography of the Civil Rights Movement." *American Quarterly*, vol. 59, no. 4, 2007, pp. 1129–57. doi: 10.1353/aq.2007.0085.

Roelstraete, Dieter. "Visible Man: Kerry James Marshall, Realist." *Kerry James Marshall: Mastry*, edited by Helen Molesworth, Rizzoli, 2016, pp. 45–56.

Sembène, Ousmane. *The Money-Order with White Genesis*. Heinemann, 1972.

Theoharis, Jeanne. "How History Got the Rosa Parks Story Wrong." *The Washington Post*, 1 Dec. 2015, washingtonpost.com/posteverything/wp/2015/12/01/how-history-got-the-rosa-parks-story-wrong/?utm_term=.593edba8685d. Accessed 24 Aug. 2018.

Theoharis, Jeanne. *The Rebellious Life of Mrs. Rosa Parks*. Beacon Press, 2014.

Wells, Monique Y. "Beauford and the Civil Rights Movement." *Les Amis de Beauford Delaney*, 23 Apr. 2010, lesamisdebeauforddelaney.blogspot.com/2010/04/beauford-and-civil-rights-movement.html. Accessed 24 Aug. 2018.

Zaborowska, Magdalena J. *James Baldwin's Turkish Decade: Erotics of Exile*. Duke UP, 2009.

PART TWO

Baldwin's Journalism and Literary Journalism

4

"To End the Racial Nightmare, and Achieve Our Country": James Baldwin and the US Civil Rights Movement

Kathy Roberts Forde

In late November 1962, *The New Yorker* magazine published James Baldwin's essay "Letter from a Region in My Mind," a penetrating indictment of white Americans' failure to recognize and address the country's long history of racial oppression, exploitation, and injustice. One month later, the small but culturally influential magazine *The Progressive* published Baldwin's short essay "Letter to My Nephew" in its special issue celebrating the centennial of the Emancipation Proclamation. Both magazines catered to white middle- and upper-class American readers—and these were exactly the readers Baldwin meant to address, a group including not only ordinary citizens but also journalists, public intellectuals, and political leaders in the highest levels of public office. When Dial Press published both essays as the book *The Fire Next Time* in early 1963, Baldwin's reading audience expanded. The book spent much of the year on *The New York Times*' Best Sellers list.

Published at a critical moment in the direct action phase of the civil rights movement—on the heels of the University of Mississippi integration crisis and immediately before the revolutionary events of the spring and summer of 1963 that included the Birmingham children's marches, black freedom protests, urban disturbances, the March on Washington, and the 16th Avenue Baptist Church bombing—Baldwin's words helped to awaken

white Americans to their responsibility for the destructive past and present
of institutionalized and individual racial discrimination against black life
in America.[1] *The Fire Next Time* and the essays that comprise it traveled
an expansive "circuit of communication" in the months following their
publication, circulating among a broad range of readers (Darnton 30). As
historian Peniel E. Joseph has noted, Baldwin was read by "everyone from
Black nationalists in Harlem and Ghana to white liberals" and "came to
represent the literary voice of an entire movement" (70). Baldwin's statement
thus contributed to a national conversation about and reckoning with the
black freedom struggle—its meanings, realities, and policy demands—
among not only ordinary Americans but also the most powerful political
leaders in the United States, including President John F. Kennedy, Attorney
General Robert F. Kennedy, and Vice President Lyndon B. Johnson. Baldwin
thus helped shape the Kennedy administration's private thinking and nascent
policies on civil rights issues in the spring and summer of 1963. The policy
work of the Kennedy administration, influenced in part by Baldwin's ideas,
ultimately led to federal civil and voting rights legislation and a partial
fulfillment of the goals of the civil rights movement.

In *The Fire Next Time*, Baldwin argued that if the United States were ever
to become the country of its aspirational ideals, black Americans must be
fully included in the national project. The process of this inclusion would be
dialogic, engaging white and black Americans in a continual conversation
through which the past and present would be constantly redescribed in the
struggle, as Baldwin put it, to "achieve our country":

> If we—and now I mean the relatively conscious whites and the relatively
> conscious blacks, who must, like lovers, insist on, or create, the
> consciousness of the others—do not falter in our duty now, we may be
> able, handful that we are, to end the racial nightmare, and achieve our
> country, and change the history of the world. (*Fire* 105)

The Fire Next Time offered a forceful interpretation, in the terms of the
period's white and black racial dualism, of what it would mean for the
United States to become a truly civil society that actually embraced and
enacted democracy, equality, freedom, and justice. It was not only a demand
and claim for national inclusion but also a powerful articulation of what the
country could and should be. In this way, Baldwin's message was of a piece
with a central message of the civil rights movement at large: the country
must begin to live by its civic ideals.

When Baldwin's essays and book appeared, few white intellectuals and
journalists writing in the popular press advocated for true social and political
equality for African Americans (Polsgrove, *Divided Minds* 155–59). His
words shocked, provoked, and challenged the dominant white American
frame for understanding race relations:

The only thing white people have that black people need is power—and no one holds power forever. White people cannot, in the generality, be taken as models of how to live. Rather, the white man is himself in sore need of new standards, which will release him from his confusion and place him once again in fruitful communion with the depths of his own being. And I repeat: the price of the liberation of the white people is the liberation of the blacks—the total liberation, in the cities, in the towns, before the law, and in the mind. (*Fire* 96–97)

James Baldwin was not a civil rights leader and activist. He was a writer living outside the spheres of political organization and public policy creation and, in fact, largely outside the country (he wrote major portions of *The Fire Next Time* in Turkey) (Zaborowska 7). His discussion of America's race problem in the *New Yorker* and *Progressive* essays and *The Fire Next Time* was not particularly political. It was historical, autobiographical, and moral in nature. It was an expression of Baldwin's "radical imagination," his capacity "to imagine the world, life and social institutions not as they [were] but as they might otherwise be," as Haiven and Khasnabish have defined the term (3). "The imagination is an intimate part of how we empathize with others," they explain, "the way we gain some sense of the forces that impact our lives, and the way we project ourselves into the future and gain inspiration and direction from the past" (4).

Baldwin offered a sharp-edged commitment to empathy as one tool for social and political change—empathy rooted in historical awareness and the recognition of contemporary institutional and personal oppressions. White people needed to be liberated from racialized thinking and their role as oppressors, past and present, just as black people needed to be liberated from unjust ideologies and systems of white supremacy. Baldwin insisted that such change, to be effected through the political process and policy creation, must be rooted in empathy one for another. Without empathy, he suggested, the American experiment was doomed. "If we do not now dare everything," Baldwin wrote as the final sentence of *The Fire Next Time*, "the fulfillment of that prophecy, recreated from the Bible in song by a slave, is upon us: *God gave Noah the rainbow sign, No more water, the fire next time!*" (106).

It was this radical dimension of Baldwin's message that cut through the noise of history and confusions of many white Americans, leading highly placed figures in the Kennedy administration as well as everyday citizens to begin to acknowledge the deep-rooted discriminatory structures of the American nation-state and the unfairly restricted political, economic, and social rights that had shaped black life in America. And it was the large-scale black protests and violent white resistance in the South—the black freedom struggle itself—that forced the urgent need for such understanding during the moment in which Baldwin wrote.

At a key moment in the civil rights struggle, James Baldwin taught white Americans—at least those who were receptive—that whiteness was as much a social category as blackness and that the nation itself had been successively built on a concept and articulation of whiteness that relied on the subjugation of the "Negro." "Color is not a human or a personal reality," Baldwin told his readers. "It is a political reality" (*Fire* 118). In his formulation, American history was the history of white imaginings and treatment of black Americans, a past "of rope, fire, torture, castration, infanticide, rape; death and humiliation"—and black endurance (112). The black freedom struggle was meant to liberate not only black but also white Americans, trapped and degraded by their own role in history and the present.

In a fundamental way, Baldwin charted the map that early whiteness studies historians in the 1990s would use to navigate the terrain of a new labor and class historiography. In the third edition of his seminal book *The Wages of Whiteness*, David R. Roediger points out that the study of whiteness was hardly a new enterprise "conceived by white scholars" (xi). Among other writers of color, James Baldwin in particular produced "searching inquiries and deep insights into whiteness" (12). Baldwin was part of a "broad Black nationalist tradition" that viewed "whiteness not as natural but nevertheless as real and as problematic in intellectual, moral and political terms" (12). Roediger and Matthew Frye Jacobson have demonstrated convincingly that European immigrants to the United States in the nineteenth and early twentieth centuries—the Irish, the Greeks, the Finns, the Italians, and other ethnic groups—were ascribed a multiplicity of racial identities apart from "whiteness." To be "white" was to lay claim not only to citizenship rights but also to other privileges, to what W. E. B. Du Bois famously termed "the public and psychological wage" of whiteness (700). In the post–Second World War national landscape, the "different colors" of whiteness and hierarchies of white privilege became, Jacobson argues, a "white-black dualism" (275). If you were an American, you were either white or black. By late 1962, the cumulative wages of whiteness had produced "a bill" Baldwin feared America was "not prepared to pay" (*Fire* 117).

"Letter from a Region in My Mind"

When it appeared in November 1962, Baldwin's *New Yorker* essay generated a cultural shockwave among readers that rippled out into the mainstream press, which reported on the essay as a publication phenomenon. The November issue of *The New Yorker* sold out within days and became a collector's item. At that time in the nearly forty-year life of *The New Yorker*, only John Hersey's "Hiroshima" and Rachel Carson's "Silent Spring" had elicited more reader response than Baldwin's "Letter from a Region in My Mind" ("Reader Response Report"). With a circulation of approximately 425,000 in 1962 ("Market Research"), the magazine had steadily expanded its readership across the decades and become what historian Mary Corey called an "enormous cultural power" in American life (7).

In letters to the *New Yorker* editors, a number of readers expressed the judgment that Baldwin's essay was as important socially and historically as Hersey's reportage on the US atomic bombing of Hiroshima (Armstrong; Crumpacker; Milman; Rosten; Totten). One reader even ordered an extra copy from the magazine's editorial office to send to President Kennedy. "It may get no further than assistant number 364," she wrote. "But then I surmise that assistant number 364 will be that much wiser if he has the wit to read Mr Baldwin!" (Rose). Many readers wrote to congratulate the magazine for its editorial courage in publishing what they considered a controversial and possibly incendiary statement on the state of race relations in America. Others wrote to urge the magazine to allow the article's reprinting in other print venues with wider circulations, such as *Reader's Digest.*[2] The goal was to awaken other Americans to racial consciousness and perhaps even action against racial discrimination and inequality. A doctor wrote that she was "deeply moved" and "irrevocably different" after having read "Mr Baldwin's testament." "He has made me see," she wrote, "in a way that all my psychiatric and psychologic and sociologic readings and experiences failed to, that my fate and his are joined, as are our salvations, if any" (Milman).

According to William Shawn, the *New Yorker* editor who edited and published the work, "It was one of only two or three things that really caused a sensation during my time at the magazine ... If you read it now, the ideas might seem like generally assumed ideas—but then he was saying things that hadn't been said before. And everybody was talking about it" (Campbell 160). But Shawn was mistaken. Baldwin did not say much that African American intellectuals had not said before. The black intellectual tradition in America reached back into the nineteenth century, as did its print culture, and its central concern was, as W. E. B. Du Bois put it, "the problem of the color-line" that came to define the twentieth century (35). Black writers like Du Bois, Thomas Fortune, Mary Church Terrell, Langston Hughes, Ralph Ellison, and Richard Wright published essays across the early and mid-twentieth century, exploring and protesting the exclusions of black citizens from the American democratic project. But there *was* something new about Baldwin's *New Yorker* essay: he was writing and speaking directly to white Americans at a decisive historical moment with a direct message of intense moral authority. When the *New Yorker* essay was published as the main feature of *The Fire Next Time* in January 1963, Baldwin's reach expanded—and continued expanding.

The news media, the movement,
and Baldwin

In late 1962 and early 1963, American news media with a national reach—newspapers like *The New York Times* and *The Washington Post*, wire services like the Associated Press and United Press International, news magazines like *Time* and *Life*, and the major broadcast networks—were just beginning to recognize the magnitude of the black freedom struggle in the South and to provide the kind of in-depth coverage that would soon stimulate national awareness (Roberts and Klibanoff). In that same moment, Baldwin's essays and book electrified not only ordinary American readers but also the news media—and reached into the powerful center of the federal government. Newspapers and news magazines wrote about the essays and the public response to them. When the book appeared, the conversation continued in reviews of the book and televised interviews and magazine profiles of Baldwin and his ideas.

Baldwin began participating in more movement events and became not only a topic of news but also a sought-after news source. His face blanketed the news landscape and his voice inflected much of the new, intensive national news coverage of events. The entertainment trade magazine *Variety* identified Baldwin's *New Yorker* essay as a key cause of rising white awareness of the urgency of African American demands for freedom and rights. Describing Baldwin's essay as "a savagely bitter upbraiding of white 'hypocrisy' about civil liberties," *Variety* said the essay was "now recognized as a kind of breakthrough to the educated classes. It thoroughly frightened much of the white community which has been complacently devoted to token gestures" ("Dixie's Hesitation Waltz" 3).

Television news broadcasts, newspapers, news magazines, books—these were the media Americans listened to, read, and responded to as they struggled to make sense of the radically new dispensations of the civil rights movement. Most American families watched national evening news broadcasts and read at least one daily newspaper. Magazines were flourishing. Magazine editors and book publishers worked together to produce authors who traversed genres of serious literature, including reportage, fiction, and essays (Abrahamson and Polsgrove 107; Polsgrove, "Magazines" 256). Following the Second World War, the US book publishing industry expanded both domestically and internationally (Luey 29–30). All of these forms of print culture and media were deeply articulated and together constituted a significant means by which a national conversation could be informed and held on the country's racial discord and problems. All of these media industries and their cultural products worked together to heighten public awareness and increase readership of Baldwin's ideas in *The Fire Next Time* through commentary and publicity. These ideas included the failure of the United States to live up to its civil ideals of freedom, equality, and justice for all by including black Americans in the democratic experiment. The responsibility of white Americans was, according to these sources, to recognize and admit their role in creating racial injustice and exclusion, and to admit the necessity for white and black Americans to work together to "end the racial nightmare, and achieve our country."

Baldwin and the Kennedys

The ideas in *The Fire Next Time* ultimately made their way deep into the heart of the Kennedy administration. Attorney General Robert F. Kennedy, brother of President John F. Kennedy, read Baldwin's *New Yorker* essay when it first appeared (Risen 50). The Kennedy brothers both read a speech that presidential adviser Chester Bowles delivered at Lincoln University in Oxford, Pennsylvania, on February 15, 1963, to commemorate the one hundred year anniversary of the Emancipation Proclamation (Bryant 369–70; Kotlowski 168). In his speech, Bowles discussed Baldwin's ideas in *The Fire Next Time*, thus explaining and honoring growing black anger and militancy in the face of segregationist resistance and the philosophy of gradualism. Racial discrimination must be ended, Bowles suggested, because it is "fundamentally wrong" and "poses a moral issue which goes to the heart of our society." Bowles thought Baldwin had it right. Without a strong moral and political response from the federal government fulfilling the promises of democratic life, America might be riven apart by racial conflict.[3] As discussed later, Baldwin himself delivered many of the ideas expressed in *The Fire Next Time* directly to the Kennedys through a telegram and a historic meeting with Attorney General Robert F. Kennedy in May 1963.

These ideas, along with the growing national outrage over violent white resistance to various movement events in Birmingham, Alabama, and Jackson, Mississippi, as well as the integration crises at the University of Mississippi and the University of Alabama, helped many in the Kennedy administration understand more clearly the urgent moral nature and meaning of the black freedom struggle—and its importance to the national well-being. In early 1963, President Kennedy submitted civil rights legislation to Congress, but beyond a plank on voting rights, it was a program with little real substance. It did not substantively address racial discrimination in education, employment, or public accommodations. Congress let it fall by the wayside and turned to other concerns (Schlesinger, *Robert Kennedy* 327–28, 346). The apathy afflicting Congress was made possible in part because civil rights leaders in the South had yet to capture the full attention of the national media. In April 1963, Southern Christian Leadership Conference strategists realized they needed an event, a crisis, that would compel the attention of the national press, the federal government, and the nation itself if the local movement were to be successful. Andrew Young, who had production experience in broadcast news and an appreciation for the power of the image in national news coverage, pushed Martin Luther King Jr. to craft both his message and dramatic movement events for the camera and the news bite. Civil rights leaders shifted their attention and activities to Birmingham, where police safety commissioner Bull Connor, with his infamous police dogs, fire hoses, and billy clubs, provided vivid images of violent white resistance to black nonviolent protest that would capture the attention of the media, the nation, and the world (Jackson 159).

In early May, several thousand school children took to the street in Birmingham with peaceful protest marches. Thousands were arrested, loaded in paddy wagons and school buses, and jailed. Birmingham authorities used high-powered fire hoses and attack dogs against the teenage marchers, who replaced the younger children. The images caught on camera, splashed across the front pages of national newspapers and played on evening news broadcasts, stunned many Americans. When President Kennedy saw an AP photo of a police dog attacking a black teenager on the front page of *The New York Times*, he said it made him "sick." Bayard Rustin called it "television's finest hour." It was the moment, King suggested, when the civil rights movement became truly national in scope (Branch, *Parting the Waters* 756–70; Dallek 594–95).

In the two weeks following the Birmingham children's marches, *The New York Times* published more stories on race than it had in the previous year. "Race, so long conceived as a distant element of nature, slow-moving as a bank of rain clouds," Taylor Branch explained, "suddenly bubbled up everywhere to sweep away the prevailing notion that passion was the enemy rather than the friend of racial goodwill" (*Pillar of Fire* 87). In Washington, it appeared, things were falling apart, the center could not hold.[4] President Kennedy was increasingly convinced that a federal law enforcing integration was needed, but he was worried that if he moved immediately it would appear as if King had forced his hand. His brother and Attorney General Robert Kennedy took on the task of trying to understand the perspectives and demands of the black protestors on the street. He wanted to know, as Branch put it, "what drove them, did they understand politics, how fine was the line between political inspiration and insurrection?" (*Pillar of Fire* 89). He began organizing meetings with various groups of black leaders and civil rights activists (Hendricks).

The Kennedys actively associated with writers and artists, and Robert Kennedy in particular was fascinated with people who achieved remarkable things in their lives. That group included James Baldwin (Schlesinger, *Robert Kennedy* 590, 814–15). After the bombings and civil disturbances in Birmingham on May 12, Baldwin sent a telegram to the Attorney General chastising his brother's administration for its lack of decisive action in securing black Americans their rights. It was a statement bristling with an outrage and moral certainty similar to *The Fire Next Time*:

> Those who bear the greatest responsibility for the chaos in Birmingham are not in Birmingham. Among those responsible are J. Edgar Hoover, Senator Eastland, the power structure which has given Bull Connor such license, and President Kennedy, who has not used the great prestige of his office as the moral forum which it can be. This crisis is neither regional nor racial. It is a matter of the national life or death. No truce can be binding until the American people and our representatives are able to accept the simple fact that the Negro is a man. (Baldwin, Telegram)

Less than two weeks later, Robert Kennedy arranged to meet Baldwin in Washington for breakfast at Kennedy's home, Hickory Hill (Leeming 222; Weatherby 219). Kennedy asked whether Baldwin thought the "Black Muslims" were important. Baldwin, who wrote about his own meeting with Elijah Muhammad in *The Fire Next Time*, said they were because they best articulated "the Negro's pain and despair" (Eckman 158). When the meeting was cut short—Baldwin's flight had been delayed and Kennedy had another meeting on his schedule—Kennedy suggested that they meet the next day in New York City at his family's apartment. He asked Baldwin to assemble a group able to speak about black needs and desires in the northern cities, where unrest about housing discrimination and school segregation was brewing (Schlesinger, *Robert Kennedy* 331).

It was, by all accounts, a disastrous and traumatic meeting. Robert Kennedy wanted to discuss public policy solutions to address race relations and black demands. Baldwin's group wanted to discuss the dire plight of blacks in American life and the urgent need not only for new policy but also for moral statements in support of black rights and equality from the President and his administration. On short order, Baldwin had arranged for a number of black intellectuals, writers, and celebrities to meet with the Attorney General, including Harry Belafonte, Lena Horne, Lorraine Hansberry, Kenneth Clark, and Clarence Jones. A few white friends also attended the gathering: Robert Park Mills, Baldwin's literary agent, and Assistant Attorney General Burke Marshall ("Persons Present"). But it was Jerome Smith, a young black Freedom Rider and civil rights activist, who took center stage and set the tone of the meeting.

Kennedy began the meeting with a précis of the administration's commitment to and record on civil rights issues. At first, guests suggested mildly that the government had, in fact, done very little and a more rigorous response was needed. Kennedy responded that the administration was doing its best and that black protest, growing in urgency, was provoking trouble and demanding a faster response than the administration could reasonably produce. "You don't have no idea what trouble is," Jerome Smith replied,

"Because I'm close to the moment where I'm ready to take up a gun." The mood was set and the meeting continued for three exhausting hours. Baldwin asked Smith whether he would consider fighting in a war for the United States. The response: "Never! Never!" Kennedy could not abide what he perceived as an unconscionable lack of patriotism. Smith chafed against Kennedy's apparent lack of empathy. When Smith said that the necessity of the meeting—having to meet with the Attorney General to discuss such matters—made him want to vomit, and Hansberry agreed, Kennedy's defenses rose so high he was no longer willing to entertain any of the suggestions his guests offered as politically feasible or meaningful. He met them with scorn. In the midst of it all, Baldwin and others urged the Attorney General and his brother, the President, to make a moral commitment to the civil rights movement in a national address (Branch, *Pillar of Fire* 809–13; Campbell 163–67; Leeming 222–25; Robinson; Schlesinger, *Journals* 191–93; Schlesinger, *Thousand Days* 962–63; Weatherby 218–27).

As Branch described the encounter, "Kennedy considered the Negroes helplessly naïve about big-time politics; they considered him just as naïve about race" (*Parting the Waters* 809–11). Years later, Kenneth Clark, the well-known African American psychologist and public intellectual, described the event as "the most intense, traumatic meeting in which I've ever taken part ... the most unrestrained interchange among adults, head-to-head, no holds barred ... the most dramatic experience I have ever had" (Schlesinger, *Robert Kennedy* 335). Although the Attorney General's various meetings with black leaders and other civil rights activists were meant to be private affairs, Baldwin and others involved discussed their meeting openly with the press. In fact, Baldwin held a press conference at his New York apartment on May 25, where Kenneth Clark served as a particularly vocal witness. Baldwin suggested that Robert Kennedy's desire to meet stemmed from the telegram Baldwin had sent him urging the President to make a moral commitment to the civil rights movement in a national statement. Baldwin said participants in the meeting "were a little shocked at the extent" of the Attorney General's "naïveté." Clark said that Kennedy was "by no means a devil. The Attorney General is clearly among the best that America has to offer on this issue." Yet, he continued, "we were unable to communicate clearly and skillfully that this was not a group of Negroes begging the white power structure to be nice to Negroes. We were trying to say that this was an emergency for our country, as Americans. This never got over" (Solet 1).

Press coverage of the meeting was extensive, with articles appearing on the front pages of various New York newspapers and national news magazines. *The New York Times* reported that Baldwin described the meeting's "exchange of views" as "caustic" yet "significant" ("3 Negro Leaders" 13). Many participants in the meeting described it as an abject failure. But Baldwin refused to view the meeting in these terms. "No one can afford to regard this as a failure," he told *Newsweek*. "We've finally opened up a dialogue. No one can expect it to be polite, but we've started" ("Kennedy and Baldwin" 19).

Interestingly, the press was intimately involved in the meeting from the very beginning. One of the participants was Henry Morgenthau III, a Boston public television producer who would tape the James Baldwin segment of the special television show *The Negro and the American Promise* in the hours following the meeting.[5] Kenneth Clark, whose participation in and witness to the meeting became a critical element of the historical record, was the interviewer and narrator of the show, which also featured interviews with Martin Luther King Jr. and Malcolm X. But it was Clark's interview with Baldwin that elicited the most widespread public response. Suggesting that the future of black Americans and the future of the nation were deeply intertwined, Clark asked Baldwin his opinion of the future of the country. In answering, Baldwin instructed white viewers to consider their own whiteness and suggested that the future of the nation lay in their hands. "It is entirely up to the American people whether or not they are going to face and deal with and embrace this stranger whom they maligned so long. What white people have to do is try and find out in their own hearts why it was necessary to have a n***er in the first place." Speaking directly to the television camera, Baldwin said, "I am not a n***er. I am a man" (*Negro and the American Promise*; "3 Negro Leaders" 13).[6] *Negro Digest* called the show "one of television's finest hours," and *The New York Times* called it "a television experience that seared the conscience of the white set owner" ("'There Is No Compromise'" 25; Gould 29). Jack Gould, the television critic for the *Times*, considered the Baldwin interview an "exclusive" for public television, given what he described as "the inadequacy" of the network news coverage of the Baldwin–Kennedy meeting (29).

According to James Reston, Washington correspondent for *The New York Times* and nationally syndicated columnist, the Kennedy brothers understood much more about "the problem" by mid-June than they had previously. "The Administration seemed to be saying that here it was doing all it could to help the Negroes in the middle of a world crisis and that nobody understood or appreciated its efforts," Reston wrote. But recent movement activities and the Attorney General's meeting with Baldwin had changed "many things" in Washington. To explain the influence of the Baldwin meeting, Reston quoted Kenneth Clark, who said, "Suddenly I looked at the Attorney General and understood that he did not understand us ... We were asking him to stop thinking about this as a special problem of a particular group and to begin to think about it as an American problem." Just three weeks after the meeting, the situation had changed, Reston claimed: "The President and his brother are thinking of it as an American problem now" (148).

Well before Reston assessed the change in the administration's understanding of the magnitude and urgency of the freedom struggle, the black press had predicted the change as inevitable. On June 8, a

Baltimore Afro-American editorial noted that the administration's failure to champion "meaningful" civil rights legislation, along with "Birmingham and mass demonstrations mushrooming in city after city in the South," revealed just how badly the Kennedys had misjudged the urgency of the domestic situation on civil rights. "Now the Kennedys know," the editorial claimed, "that nice-sounding words no longer satisfy." James Baldwin's meeting with Robert Kennedy had helped the Kennedy brothers come to this realization. "If it served no other purpose than this," the *Afro-American* claimed, "the Baldwin conference was of great value" ("Now the Kennedys Know" 4).

Several days after the Baldwin–Kennedy meeting, press reports began to speculate that the Kennedy administration would soon seek rapid congressional action on civil rights legislation. Most made reference to the Attorney General's meeting with Baldwin and his shock at the charges of an inadequate response from the administration. In a column devoted to President Kennedy's new civil rights legislation and his intended "major television address to the nation concerning the crisis," William V. Shannon of the *New York Post* noted the administration's remarkable new action on the civil rights front. Robert Kennedy's meeting with Baldwin and "other Negro intellectuals played a part in changing the Administration's approach," he wrote. "Although the meeting went badly and Kennedy became angry at the time, he has turned his anger to constructive use" (Shannon; Wilson).

The meeting did anger Robert Kennedy—and it ripped him apart. It was a defining moment in his political life, when he began to understand more deeply the plight of black Americans and to make a strong commitment to civil rights. In a column published just days after the meeting, James Wechsler noted that Kennedy's "response on reflection could be a large clue to the size of the man" (30). Biographers and historians have written about the implications of this meeting in Robert Kennedy's political maturation and growth. "As an authentic disaster," Branch wrote, "the Baldwin meeting made Robert Kennedy a pioneer in the raw, interracial encounters of the 1960s. Hard upon Birmingham and his previous ordeals in civil rights, the experience knocked the Attorney General off balance. What was intensely personal no longer seemed so distinct from policy, not public from private" (*Parting the Waters* 813). For Schlesinger, the exchange eventually led Kennedy, after a cooling-off period, "to grasp as from the inside the nature of black anguish. He resented the experience, but it pierced him all the same. His tormentors made no sense; but in a way they made all sense. It was another stage in education" (*Robert Kennedy* 335).

It was after this meeting, Schlesinger noted in the journals he kept during his days in the Kennedy White House, that the government picked up the pace of its reaction to the civil rights movement. He drew a straight line from the Robert Kennedy–James Baldwin encounter to the creation of the civil rights legislation that President Kennedy would present that June and that Lyndon B. Johnson would, after Kennedy's assassination, help push through Congress (Schlesinger, *Journals* 191–93).

Conclusion

In the spring of 1963, the orbits of James Baldwin and Robert Kennedy overlapped repeatedly as both responded to momentous events. When Baldwin met with Kennedy in late May, he was at the height of his media celebrity as the literary voice of the movement, having appeared just weeks prior on the cover of *Time* magazine, in a long photo spread in *Life* magazine, and in nationally televised interviews ("At the Root of the Negro Problem" 26–27; "At a Crucial Time" 81–90). This coverage gave Baldwin yet another platform for articulating the views expressed so powerfully and poignantly in *The Fire Next Time*. *The Fire Next Time* and the two magazine essays that comprised it did not simply circulate quietly among readers across the nation. Baldwin's work was a statement of such moral force and persuasive substance—and articulated by a person elevated to such national prominence—that it inflected a great swath of public discourse in America in its historical moment.

"The awesome power of race as an ideology," Jacobson has written, "resides precisely in its ability to pass as a feature of the natural landscape" (10). Baldwin helped Robert Kennedy and those around him to see whiteness as a problem and barrier in achieving racial justice in the United States. Baldwin's words in *The Fire Next Time*, his statements to the press, and his telegram to and meeting with Robert Kennedy influenced both ordinary citizens' and the Kennedy administration's ideas about racial injustice and whiteness during a critical period of the civil rights movement. His words helped many Americans understand and acknowledge that black Americans had been unjustly excluded from the nation's democratic community; that a truly democratic and civil society could not be achieved with racial injustice at its core; and that embracing solidarity across racial lines was the only way for Americans "to end the racial nightmare, and achieve our country" (Baldwin, *Fire* 105).

On May 30, 1963, Vice President Lyndon B. Johnson gave a Memorial Day address at Gettysburg. "The Negro today asks justice," he said. "We do not answer him—we do not answer those who lie beneath this soil—when we reply to the Negro by asking, 'Patience'" (Branch, *Pillar of Fire* 92). On June 3, 1963, in a long conversation in which he quoted Baldwin in *The Fire Next Time*, Johnson advised Ted Sorensen, a top aide to President Kennedy, that the administration's civil rights efforts were failing and that the President should give a public speech making "a moral commitment" to "the Baldwins and to the Kings" of the nation (Lawson 170).[7] On June 11, President Kennedy famously addressed the nation about that day's troubling events at the University of Alabama, where Governor George Wallace had refused to allow two black students to enter the school until National Guardsmen forced his hand. Promising to send a strong civil rights bill to Congress, he finally made the moral commitment Johnson, his brother, and Baldwin had urged him to make (Branch, *Pillar of Fire* 91–95; Lawson 170).

Acknowledgment

An earlier version of this chapter appeared as "*The Fire Next Time* in the Civil Sphere: Literary Journalism and Justice in America 1963," special issue on ethics and literary journalism, *Journalism: Theory, Practice and Criticism*, vol. 15, no. 5, Spring 2014, pp. 570–85. This research received funding from the Office of the Provost's Humanities Grant Program and the College of Mass Communications and Information Studies' Faculty Development Stimulus Grant, both at the University of South Carolina.

Notes

1 Robert Park Mills, Baldwin's literary agent, wrote to Milton Greenstein of *The New Yorker*, noting the Dial Press publication date for *The Fire Next Time* as January 21, 1963.

2 See reader letters to *New Yorker* editors and James Baldwin, New Yorker Records, box 1000, folders 1–4.

3 Two versions of the speech exist: a manuscript version with penciled deletions and additions in Chester Bowles's personal papers and an official version recorded in the Congressional Record. Bowles's personal version, which appears to be edited for presentation as the Lincoln University speech, shows a deletion mark through the reference to the 1960 Democratic platform's promises to end racial segregation and civil rights violations.

4 An allusion to the poem "The Second Coming" by William Butler Yeats: "Things fall apart; the centre cannot hold."

5 The show was produced by Boston public television station WGBH and was aired on National Educational Television (the predecessor of PBS) across several weeks in the summer of 1963.

6 The show consisted of interviews taped by Kenneth Clark in separate sessions between May 24 and June 4, 1963.

7 Lawson provides the transcript of the telephone conversation recording in the prepresidential files of the Lyndon B. Johnson Presidential Library.

Works Cited

Abrahamson, David, and Carol Polsgrove. "The Right Niche: Consumer Magazines and Advertisers." Nord, Rubin, and Schudson, pp. 107–18.

Armstrong, Eunice. Letter to Editor, *The New Yorker*. 19 Nov. 1962. New Yorker Records, box 1000, folders 1–4.

"At a Crucial Time a Negro Talks Tough: 'There's a Bill Due That Has to Be Paid.'" *Life*, 24 May 1963, pp. 81–90.

"At the Root of the Negro Problem." *Time*, 17 May 1963, pp. 26–27.

Baldwin, James. *The Fire Next Time*. 1963. Vintage International, 1993.

Baldwin, James. "Letter from a Region in My Mind." *The New Yorker*, 17 Nov. 1962. pp. 59–144.

Baldwin, James. "Letter to My Nephew." *The Progressive*, Dec. 1962, pp. 19–20.

Baldwin, James. Telegram to Attorney General Robert Kennedy. Robert Park Mills Papers, box 2, folder 2.

Bowles, Chester. "Emancipation: The Record and the Challenge." Chester Bowles Papers, Yale U Library, box 314, folder 762.

Bowles, Chester. "Emancipation: The Record and the Challenge." *Congressional Record*, daily ed., 25 Mar. 1963, pp. S4,850–53.

Branch, Taylor. *Parting the Waters: America in the King Years, 1954–63*. Simon and Schuster, 1988.

Branch, Taylor. *Pillar of Fire: America in the King Years, 1963–65*. Simon and Schuster, 1998.

Bryant, Nick. *The Bystander: John F. Kennedy and the Struggle for Black Equality*. Basic Books, 2006.

Campbell, James. *Talking at the Gates: A Life of James Baldwin*. U of California P, 1991.

Corey, Mary F. *The World through a Monocle: "The New Yorker" at Midcentury*. Harvard UP, 1999.

Crumpacker, Rose Turner. Letter to William Shawn. 7 Dec. 1962. New Yorker Records, box 1000, folders 1–4.

Dallek, Robert. *An Unfinished Life: John F. Kennedy, 1917–1963*. Little, Brown and Company, 2003.

Darnton, Robert. "What Is the History of Books?" *Reading in America: Literature & Social History*, edited by Cathy N. Davidson, Johns Hopkins UP, 1989, pp. 27–52.

"Dixie's Hesitation Waltz: You Lead, We Might Follow." *Variety*, 29 May 1963, p. 3.

Du Bois, W. E. B. *Black Reconstruction in America, 1860–1880*. 1935. Free Press, 1995.

Eckman, Fern Marja. *The Furious Passage of James Baldwin*. Popular Library, 1966.

Gould, Jack. "TV: Challenge on Racism: James Baldwin Puts Problem Squarely in the Laps of All Americans." *The New York Times*, 30 May 1963, p. 29.

Haiven, Max, and Alex Khasnabish. *The Radical Imagination: Social Movement Research in the Age of Austerity*. Zed Books, 2014.

Hendricks, Alfred T. "RFK Session with Negroes Fails: Baldwin." *New York Post*, 25 May 1963. Robert Park Mills Papers, box 3, folder 12.

Jackson, Thomas F. *From Civil Rights to Human Rights: Martin Luther King, Jr., and the Struggle for Economic Justice*. U of Pennsylvania P, 2007.

Jacobson, Matthew Frye. *Whiteness of a Different Color: European Immigrants and the Alchemy of Race*. Harvard UP, 1999.

Joseph, Peniel E. *Waiting 'Til the Midnight Hour: A Narrative History of Black Power in America*. Henry Holt, 2006.

"Kennedy and Baldwin: The Gulf." *Newsweek*, 3 June 1963, p. 19.

Kotlowski, Dean. "With All Deliberate Delay: Kennedy, Johnson, and School Desegregation." *Journal of Policy History*, vol. 17, no. 2, 2005, pp. 155–92.

Lawson, Steven F. "'I Got It from *The New York Times*': Lyndon Johnson and the Kennedy Civil Rights Program." *Journal of Negro History*, vol. 67, no. 2, 1982, pp. 159–73. doi: 10.2307/2717574.

Leeming, David. *James Baldwin: A Biography*. Alfred A. Knopf, 1994.

Luey, Beth. "The Organization of the Book Publishing Industry." Nord, Rubin, and Schudson, pp. 29–54.

"Market Research on *The New Yorker*." New Yorker Records, box 1324, folder 5.

Mills, Robert Park. Letter to Milton Greenstein. 13 Dec. 1962. Robert Park Mills Papers, box 3, folder 1.

Milman, Doris H. Letter to Editor, *The New Yorker*. 1 Dec. 1962. New Yorker Records, box 1000, folder 3.

The Negro and the American Promise. Produced by Henry Morgenthau III. WGBH, 1963, pbs.org/video/american-experience-james-baldwin-from-the-negro-and-the-american-promise/. Accessed 24 Aug. 2018.

New Yorker Records. Manuscripts and Archives Division, New York Public Library.

Nord, David Paul, Joan Shelley Rubin, and Michael Schudson, editors. *The Enduring Book: Print Culture in Postwar America*. University of North Carolina Press, 2009. Vol. 5 of *A History of the Book in America*, general editor, David D. Hall.

"Now the Kennedys Know." *Baltimore Afro-American*, 8 June 1963, p. 4.

"Persons Present at the May 24 Meeting with Attorney General Robert Kennedy and Assistant Attorney General Burke Marshall." Robert Park Mills Papers, box 3, folder 12.

Polsgrove, Carol. *Divided Minds: Intellectuals and the Civil Rights Movement*. W. W. Norton, 2001.

Polsgrove, Carol. "Magazines and the Making of Authors." Nord, Rubin, and Schudson, pp. 256–68.

"Reader Response Report." Karen Durbin to Mr. Hofeller, 23 Jan. 1968. New Yorker Records, box 966, folder 5.

Reston, James. "No Longer a 'Problem' but a Revolution." *The New York Times*, 16 June 1963, p. 148.

Risen, Clay. *The Bill of the Century: The Epic Battle for the Civil Rights Act*. Bloomsbury Press, 2014.

Robert Park Mills Papers. Harry Ransom Humanities Research Center, U of Texas at Austin.

Roberts, Gene, and Hank Klibanoff. *The Race Beat: The Press, the Civil Rights Struggle, and the Awakening of a Nation*. Alfred A. Knopf, 2007.

Robinson, Layhmond. "Robert Kennedy Consults Negroes Here about North." *The New York Times*, 25 May 1963, p. 1.

Roediger, David R. *The Wages of Whiteness: Race and the Making of the American Working Class*. Verso, 2007.

Rose, Sandra. Letter to Editor, *The New Yorker*. 27 Nov. 1962. New Yorker Records, box 1000, folder 4.

Rosten, Norman. Letter to Editor, *The New Yorker*. New Yorker Records, box 1000, folder 4.

Schlesinger, Arthur M., Jr. *Journals: 1952–2000*. Penguin Press, 2007.

Schlesinger, Arthur M., Jr. *Robert Kennedy and His Times*. 1978. Houghton Mifflin, 2002.

Schlesinger, Arthur M., Jr. *A Thousand Days: John F. Kennedy in the White House*. Houghton Mifflin, 2002.

Shannon, William V. "JFK and Rights." *New York Post*, 9 June 1963. Robert Park Mills Papers, box 3, folder 12.

Solet, Sue. "N.Y. Negroes and Bobby – Both Shocked." *New York Herald Tribune*, 26 May 1963, p. 1.

"'There Is No Compromise': Total Freedom or Total Oppression." *Negro Digest*, Oct. 1963, pp. 25–31. Transcript of the Baldwin interview in *The Negro and the American Promise*, produced by Henry Morgenthau III, WGBH, 1963.

"3 Negro Leaders on TV Hold Kennedy Leadership Inadequate." *The New York Times*, 25 June 1963, p. 13.

Totten, Lillian. Letter to Editor, *The New Yorker*. 1 Dec. 1962. New Yorker Records, box 1000, folders 1–4.

Weatherby, W. J. *James Baldwin: Artist on Fire*. Donald I. Fine, 1989.

Wechsler, James A. "RFK & Baldwin." *New York Post*, 28 May 1963, p. 30.

Wilson, Victor. "For Bobby Next: Bias in Theater." *New York Herald Tribune*, 27 May 1963, p. 1.

Zaborowska, Magdalena J. *James Baldwin's Turkish Decade: Erotics of Exile*. Duke UP, 2009.

5

The Documentary Tradition in James Baldwin's *Écriture Vérité*

Isabelle Meuret

The significance of Baldwin today

Recent research has established the major role played by African American writers in developing literary journalism (Maguire 11–12). While Barbara Foley has pointed to an important documentary tradition based on black experience that should be acknowledged as a legitimate forebear of literary journalism ("History"; *Telling the Truth*), a vast corpus still begs for further exploration. Scholars have started to repair that glaring omission in crediting the nonfiction of Richard Wright (Dow, "Unreading"), Langston Hughes (Roiland), and James Baldwin (Forde, "Communication"; Forde, *Fire*; Dow, "Reading") as paving the way for the genre. Notwithstanding the abundance of exegesis on Baldwin—as a novelist, an essayist, a spokesman for the civil rights movement—his texts can still benefit from a reexamination in light of the many documentary modes Baldwin deployed. Besides his seminal novels, short stories, and plays, Baldwin penned powerful nonfiction, critical essays, reviews, and journalistic texts. In addition to his better-known nonfiction texts, most prominently *The Fire Next Time* (1963), Baldwin also tried his hand at risky ventures that involved either collaborative or investigative work. By way of illustration, *Nothing Personal* (1964), a photo-text with Richard Avedon, and *The Evidence of Things Not Seen* (1985), an investigation of the Atlanta child murders, are just a few examples of his contributions that document the African American experience.

The ubiquitous presence of Baldwin in the academic and cultural landscape today must be credited to a timely concurrence of events: international conferences devoted to the transatlantic author, first-time publications of his nonfiction in translation,[1] the release amid a blaze of publicity of Raoul Peck's widely acclaimed documentary *I Am Not Your Negro* (2016), and the recent acquisition of Baldwin's archive by the Schomburg Center for Research in Black Culture in New York (Schuessler). The serendipitous resonance of Baldwin's words is also due to major African American voices routinely praising Baldwin, among them Toni Morrison and Ta-Nehisi Coates, to which must be added the wider climate of obscene bigotry that shocks Americans at home and impacts consciences abroad. Across the globe, screens have been flashing with images of white supremacy and blatant racism. Police brutality against African Americans and the shameful exposition of their slain bodies reminiscent of lynchings have us looking for artists and thinkers to make sense of the pervasive insanity. In contemporary circumstances, Baldwin's words are a welcome *pharmakon* against heinous and hideous crimes. The poet-prophet's deft dovetailing of race and rage is his conduit to a radical imagination that sets us free from essentialist shackles. As Alice Mikal Craven and William E. Dow make clear in the foreword to this volume, revolutionary thinking fused with narrative prowess underpins Baldwin's creative process.

Baldwin's nonfiction has been scrutinized extensively, positing him as a true innovator in literary journalism. However, this claim still needs further exploration for a number of reasons. First, Baldwin's perennial insistence on being a witness is a solemn profession of faith in verity, a creed to which his writing holds tenaciously. His nonfiction abides by the deontological tenets of reportage, which even made him critical of "New Journalism." While penning *The Evidence of Things Not Seen*, he confessed his resistance to fictionalizing the story, torn between ethic and aesthetic tensions (Estes 272). This chapter intends to unpack his reservations and elucidate his dilemmas, in particular when it comes to the mechanics of reconstructing reality. Second, aside from his impressive production as a writer of fiction and nonfiction, Baldwin's life and times gain from being apprehended in a holistic manner. Baldwin was a performer of interviews, which shaped his public persona and accelerated his rise to prominence. He has been the subject of a number of documentaries, including *Take This Hammer* (1963), *I Heard It through the Grapevine* (1982), *The Price of the Ticket* (1989), and *I Am Not Your Negro* (2016). With hindsight, Baldwin's versatility calls for a comprehensive approach to his work on par with his prolific existence and his radical imagination. Such a panoptic stance is best encapsulated in what I venture to call *écriture vérité*, a conceptual proposition that posits Baldwin's oeuvre as a series of sequence shots that exceed the frame of his written production.

Racial nation, radical imagination

"Practically, black emancipation," Manning Marable notes, "occurred not by fiat, but by the direct actions of the slaves themselves" (4). Paradoxically, the implementation of racial segregation was made legal by the Supreme Court in 1896 (8). Today, Michelle Alexander argues, "new" Jim Crow laws perpetuate this institutional apartheid and have moved the color line from within society to behind bars. Alexander traces the genealogy of "a racial caste system based entirely on exploitation (slavery), to one based largely on subordination (Jim Crow), to one defined by marginalization (mass incarceration)" (219).[2] The twentieth century certainly witnessed some major economic and social improvements, with the National Association for the Advancement of Colored People (NAACP), the Nation of Islam, and the Black Panther Party pushing in favor of provocative action, with varying intentions and degrees of success. Other actors, albeit lesser known, must be hailed for generating politically active communities and initiating liberatory social movements. Robin D. G. Kelley's *Freedom Dreams: The Black Radical Imagination* (2002) is a powerful and grateful nod to those who audaciously imagined new worlds, without necessarily reaping the benefits of their bold visions. Also, Baldwin significantly left an unfinished tribute to heroes of black activism—Medgar Evers, Malcolm X, Martin Luther King Jr.—who were all assassinated, sacrificed for their major interventions toward a more egalitarian society: *Remembering This House* (unpublished) became Peck's cue to *I Am Not Your Negro*, Baldwin's unwritten book unto film.

Baldwin shared with his readers true stories learned under different climes. In *The Radical Imagination* (2014), Max Haiven and Alex Khasnabish argue that the imagination is fundamentally a collective, or dialogical, process, as it rests on "shared experiences, language, stories, ideas, art and theory" (4). It must be envisaged from a locational standpoint, as subjects are "embodied in a racist, sexist, and oppressive society" but also transversally as "they struggle with the power relationships that intersect them." In other words, "radical imagination" is a joint venture constantly "reweaving itself" relative to "people, institutions, and forms of power" around the oppressed (Khasnabish and Haiven 411). Beyond his ruminations which were conceived on the premises of blackness and bitterness, it can be argued that Baldwin's endeavors were suffused with an "ability to imagine the world, life and social institutions not as they are but as they might otherwise be" (Haiven and Khasnabish, *Radical Imagination* 3). Crucially, Baldwin did not content himself with dreams of a better future but relentlessly probed the past, examined the present, and deconstructed received ideas in a determinedly diachronic perspective. This, if we follow Haiven and Khasnabish's rationale, is a profoundly radical attitude, since Baldwin was unremittingly pulling up evil roots from the American historic soil and social fabric. While not included in Kelley's study on marginalized freedom dreamers, Baldwin nevertheless remains a highly inspirational figure.

Neither on the side of nonviolence nor on the side of guerrilla movements, Baldwin's engagement in civil rights became radical in the 1960s, despite failed attempts at joining forces with his Black Power brothers (Field, *All Those Strangers* 66; Field, "Looking" 460). Baldwin's camera-eye encompassed transatlantic swerves and captured images of decisive moments, which were later translated into a language strengthened by Black Power-inspired radical rhetoric, in which his growing disillusionment after the assassinations of Martin Luther King Jr. and Malcolm X is palpable (Field, "Looking" 466–67). And while Baldwin infused his texts with carefully crafted filmic references, others used their cameras to capture the meaning of Baldwin. Like Fontaine and Harley before her, Thorsen's haunting tribute, *The Price of the Ticket*, was originally devised as a *cinéma vérité* project. Much earlier, poet and director Richard O. Moore resorted to these freshly minted techniques in his 1963 film featuring Baldwin in San Francisco. As its evocative title indicates, *Take This Hammer* honors Baldwin's insistence on destroying the veneer of hypocrisy and breaking down barriers to a radical consciousness. Sadly, sequences containing incendiary words proffered by disaffected black youths were cut from the original footage to suit audiences, a violation which infuriated Baldwin. The KQED producers, disturbed by "the preponderance of black rage being expressed," vetoed inflammatory segments they deemed detrimental for the National Educational Television viewers for whom the film was intended. Baldwin's willingness to show "the real situation of Negroes" in San Francisco thus suffered from a montage that obliterated vital evidence—"a very painful compromise"—which Moore later regretted (*The Making of* Take This Hammer).

In an interview with François Bondy in 1964, Baldwin wondered about America's capacity "to deal with what really happened in the country and what is really happening there now" (Baldwin, Interview 15). And in the eloquent monologue completing the aforementioned *Take This Hammer*, filmed the year before, Baldwin delivers a dramatic rant in which he accuses white people of inventing the "n***er." He dexterously reverses the roles and thereby piques his white interlocutor:

> We have invented the n***er. I have been invented. White people have invented him ... But if I'm not the n***er, then who is the n***er? The n***er is necessary. Not necessary to me. It must be necessary to you. So, I give you your problem back. You're the n***er, baby. It isn't me. (Baldwin qtd. in Moore)

Here is Baldwin at his best, realigning the pronouns—we, I, him, me, you—blurring distances and turning the tables, forcefully imposing *rapprochement* and distance, alienation and sodality. Almost twenty years later, traveling the roads of America from Atlanta to Newark with his brother David, as recounted in *I Heard It through the Grapevine*, Baldwin shows a sense of hopelessness, while claiming that liberation will come from the next generations. Despite railing against systematic racial objectification, Baldwin converts negative experience into positive change, using emotions as the most effective ammunition for "communicative interaction" (Santa Ana 93–95, 96). For radical consciousness to be productive, a collective vision must be imagined. The rage and compassion which suffuse Baldwin's revolutionary discourse (102) needs to be cemented by our "being-in-common," a tenet central to *écriture vérité* and commensurate with a profoundly humanistic aspiration.

Baldwin's writing, in particular his nonfiction, partakes of a lifetime project that, paradoxically, yet momentarily, had him excluded from the pantheon of black dissenters. Kelley's *Freedom Dreams* conspicuously ignores Baldwin in his nonetheless comprehensive evaluation of revolutionary, albeit marginalized, African American thinkers and activists. While he does not provide any explanation for this blatant absence, Kelley later suggested, on the occasion of a televised discussion of the author's black radicalism, that Baldwin was not so much the product of the American civil rights movement but rather of the Algerian revolution and anticolonialism, as he was then mostly residing in France ("Writings").[3] This assertion begs the question of the porosity of our experiences, the fluidity of our identities. Douglas Field would reject such a claim, as he believes Baldwin's time "with 'les misérables' (Algerians) was a blatant rewriting of his first years in Paris," which he supposedly polished with a radical veneer to reinforce his political engagement (*All Those Strangers* 74). Cosmopolitanism certainly has the virtue of augmenting perspective, and Baldwin's foreign encounters impacted and expanded his worldview, but probably not to such an extent that they diminished his sense of being an African American from Harlem. Radical he was, though, Kelley hastened to add, precisely due to the power of his imagination: despite its dystopian conclusive notes, *The Fire Next Time* is visionary in its ambition to unite people across color and gender, and in its creation of a sense of possibility and empowerment ("Writings"). Baldwin's alternative vision, informed by a transnational positioning, is one focus of this chapter.

Écriture vérité

In *The Devil Finds Work* (1975), a young Baldwin confides his grief about realizing his father's aversion to him, "this hatred proving ... more resounding than real" (481), a phrase that describes how Baldwin's heritage can be read today. His heritage is a resonance chamber in which his words echo the past, strike a particular chord with the present, and energize the future. Bouncing back and forth between America and Europe, Baldwin inflamed readers, and his message gained in amplitude and latitude. *Écriture vérité* is not just a stylistic consideration; it also proves to be a useful tool for parsing Baldwin's oeuvre. Although hints of *cinéma vérité* can be traced in previous Baldwin criticism (Porter 33), the potential of such a technique has not yet been thoroughly explored across generic borders. The *écriture vérité* analogy offers an original prism to consider Baldwin's oeuvre and authorial presence, and to problematize issues similar to those raised by its filmic counterpart. *Écriture vérité* is alternately a tentative representation and interrogation of reality and truth, and possibly an urge for direct action. The French phrase *action directe* is leavened with a particularly violent ferment, as revolutionists and far-left anarchists had been promoting terrorist action since the early twentieth century. There is no such violence in Baldwin's writing, but a tipping point came in 1956 when the face of Dorothy Counts, harassed by mobs "as she approached the halls of learning, with history, jeering at her back," filled him with fire and fury. "I could, simply, no longer sit around in Paris discussing the Algerian and the black American Problem" ("No Name" 383), Baldwin confessed.

Baldwin's radical imagination eventuates from a desire to bring to the documentary tradition an immediacy and urgency that it crucially lacked. Foley shows that black writers have always aimed at "conveying their visions of historical reality and potentiality" ("History" 402). Whichever documentary mode was chosen, the purpose was to resist mythologization and to patently reveal the actuality, veracity, and plurality of truths. Witnessing events and grasping a sense of remote realities are essential to preserve memories, but with Baldwin they call for a provocative engagement with those realities. *Cinéma vérité* revolutionized the way images and words move us and make us move. Likewise, *écriture vérité* may be vindicated on such tangible promises of agitation. Galvanized by the "unutterable pride, tension, and anguish" in Count's expression, Baldwin goes back not just to America; he aims for the South. That experience, of being confronted with unbearable images from home, and of connecting with his people, made him realize "how deep and strangling were [his] fears, how manifold and mighty [his] limits" and, most importantly, that he "should learn to live, every day, both within his limits and beyond them" ("No Name" 384). Baldwin trespasses from an enunciative onto a performative space. He lacked the emotional bond, a deficiency he himself deplored, that "organic connection between [one's] public stance and [one's] private life" (385), which preempts collective action.

Literary journalism documents reality and induces feelings resulting from experiences shared in that reality, often leaving a lasting impression on readers. Starting from an objective reality, the subjective camera-eye of the writer captures events and scenes that will shatter certainties and possibly elicit reactions. Baldwin's radical imagination is articulated within the conceptual and operational frame of *écriture vérité* as it entails a rendition, mediation, and transformation of reality. *Écriture vérité* offers a wider prism for probing the depths of Baldwin's oeuvre in terms of production, perception, and reception, all three processes being connected, rather than separated, on a creative continuum. Dabbling with various genres, crossing geographic borders, living in multiple cultural milieus, the adaptable Baldwin was an expert at taking wide-angle shots and guiding readers on a journey into the realities he exposed. Devising such a discerning model is contingent upon the controversies that accompanied the development of *cinéma vérité*.[4] The 1960s saw technological advances that were deemed pivotal to the evolution of filmmaking: the freedom to use hand-held cameras at close range and to record the voices of the protagonists defined this new cinema whose "potential was electrifying" (Leacock qtd. in Wintonick). However, opinions differed as to the specificities of *cinéma vérité*, and two schools rapidly diverged over an alleged "truth" and the role of a purportedly "spontaneous" camera.[5] Some supported the all-important camera recording facts, capturing the internal drama of a given situation (Drew, Pennebaker, Maysles, Leacock), while others, the partisans of a more reflexive and interventionist attitude, claimed that editing was fundamental (Flaherty, Rouch).

Two essential lessons are to be taken from this departure from traditional cinema, which scrutinize Baldwin's nonfiction. First, *cinéma vérité* is intrinsically a transatlantic movement, as its themes, techniques, and tools emanated from and circulated between two continents. The international collaboration was unique and fertile, a point admirably presented in Wintonick's *Cinéma-Vérité: Defining the Moment* (1999), which highlights the connections between those who left their mark on the genre and deepened its methods. Contentions around methods existed, but those contentions produced joint ventures and led to inspirational breakthroughs.[6] The cross-fertilization of experiences resulted in a reconfiguration of the "cinema of the real," which raised questions about the development of documentary cinema. Those experiences equally triggered a debate around the creative process and its claims for authenticity. While Robert Flaherty's concern was on *revelation* (seeing what the camera could discover), John Grierson's was on *creation*, or the imaginative treatment of actuality (editing what the camera captured) (Ellis 5). The attendant questions posed in the context of film production—fact vs. fiction, ethics vs. aesthetics, objectivity vs. subjectivity, the porosity of borders with other disciplines (ethnography, anthropology, sociology, history), and the interaction between the protagonists (authors, actors, technicians, viewers)—are identical to those with which literary journalism is grappling. Baldwin's *écriture vérité* is imbued with a deft combination of perceptive observation (revelation) and participative intervention (creation).

The second lesson concerning Baldwin's *écriture vérité* has to do with the sense of purpose. Despite divergences in practices, directors concurred when it came to intentionality. The gist of their approach was to trust the camera and to learn how to see the actuality before their eyes. There was no fabrication or forging of content. The ultimate barrier between characters and director dissolved. *Cinéma vérité* provided access to *human* experience, with filmmakers differing only on the role they assumed with that camera, either unobtrusive (discovery) or active (montage). The innovation resided in the sense of possibility that existed within and beyond the frame of the filmed reality. On that particular account, Morin conceptualized *cinéma vérité* as "a cinema that depends on reality—lived, recorded, or camera-induced" and preeminently noted that "there [was] no longer an author in the sense of a director; the author is the cameraman, the interviewer, the interviewee, chance, event, all of them at once. There is no longer any author in the conventional sense" (Morin, "Edgar Morin"; my trans.). This is paramount for understanding agency and dialogism in Baldwin's *écriture vérité*.[7] The author is no longer the only conduit to the story, but one out of many that have the capacity to give and to shift direction. Henceforth, the power of imagination significantly lies also with the receptors—readers—who may act upon said reality. Morin pivotally suggested that viewers welcomed the idea of a minor author, provided *they* took on a major role. Consequently, the idea that denouement might take place *out* of the story is incredibly empowering. Tellingly, the preferred appellation of "direct cinema" morphed into "radical" and even "militant cinema."

Beyond the realization that viewers or readers are granted agency, actors in the story have also gained entitlement to authority. Indeed, Morin aptly added that "*cinéma vérité* is looking for human beings who would be, in front of the camera and if only for a moment, the authors of their own existence." From these audacious propositions, it can be inferred that some of the major advances in *cinéma vérité*, both in terms of method and purpose, lie in its collaborative efforts and its democratizing endeavors. Most significantly, Morin's theorization of *cinéma vérité* rests on a dual articulation of *alienation* and *fraternization*, and proves a cogent model to explore the ethical potential of Baldwin's aesthetic choices. By *alienation* Morin means taking distance from ourselves; by *fraternization* he refers to a momentum toward, or a surge of sympathy for, the other(s). Baldwin's covenant of truth seeking is alternately implemented through detachment and proximity, which his transatlantic perspective fostered. Alienation is thus a linchpin of *cinéma vérité*, and it implicitly calls for brotherhood. Indeed, Graff insists that the heated polemics that interrogated the absence of filter between film and viewers were part and parcel of *cinéma vérité*. Controversies and confrontations were central to a cinema that posited truth as a dialectical process premised on a dynamic exchange between directors, actors, film, and audience (*Cinéma-vérité* 21–22). Baldwin's *écriture vérité* is in accordance with the guiding principles of its cinematic counterpart, revisited with a radical twist.

Fragments of reality, figments of truth

A. Russell Brooks argues that Baldwin was "uncompromisingly radical, not in the widely used sense of *extreme* but in the sense of *fundamental*," relentlessly looking for the reasons behind a given reality and probing for evidence thereof (126). Brooks compares Baldwin's "radical truth" to a Socratic search for facts that expands knowledge and also demands a questioning of that very truth.[8] In discussing Baldwin's work as a film critic, Ryan Jay Friedman notes that his approach to interpretation is similar to the reviews typical of the *Cahiers du cinéma* in the 1960s (390). I would even speculate that Baldwin was aware of *cinéma vérité* and possibly digested its tenets and aspirations.[9] Friedman points to the author's insightful analysis of film images that "have the power viscerally to manifest ethical 'truths' that American narrative films otherwise tend to evade" (385). Through such dramatization, he intimates, Baldwin illuminates the effects of collision and collusion resulting from "true intersubjective communion" (386). Baldwin resorts to "tropes of violent impact and energy transfer," which percolate from "indelible moments" and affect the viewers' consciousness (388). "Indelible moments" in cinema and, arguably, latent images in text participate in a revelatory process that makes reality legible and unforgettable.

Such epiphanies—"The sea rises, the light fails, lovers cling to each other, and children cling to us. The moment we cease to hold each other, the moment we break faith with one another, the sea engulfs us and the light goes out" (Baldwin and Avedon, part 4)—are climactic instants generating affinities between subjects. In these lines, Baldwin lets the forces at play interact and generate prophetic truths. The writer is an inconspicuous witness of events and transcends reality. Conversely, he may take on a more interventionist posture, as one among other participants in the making of the story, albeit as a mediator rather than as an author. The fragments of reality collected in Baldwin's literary journalism—be it, for instance, his coverage of the Conference of Negro-African Writers and Artists in Paris (1956) or his encounter with Martin Luther King Jr. in Atlanta (1961)—exemplify such situations created from impressions and interactions. Baldwin is party to a negotiation of reality, from which he draws portraits, collects observations, and divulges malaises. The resulting hall of mirrors creates competing versions of or dissenting opinions on reality. In so doing, Baldwin reconciles revelatory and creative impetuses and leaves the inconclusive present open for speculation. Baldwin's writing urges us to focus not so much on the narrative but rather on the chemistry between real characters, in and outside the text. In these examples, he is the attentive journalist alternately hopping on the stage and retiring behind the scenes, breaking the fourth wall, dissolving delusions, and offering a chance to all—characters and readers— to take a stand.

Whereas the dual "conception and periodization" of *cinéma vérité* based on the technological premises presented above is generally accepted, Adam Knee and Charles Musser propose a revision of such articulations. They posit the year 1968 as a "watershed" moment that tolled the knell of "white male hegemony in documentary film-making" (24), a postulation deduced from their thorough examination of William Greaves's pioneering documentary work on the African American experience. Greaves embraced and advanced the *cinéma vérité* he experimented with while working at the National Film Board of Canada. Although I have found no evidence of an actual encounter or collaboration between Greaves and Baldwin, chances are that the two were aware of each other.[10] Originally a black performing artist from Harlem, Greaves was in New York in 1968 to direct *Symbiopsychotaxiplasm: Take One*, a creatively and technically audacious film based on the improvisation and interaction with a crew of mixed-race men and women (20).[11] Not incidentally, Greaves then also started to host *Black Journal*, the first African American current affairs program, which was broadcast on public television from 1968 to 1970. Such forays into experimental and documentary filmmaking parallel Baldwin's tendentious modes of expression and strident calls for liberation from white domination at the time, which texts such as "White Racism or World Community?" (1968) and "The Price May Be Too High" (1969) aptly illustrate.

"White Racism or World Community?" delivered at the assembly of the World Council of Churches in Sweden, while Baldwin himself was the target of radical activists in America, sounds like a provocation: "I am saying that when a person, when a people, are able to persuade themselves that another group or breed of men are less than men, they themselves become less than men and have made it almost impossible for themselves to confront reality and to change it" (755). According to Jeffrey Santa Ana, "Baldwin posits a dialectical relationship between human feeling and social fragmentation from which the contradiction of radical consciousness emerges for the racialized minority subject" (93). I would argue that Baldwin's perspective is dialogical rather than dialectical, in the Bakhtinian sense of the term. In this particular sermon, he opens windows onto other realities—South Africa, South Asia—initiating a conversation, reaching out to third parties to shed light on a given situation. Baldwin is emulating, or anticipating, some of the groundbreaking techniques devised by Greaves. In *Symbiopsychotaxiplasm: Take One*, Greaves occasionally shows several films running parallel, "not exactly through split screens but by means of a black matte, as if in a photo album, that gives the multiple screens multiple windows" (Brody). It also contains audacious segments filmed by the crew, about which Greaves is unaware, and in which they discuss the film and its director. Baldwin's hard-hitting *écriture vérité* is congruent with Greaves's innovative and insufficiently acknowledged experiments in documentary cinema when he engages in conversations with blacks and whites, or dabbles with a wide range of creative genres.

For Baldwin, the fear of confronting "our national self" results in the country's compulsive, obsessive, and counterproductive categorization of individuals *ad absurdum* (Collier 136). While resisting the homogenizing or totalizing view that blackness is a "great big monolith" or "abstraction" (Baldwin, Interview 13), Baldwin vehemently opposes the division of individuals into categories. His personal experiences in adversity always impacted his sense of himself and his relationship to others, as Horace A. Porter argues (166). Baldwin's black perspective took different shades as soon as he no longer perceived of himself as just a "Negro" and strived to adopt "a trans-racial and an androgynous vision of human possibility" (171). However, a radical tone also erupts in the aforementioned "The Price May Be Too High," written precisely in the context of his own disappointing experience as a screenwriter with Columbia Pictures. Baldwin interrogates a racist film industry, in which "the question is not whether black and white artists can work together" but "whether or not black and white *citizens* can," thereby eroding the line between art and life. By the same token, when he labels whites "pawns" and calls blacks "victims" of a systemic racism, he places them on an equal footing. Lashing out against the contempt of those who have been "married to the lie of white supremacy too long" (*Cross of Redemption* 86), he points to a travestied reality for which everyone ends up being held accountable, and where roles could be reversed.

Baldwin's engagement with white Americans was essential and must be viewed as an all-embracing strategy to come to terms with the country's paradoxes and to debunk its perennial myths (Collier 135). But rather than holding up a mirror to white Americans, he opts for a fragmentation of perspectives aimed at dissolving a black-and-white duality into multiple points of view. This anticipates the Nancean case for a "different alterity," which posits a fertile coexistence, not the pitting of individuals and communities against each other and themselves. Sense-making, and possibly truth, is revealed in this coalescence of multiple subjectivities; it is predicated upon "compossibility," the concurrent constellation and fragmentation of units which constitute our worlds (Conley 89). Space is created for a "singular plurality" that shuns any attempt at essentializing others. Nancy champions a radical new ethic relying upon the primacy of relation, or "compearance," which pulverizes the *same* and *other* dichotomy (Watkin 50, 53). "Truth is being-*such*," Nancy argues, while "sense is the movement of being-*toward*" (12). Baldwin's *écriture vérité* is predicated upon this momentum toward the other (being-*toward*), which nourishes his inner experience. Self-reflexivity (alienation) is then conducive to a creative movement prompted by a connection imperative (fraternization) and which eventuates in moments of truth. As an emanation of imagined combinations of segments of reality, sense-making allows for constant reconfigurations of our views and depends, more fundamentally, on the capacities of humans to connect with each other (Conley 88). In shifting perspectives and eliciting a large palette of emotions, Baldwin, "faced with a myriad contradictions," deconstructs them and reasserts "life's inescapable complexity" (Field, "Looking" 473). Published twenty years apart, the two texts discussed below show that the "compossibility" hinted at in the former is more forcibly or even militantly urged upon the reader in the latter.

Nothing Personal, the sentience of things unseen

In *Telling the Truth*, Foley showcases African American novelists, among them Baldwin, whose factual fictions and self-referential autobiographies served as authenticating testaments to challenge the objectification of racial ideologies through "empirical validation" (26). In a similar vein, Mas'ud Zavarzadeh clarifies the meaning of nonfiction as "determined by its phenomenalistic, non-endorsive use of fact" and composed of "a self-verifying system" of documents that reflect the experiential world and testify to its authenticity. Zavarzadeh also makes the important point that such evidence "leads the reader to the outside world" (85, 98), thereby connecting the text to its real context and opening avenues for cogitating on truth claims. This overture is an invitation to communicate with, and thus consider, the other. When it comes to films, Jack Ellis reminds us that "documentary" originally meant "a lesson; an admonition, a warning," serving either as information or proof. Dealing with matters of public concern, albeit taken from private situations, documentaries are always "purposive" (Ellis 7). In advocating causes, they aim to enlighten, possibly to arouse sympathy and to prompt action (2–3). While documentaries derive their persuasive power from authentic material from the past, they are also reliant on their visibility in the present moment (Gauthier 8). Consequently, the veracity of a document rests on its being a fragment from the real, not necessarily a claim to truth (13, 14).

In an oft-quoted interview, Baldwin mentions his fascination with "a certain *optic*—a process of seeing things" (Elgrably and Plimpton 248). In another instance, he affirms that "a movie is, literally, a series of images, and what one *sees* in a movie can really be taken, beyond its stammering or misleading dialogue, as the key to what the movie is actually involved in saying" (Baldwin, "Carmen Jones" 38). *Nothing Personal*, Baldwin and Avedon's intermedial project, is an "interpretation" or "profound evocation of the truth of the times," as Hilton Als explains in his essay accompanying the new edition of the photo-text (*The Way We Live Now*, 2017).[12] Baldwin uses his *cinema-stylo* (camera-pen) to facilitate the passage from the sensible to the intelligible, without much interference. In the tormented switch from experience to essence, a singular perception opens itself to the universality of sense (Robert 149). Baldwin's "elegiac, crystal-clear text" leads us to a discomfort zone, a darkroom where perception requires adjustments, where the full picture reveals itself progressively (Als). His musings start with a succession of images flashing on the television screen, commercials instilling desire and anxiety, mythologies inducing reflections on other, more profound myths about the American Dream. Words are latent images disclosing past experience, illuminating the present, and providing glimpses of the future. In "The Creative Process," Baldwin anticipates when he writes, "society must accept some things as real; but [the artist] must always know that the visible reality hides a deeper one, and that all our action and all our achievement rests on things unseen" (670).

Nothing Personal is a revelation or Heideggerian *alētheia* (Nancy 16) elicited by the juxtaposition of text and image, more on the side of "truth-disclosure" than "truth-adequation," to use Todorov's apt terminology. The reader thus consents to an interpretation of events, where truth is conveyed intersubjectively, that is through access to an experience rather than to facts (Todorov 122–23). Baldwin accuses, "what the system does to the subjugated is to destroy his sense of reality" ("American Dream" 714), hence the urgency to shatter narratives that ignore the plight of African Americans. *Écriture vérité* questions our legitimacy as observers of a given reality and our willingness to address "this rigid refusal to look at ourselves" (Baldwin, "Lockridge" 593; also qtd. in Thomas 6). As a counterpoint to Avedon's photographs, Baldwin's words read as negatives revealing a different picture. They make sense by themselves, in their own arrangement, and tell another story too, when read in connection to Avedon's shots. Below the surface of the text lurks an intention, and the reader cannot be content with its face value: "the truth cannot be told, even about one's attitudes: we live by lies" (*Nothing Personal*, part 2). Baldwin and Avedon's book unveils disturbing truths. "To the force of Avedon's disciplined, revelatory photographic performances," Sara Blair eloquently sums up when she remarks that, "Baldwin juxtaposes his stance as a subjective documentary observer; in tandem, text and images deploy the tragic sensibility as a form of political agency" (186). He excavates souvenirs that lie dormant in the depths of his experience and transforms experience into testimony.

Baldwin's perceptive text, a poetic and poietic diatribe, combined with Avedon's pictures, unfolds its emotional charge "on a confrontational or frictional stance" (Blair 188). Baldwin's sentience remarkably captures the pain and anguish that comes from confronting a changing reality. He nevertheless reaffirms the interconnectedness of our lives and expresses his faith in "the human heritage" and his hope for the future, as "nothing is fixed, forever and forever and forever, it is not fixed" (*Nothing Personal*, part 4). Avedon's photos are unconventional, and Baldwin's words are speculative. The book itself is an affirmation that diverse trajectories, thanks to a providential collaboration—their work on the *Magpie*, a literary magazine—may produce stunning material.[13] As for the title, *Nothing Personal* is a double entendre that reads like a caveat against offensive divulgations and points to the absence of singularity (nothing is personal) or to a commanding view (if such is the case, then everything is plural, belongs to anyone, and concerns us all). Als's essay continues the conversation and convocation. He takes another look at Baldwin and Avedon's joint venture and reminisces about his encounter with both of them. Going through the appropriately named "contact sheets" excluded from the original volume, Als confesses his emotion at discovering the "reality" and "intimacy" of unseen shots: "What Avedon and Baldwin shared ... was an imagination that was not so much informed by reality as inseparable from it." A supporting actor in their lives, Als produces further evidence to illuminate and solidify the eminence of their work.

Patency and potency:
The Evidence of Things Not Seen

"It was something quite beyond my imagination," Baldwin confided, this horrendous *fait divers*. "I couldn't fictionalize the story of the Atlanta murders. It's beyond my province and would be very close to blasphemy," he concluded (Estes 272). The meaning Baldwin confers to the verb "fictionalize" poses a moral question, as creative techniques are deemed out of place with regard to the gravity of the situation. Any pretension to elegance in the face of atrocities, in particular the harrowing case of murdered children, would be tantamount to adding insult to injury. The task at hand is to focus on a specific event and to produce evidence, not to indulge in aesthetic considerations fashioned after brute facts. Baldwin takes a closer look at a dark reality unfolding in a context tainted by race relations. He challenges our skewed perspectives and biased views, our "ability to perceive ... at once tyrannized by our expectations" (*Evidence* 1). This is obvious, he suggests, as "much had been made of the fact (assuming it to *be* a fact) that Wayne Williams [the suspect] denied knowing any of the victims, yet was photographed in proximity to some of them" and that nobody had "associated Wayne Williams with the Terror until he was placed under *open surveillance*" (77). Baldwin collects evidence, and the absence thereof, to expose the absurd conclusions of a case whose elucidation amounts to a *trompe l'oeil*. Documenting the case means interviewing relatives, attending court hearings, getting a sense of the city. Baldwin does not arbitrarily extrapolate from facts. He spends time in Atlanta to explore the pervasive racism that may have led to a mockery of justice.

Baldwin shies away from New Journalistic techniques, inappropriate in the case of such a tragedy, which would amount to an "occasion for the exhibition of [your] virtuosity" (Estes 272). New Journalism in particular, as practiced by the likes of Tom Wolfe or Truman Capote, is characterized by its stylistic experiments with language for aesthetic ends. Baldwin refuses to hone his literary tools for they would get in the way of his moral purpose, although the choice of *le mot juste*, Susan Greenberg has shown, is more than aesthetic choice; it is also an ethical matter (527). Inasmuch as some proponents of *cinéma vérité* believed that a moral stance was essential in order to approach truth, those who favored what came to be better known as "direct cinema" saw technique as the pivotal element in the quest for truth. Baldwin writes as a faithful documentarian avoiding "predetermined outcomes" (Geiger 159). In his portrayal of the author as a "literary reporter," Derrick Bell, with Janet Dewart Bell, specify that "Baldwin eschews a search for clues and, instead, undertakes an exploration for truths. Once engaged, he follows his own leads, relying on personal perception and a probing intellect" (vii). Leaning on past and present events, convoking a number of comparisons and similes—the treatment of Indians in America (*Evidence* 42), the situation of Coloreds in South Africa (6, 28–29), the Europeans' complicity in slavery (81), the plight of Algerians in France, or starving Irish at the hands of the British (91)—Baldwin convenes a wider assembly and hopes to spark outrage. Baldwin's all-embracing, panoptic strategy aims at reducing any objectifying gaze.

While suspicious of the creative liberties of New Journalism, Baldwin is a talented reporter strongly attached to his reader by a pact guaranteeing the veracity of information, expressed in a form infused with substance and style (Dow, "Reading" 130). *The Evidence of Things Not Seen* is replete with details of felt lives, with proof that Baldwin met the families of the victims and the accused, spent time at the crime scenes, consulted documents, and confronted inconsistencies. But like a *cinéma vérité* director, he uses his camera-eye to make the most of the visible reality and fills the gaps with additional observations, in a creative manner similar to that of Jean Rouch, who relied on his editors to capture and salvage what escaped the frame. Totally immersed in the story, the ethnologist infiltrated a community and was the "human hinge of a technological revolution" (Colleyn 11; my trans.). Likewise, Baldwin penetrates the reality of the South and becomes a vital link between said reality and the outside world. By his own admission, Baldwin conceded that, "[he] had been doing what every writer, unconsciously, is always doing: a writer is never listening to what is being said, he is never listening to what is being told. He is listening to what is *not* being told, which means that he is trying to discover the purpose of the communication" (*Evidence* 95). This, coupled with his awareness that reality always conceals a more profound, invisible truth, reads like the author's clairvoyant manifesto of *écriture vérité*, in his own terms.

Throughout the investigation, Baldwin's increasingly revolted voice takes on a judgmental position. His damning indictment of America's Manifest Destiny, which he equates with "calculated and deliberate genocide," a "legend [that] has obliterated the truth" and hijacked "the American imagination" in suggesting that some are less human than others, runs parallel to the searing criticism against the murder case under scrutiny (*Evidence* 42). Aware of "the different vantage points from which our lives are apprehended," he even relinquishes the word "perception" (54), a problematic concept, as reality does not look the same for each one of us. In doubt, Baldwin self-reflectively shares his own compunctions about investigating the case. But whereas one tends to unwillingly obliterate a trauma—"one blots it out"— writing remains a saving grace (xiii). "My memory stammers: but my soul is a witness" (xv) reads like a pact through which Baldwin's own latent images of black persecution and humiliation resurface, proposing a new ethic of seeing. The fear of a collective amnesia, of forgetting "that terror which the memory repudiates ... the terror of being destroyed" (xiii–xiv) permeates his *écriture vérité* and aims for a radical climax in his exhortation to remember. His *cri de coeur* is that of "the Black preacher ... our first warrior, *terrorist*, or *guerrilla*" (82). Beyond revelation, he takes on a more assertive posture, that of a radical lecturer who adamantly refuses victimization and enunciates implacable truths.

Direct action through reconciliation

Beyond the purely aesthetic proclivity to indulge in the possibilities of an *écriture vérité*, my intention has been to expand on Baldwin's imaginative forays out of a region in his mind. *Écriture vérité* proves a solid paradigm integrative of both method (aesthetic tools and techniques) and purpose (ethical processes and intentions) to understand Baldwin's multifaceted profile and kaleidoscopic oeuvre. Moving beyond the *revelation* and *creation* impulses that polarized *cinéma vérité* filmmakers, Greaves opened a third way by crossing yet another line, showing parallel scripts and featuring a mixed-race cast in his film. Likewise, betting on Morin's brotherhood, or anticipating Nancy's communality, Baldwin's *écriture vérité* creates a new radical imagination. By his own account, he forebodes the difficulty of coming to terms with antagonisms:

the forces are there, we cannot will them away. All we can do is learn to live with them. And we cannot learn this unless we are willing to tell the truth about ourselves, and the truth about us is always at variance with what we wish to be. The human effort is to bring these two realities into a relationship resembling *reconciliation*. (Baldwin, "Creative Process" 671; emphasis added)

According to Graff, an appeal to fraternization is the essential breaking point of *cinéma vérité* with tradition. After an inevitable identification with characters, viewers become aware of the social personas crafted by these characters, and they will drop the masks to live a more authentic life favoring solidarity (*Cinéma-vérité* 46–47). In the final analysis, *revelation* and *creation* move toward *reconciliation*.

Adepts of "direct cinema" believed in the status of the artist as an activist. The polemics that pitted those who preferred the term *cinéma vérité* to "direct cinema" followed transcultural contamination and cross-fertilization. Transatlantic contacts between filmmakers and a fertile terrain for the production and distribution of their films were stimulating on several accounts. First, because the evolution of the documentary tradition was rejuvenated and reinvented by the many directors whose creative potential was maximized by technological innovations and, second, because "direct cinema" took a radical turn, with its unmediated approach to reality. Viewers become witnesses by proxy, vicariously participating in the lives of others, to whose dire situations they can relate, although their connection is only imagined (Geiger 154). Sidestepping from the scene, handing over his camera to his crew or actors, the director opens the sense of possibilities, and agency becomes a collective affair. Radical imagination eventuates into direct action, provided the previous stages of sentience and perception have been thoroughly integrated. "Direct action is what is demanded," Baldwin stated (Baldwin, Worsthorne, and Magee 120), and his "rhetoric of accusation and condemnation" supported such exhortation (Porter 158). Baldwin's *écriture vérité* emulates revolutionary cinematic techniques used to document and probe reality, and to access truth. Its emphatic force is predicated upon a passage from patency to potency.

From an early age Baldwin took refuge in reading and writing, a safe space from the violence of the streets of Harlem and his responsibilities at home, where family obligations and the care of siblings conditioned his "being-toward" or "being-toward-more-than-one," a position gained "even at the heart of solitude" (Nancy 88). Baldwin's internal ruminations in *Nothing Personal* nevertheless display a sense of community. The inevitability of our "being-in-common" is manifest in his own admission that "all lives are connected to other lives" (*Nothing Personal*, part 3). He tells stories from the past—the "mighty heritage"—and proposes another way of seeing, "descending, as it were, into the eyes of my father and my mother" (part 4).

In reaching for the roots of society's contradictions, Baldwin attacks the very causes of institutionalized racism. In reawakening a singular sedimented language suffused with plural experiences, he builds bridges for further "compossibility." "The moment we cease to hold each other, the moment we break faith with one another, the sea engulfs us and the light goes out" (part 4), he warns. Intriguingly, his peroration is followed by a picture of the members of the Student Nonviolent Coordinating Committee in Atlanta, where he would later carry out his investigation of the murdered children. As if indeed darkness had returned and confidence vanished. A sense of urgency pervades the text, as Baldwin is repeatedly calling for light without which "we will perish" (part 4).

In *The Evidence of Things Not Seen*, published some twenty years later, his tone is more confrontational and his role more directional. He collects elements from the somber reality of Atlanta and obstinately zooms in and out of the frame to integrate an abundance of asides that complete the picture and complicate the story. The patency of the evidence gleaned is leverage on the potency of his message, which is increasingly inclusive and accusatory. Baldwin's impressive knowledge of past and current histories and his powerful rhetoric are strategic ploys to reach out to individuals and include them in a responsible project. Baldwin's sense of the world shows in his highly sensitive, sensible, sensual writing. And sensational he is today, as his work is reprinted, rediscovered, and revered. With extremism and nationalism rampant in the Western world, the poet-prophet is compulsory reading, not only in America but significantly in Europe too. This is a vital part of Baldwin's legacy: to keep on confronting racial terror and bigotry. Because, as Kelley rightfully notes, "struggle is par for the course when our dreams go into action" (*Freedom Dreams* 198). *Écriture vérité* is a demanding process that calls for a multifaceted approach to reality and whose pointedness is resolutely *reconciliatory*. And yet Baldwin "refuse[s], absolutely, to speak from the point of view of the victim [as it] corroborates, simply, the reality of the chains that bind him ... and ... consoles the jailer, the keeper of the keys" (*Evidence* 78). In a radical move to shake the dungeon, Baldwin takes the keys to the house and lets his people go.

Notes

1   By way of illustration, Christian Bourgois éditions in France recently published a French translation of essays originally released in US magazines and newspapers between 1960 and 1985. See Baldwin, *Retour dans l'oeil du cyclone*.

2   Alexander argues that, like Jim Crow, mass incarceration is an institution that "serves to define the meaning and significance of race in America" (200). "New" implies that there are both similarities and differences between the

racial caste system today and the segregation laws of the past. Chapter 5, "The New Jim Crow" (178–220), specifically addresses these "parallels" (for example, legalized discrimination, political disenfranchisement, exclusion from juries, racial segregation) and the "limits of the analogy" (absence of overt racial hostility, white victims of the racial caste system, black support of tough policies).

3   Robin D. G. Kelley discussed Baldwin in 2002, on a live television program ("The Writings of James Baldwin"). On that particular subject, Baldwin did indeed write about the conditions of Algerians in Paris, and his own identity in relation to Algerians, but always with a view to his own African American background and with an emphasis on their fundamental differences. He also humbly confessed to being "almost ignorant of the details of the Algerian-French complexity." See Baldwin, "No Name" 366–67, 377. Note that Kelley's book is first and foremost on freedom dreamers and the achievements of lesser known activists. Dr. King, Malcolm X, and Amiri Baraka are featured in the book, but there is no mention of Baldwin, hence my remark.

4   *Cinéma vérité* emerged, flourished, and sparked controversy in France in the early 1960s. The genre was all the rage at the time and was eventually subsumed under the "direct cinema" moniker in Europe, while the Americans stuck with the *cinéma vérité* designation (Brault qtd. in Wintonick). Pioneers, essentially from North America, Britain, and France, brought their own expertise to this groundbreaking cinema. Without the technological innovations of the Canadians, French ethnographer Jean Rouch would never have taken to it. Neither would John Grierson, a Scottish filmmaker, have developed the British documentary movement. Note that Rouch is hailed as the inventor of *cinéma vérité* in France, a term he borrowed from, and used as a tribute to, the Russian Dziga Vertov. Together with Edgar Morin, Rouch made *Chronique d'un été* in 1961, which revolutionized filmmaking. The technological innovations led Rouch to develop immersion in cinema. The genre was occasionally called a misnomer, Séverine Graff explains, as some failed to consider its historicity. Graff's book provides a detailed framework to understand the archeology, taxonomy, and dissensions around *cinéma vérité*. See Graff, *Le cinéma-vérité*. For detailed inventories of the many designations of *cinéma vérité*, see Issari and Paul; Graff, "'Cinéma-vérité'"; and Ellis.

5   The term is used by Jonas Mekas in "New York Letter: Towards a Spontaneous Camera." In this article, Mekas discusses the "new American wave" and independent filmmakers, whose "films reveal an open ear and an open eye for timely, contemporary reality … And since their most passionate obsession is to capture life in its most free and spontaneous flight … these films could be described as a *spontaneous cinema*" (118–19).

6   Leading journals echoed the fiery debates of experts who fueled the feuds but, more vitally, also helped finetune the principles of a revolutionizing invention, later distillated in a number of variations, from "cinéma vérité" (France) to "direct cinema" (United States), "candid cinema" (Canada), or "free cinema" (Britain). A new synchronizing technology, called Nagra, made it possible to film and record action without interruption as of 1958. See Ellis 219.

7   Dialogism should be understood in the Bakhtinian sense, as a polyphony of
    voices that create space for interaction and collectively provide elements—
    albeit contradictory and subversive—to create meaning. See Bakhtin.

8   On Baldwin's links to Socrates, see also Schlosser.

9   My assumptions are only tentative but worth sharing. First, Baldwin was
    the subject of *Take This Hammer* (1963), a documentary in which Moore
    acknowledges the use of the brand new and revolutionary *cinéma vérité*
    techniques of the time (see *The Making of* Take This Hammer). Second, there
    is every indication that Baldwin, as a film critic, may have been aware of this
    movement, which French cinema journals regularly featured in their pages, in
    particular of Jean Rouch's documentaries, which often had Africans as central
    subjects. Third, I am also tempted to surmise that Baldwin may have known the
    work of William Greaves, the first prominent African American *cinéma vérité*
    director, a pioneering documentarist originally from Harlem. Both Baldwin
    and Greaves were listed as scheduled attendees in "Famous Blacks to Attend
    Festival in Nigeria" (the Second World Black and African Festival of Arts and
    Culture [FESTAC] in Lagos, Nigeria, from January 15 to February 12, 1977),
    but Baldwin did not attend, as confirmed by *The Washington Post* (Randal).

10 William Greaves does mention Baldwin in an interview with Ken Paulson on
    Speaking Freely.

11 Greaves hosted *Black Journal*, a major news program that was broadcasted
    from 1968 to 1970. Baldwin never featured in *Black Journal*, but artists such
    as James Brown, Nina Simone, and Nikki Giovanni and prominent black
    leaders such as Huey P. Newton, Stokely Carmichael, Elijah Muhammad,
    and Jesse Jackson did. *Black Journal* was a "landmark in American broadcast
    history as the first nationally-televised, regularly-scheduled African American
    public affairs program" and had a prominently African American production
    team, a first at a particularly volatile moment in the period of the civil rights
    and black liberation movements ("Black Journal").

12 The booklet pages are not numbered, so all following quotations simply refer
    to Als.

13 *The Magpie* was launched at the DeWitt Clinton High School in the Bronx.

Works Cited

Alexander, Michelle. *The New Jim Crow: Mass Incarceration in the Age of
    Colorblindness*. New Press, 2012.
Als, Hilton. *The Way We Live Now*. Taschen, 2017.
Bakhtin, Mikhail. *The Dialogic Imagination: Four Essays*. U of Texas P, 1981.
Baldwin, James. "The American Dream and the American Negro." Baldwin,
    Collected Essays, pp. 714–19.
Baldwin, James. "*Carmen Jones*: The Dark Is Light Enough." Baldwin, *Collected
    Essays*, pp. 35–41.

Baldwin, James. *Collected Essays*. Edited by Toni Morrison, Library of America, 1998.

Baldwin, James. "The Creative Process." Baldwin, *Collected Essays*, pp. 669–72.

Baldwin, James. *The Cross of Redemption: Uncollected Writings*, edited and with an introduction by Randall Kenan, Knopf Doubleday, 2010.

Baldwin, James. *The Devil Finds Work*. Baldwin, *Collected Essays*, pp. 477–572.

Baldwin, James. *The Evidence of Things Not Seen*. 1985. Henry Holt, 1995.

Baldwin, James. Interview by François Bondy. *Transition*, no. 12, Jan.–Feb. 1964, pp. 12–19.

Baldwin, James. "Lockridge: 'The American Myth.'" Baldwin, *Collected Essays*, pp. 588–93.

Baldwin, James. "No Name in the Street." Baldwin, *Collected Essays*, pp. 349–476.

Baldwin, James. "The Price May Be Too High." Baldwin, *Cross of Redemption*, pp. 105–08.

Baldwin, James. *Retour dans l'oeil du cyclone*. Christian Bourgois, 2015.

Baldwin, James. "White Racism or World Community?" Baldwin, *Collected Essays*, pp. 749–56.

Baldwin, James, and Richard Avedon. *Nothing Personal*. 1964. Taschen, 2017.

Baldwin, James, Peregrine Worsthorne, and Bryan Magee. "A Television Conversation." Standley and Pratt, pp. 113–26. Originally published in *Encounter*, no. 39, Sept. 1972, pp. 27–33.

Bell, Derrick, and Janet Dewart Bell. Foreword. *The Evidence of Things Not Seen*, by James Baldwin, Henry Holt, 1995, pp. vii–xii.

"Black Journal: Archive 1968–1970." *California Newsreel*, newsreel.org/video/BLACK-JOURNAL.

Blair, Sara. *Harlem Crossroads: Black Writers and the Photograph in the Twentieth Century*. Princeton UP, 2008.

Brody, Richard. "The Daring, Original, and Overlooked 'Symbiopsychotaxiplasm: Take One.'" *The New Yorker*, 5 Feb. 2015, newyorker.com/culture/richard-brody/daring-original-overlooked-symbiopsychotaxiplasm-take-one. Accessed 24 Aug. 2018.

Brooks, A. Russell. "James Baldwin as Poet-Prophet." *James Baldwin: A Critical Evaluation*, edited by Therman B. O'Daniel, Howard UP, 1977, pp. 126–34.

Cinéma-Vérité: Defining the Moment. Directed by Peter Wintonick. National Film Board of Canada, 1999.

Colleyn, Jean-Paul. *Jean Rouch: Cinéma et anthropologie*. Cahiers du Cinéma, 2009.

Collier, Eugenia W. "Thematic Patterns in Baldwin's Essays." *James Baldwin: A Critical Evaluation*, edited by Therman B. O'Daniel, Howard UP, 1977, pp. 135–40.

Conley, Verena Andermatt. "Nancy's Worlds." *Diacritics*, vol. 42, no. 2, 2014, pp. 84–99. doi: 10.1353/dia.2014.0008.

Dow, William. "Reading Otherwise: Literary Journalism as an Aesthetic Narrative Cosmopolitanism." *Literary Journalism Studies*, vol. 8, no. 2, Fall 2016, pp. 118–36.

Dow, William. "Unreading Modernism: Richard Wright's Literary Journalism." *Literary Journalism Studies*, vol. 5, no. 2, Fall 2013, pp. 59–89.

Elgrably, Jordan, and George Plimpton. "The Art of Fiction LXXVIII: James Baldwin." Standley and Pratt, pp. 232–54.

Ellis, Jack C. *The Documentary Idea: A Critical History of English-Language Documentary Film and Video*. Prentice Hall, 1989.

Estes, David C. "An Interview with James Baldwin." Standley and Pratt, pp. 270–80.

"Famous Blacks to Attend Festival in Nigeria." *Jet*, vol. 50, no. 15, 1 July 1976, p. 26.

Field, Douglas. *All Those Strangers: The Art and Lives of James Baldwin*. Oxford UP, 2015.

Field, Douglas. "Looking for Jimmy Baldwin: Sex, Privacy, and Black Nationalist Fervor." *Callaloo*, vol. 27, no. 2, 2004, pp. 457–80.

Foley, Barbara. "History, Fiction, and the Ground Between: The Uses of the Documentary Mode in Black Literature." *PMLA*, vol. 95, no. 3, May 1980, pp. 389–403. doi: 10.2307/461880.

Foley, Barbara. *Telling the Truth: The Theory and Practice of Documentary Fiction*. Cornell UP, 1986.

Forde, Kathy Roberts. "Communication and the Civil Sphere: Discovering Civil Society in Journalism Studies." *Civil Sphere Theory in Media History and Communication Scholarship*, special issue of *Journal of Communication Inquiry*, vol. 39, no. 2, 2015, pp. 113–24. doi: 10.1177/0196859915580849.

Forde, Kathy Roberts. "*The Fire Next Time* in the Civil Sphere: Literary Journalism and Justice in America 1963." *Literary Journalism and Ethics*, special issue of *Journalism: Theory, Practice and Criticism*, vol. 15, no. 5, Spring 2014, pp. 570–85. doi: 10.1177/1464884914523094.

Friedman, Ryan Jay. "'Enough Force to Shatter the Tale to Fragments': Ethics and Textual Analysis in James Baldwin's Film Theory." *ELH*, vol. 77, no. 2, Summer 2010, pp. 385–412. doi: 10.1353/elh.0.0088.

Gauthier, Guy. *Le documentaire, un autre cinéma*. Armand Colin, 2011.

Geiger, Jeffrey. *American Documentary Film: Projecting the Nation*. Edinburgh UP, 2011.

Graff, Séverine. "'Cinéma-vérité' ou 'cinéma-direct': Hasard terminologique ou paradigme théorique?" *Décadrages*, no. 18, 2011, pp. 32–46. journals.openedition.org/decadrages/215. Accessed 3 Sept. 2018.

Graff, Séverine. *Le cinéma-vérité: Films et controverses*. Presses Universitaires de Rennes, 2014.

Greaves, William. Interview by Ken Paulson. *Speaking Freely*, First Amendment Center, 30 July 2002. *YouTube*, uploaded by Newseum, 28 Mar. 2016, youtube.com/watch?v=dDvexn973Hc. Accessed 24 Aug. 2018.

Greenberg, Susan. "The Ethics of Narrative: A Return to the Source." *Journalism*, vol. 15, no. 5, 2014, pp. 517–32.

Haiven, Max, and Alex Khasnabish. *The Radical Imagination: Social Movement Research in the Age of Austerity*. Fernwood Publishing/Zed Books, 2014.

Henderson, A. Scott, and P. L. Thomas, editors. *James Baldwin: Challenging Authors*. Sense Publishers, 2014. Critical Literacy Teaching Series: Challenging Authors and Genre.

I Am Not Your Negro. Directed by Raoul Peck. Velvet Film and Velvet Film SAS, 2016.

I Heard It through the Grapevine. Directed by Dick Fontaine and Pat Harley. Living Archives, 1982.

Issari, M. Ali, and Doris A. Paul. *What Is Cinéma Vérité?* Scarecrow Press, 1979.

James Baldwin: The Price of the Ticket. Directed by Karen Thorsen. Maysles Films, 1989.

Kelley, Robin D. G. *Freedom Dreams: The Black Radical Imagination*. Beacon Press, 2002.

Kelley, Robin D. G. "The Writings of James Baldwin." *C-SPAN*, Washington, DC, 16 June 2002.

Khasnabish, Alex, and Max Haiven. "Convoking the Radical Imagination: Social Movement Research, Dialogic Methodologies, and Scholarly Vocations." *Cultural Studies, Critical Methodologies*, vol. 12, no. 5, 2012, pp. 408–21. doi: 10.1177/1532708612453126.

Knee, Adam, and Charles Musser. "William Greaves, Documentary Film-Making, and the African-American Experience." *Film Quarterly*, vol. 45, no. 3, Spring 1992, pp. 13–25. doi: 10.2307/1213220.

Maguire, Roberta. "African American Literary Journalism: Extensions and Elaborations." *Literary Journalism Studies*, vol. 5, no. 2, Fall 2013, pp. 8–14.

The Making of Take This Hammer. Produced by Alex Cherian. San Francisco State University and WNET.ORG, 2013. *DIVA*, San Francisco State University, diva.sfsu.edu/collections/sfbatv/bundles/210522. Accessed 24 Aug. 2018.

Marable, Manning. *Race, Reform and Rebellion: The Second Reconstruction in Black America, 1945–1982*. UP of Mississippi, 1986.

Mekas, Jonas. "New York Letter: Towards a Spontaneous Cinema." *Sight and Sound*, vol. 28, no. 3–4, Summer and Autumn 1959, pp. 118–21.

Morin, Edgar. "Edgar Morin à propos de cinéma vérité." *Un certain regard*, Office National de Radiodiffusion Télévision Française, 16 Jan. 1966. Institut National de l'Audiovisuel, ina.fr/video/I08015623. Accessed 24 Aug. 2018.

Nancy, Jean-Luc. *The Sense of the World*. U of Minnesota P, 1997.

Porter, Horace A. *Stealing the Fire: The Art and Protest of James Baldwin*. Wesleyan UP, 1989.

Randal, Jonathan C. "African Festival: Protecting Values." *The Washington Post*, 15 Jan. 1977. washingtonpost.com/archive/lifestyle/1977/01/15/african-festival-protecting-values/5b157423-c6a4-4905-8627-7932fdedce6d/?utm_term=.d33c98f0aa02. Accessed 30 Aug. 2018.

Robert, Frank. "Ecriture et vérité." *Revue internationale de philosophie*, no. 244, 2008, pp. 149–66, cairn.info/revue-internationale-de-philosophie-2008-2-page-149.htm. Accessed 24 Aug. 2018.

Roiland, Joshua M. "'Just People' Are Just People: Langston Hughes and the Populist Power of African American Literary Journalism." *African American Literary Journalism Studies*, special issue of *Literary Journalism Studies*, vol. 5, no. 2, Fall 2013, pp. 15–35.

Santa Ana, Jeffrey. "Feeling in Radical Consciousness." Henderson and Thomas, pp. 91–104.

Schlosser, Joel Alden. "Socrates in a Different Key: James Baldwin and Race in America." *Political Research Quarterly*, vol. 66, no. 3, 2013, pp. 487–99. doi: 10.1177/1065912912451352.

Schuessler, Jennifer. "James Baldwin's Archive, Long Hidden, Comes (Mostly) into View." *The New York Times*, 12 Apr. 2017, nytimes.com/2017/04/12/arts/james-baldwins-archive-long-hidden-comes-mostly-into-view.html. Accessed 24 Aug. 2018.

Standley, Fred L., and Louis H. Pratt, editors. *Conversations with James Baldwin*. UP of Mississippi, 1989.

Symbiopsychotaxiplasm: Take One. Directed by William Greaves. Janus Films, 1968.

Take This Hammer. Directed by Richard O. Moore. KQED Film Unit, San Francisco, 1963. *DIVA*, San Francisco State University, diva.sfsu.edu/collections/sfbatv/bundles/187041. Accessed 24 Aug. 2018.

Thomas, P. L. Introduction. Henderson and Thomas, pp. 1–7.

Todorov, Tzvetan. *The Morals of History*. Translated by Alyson Waters, U of Minnesota P, 1995.

Watkin, Christopher. "A Different Alterity: Jean-Luc Nancy's 'Singular Plural.'" *Paragraph*, vol. 30, no. 2, July 2007, pp. 50–64. doi: 10.1353/prg.2007.0026.

Zavarzadeh, Mas'ud. *The Mythopoeic Reality: The Postwar American Nonfiction Novel*. U of Illinois P, 1976.

6

Journeys of the "I" in James Baldwin's Literary-Journalistic Essays

William E. Dow

The first person is the most terrifying view of all.
—JAMES BALDWIN

James Baldwin is an unrecognized player in the history of African American literary journalism, a narrative form that combines the reportorial and truth-telling covenants of traditional journalism with techniques most commonly associated with fiction.[1] Primarily seen as a novelist or essayist, he has rarely been studied as a journalist or placed in an African American tradition of journalism or literary journalism. And yet, as many of his "essays" and journalistic pieces attest, he is part of a rich lineage of African American writers who have since the mid-nineteenth century produced much important literary journalism. These writers include Frederick Douglass, Alice Childress, Zora Neale Hurston, Nella Larsen, Langston Hughes, Richard Wright, Ann Petry, Isabel Wilkerson, Ta-Nehisi Coates, and Claudia Rankine.[2] In what follows, I argue that Baldwin's first-person narratives are crucial to understanding his forms of literary journalism and his versions of "the lyric essay."[3] Accordingly, Baldwin's "I" prompts us to understand his function as a writer bringing together or *pairing* literature and journalism—in ways and under a certain African American literary-journalistic tradition that have gone largely unrecognized by Baldwin critics.

In fact, extant Baldwin scholarship is still largely bifurcated between Baldwin's essays and his fiction, his political advocacy and his literary art.[4] This scholarship pays scant attention to his hybridic experimental progress and literary-journalistic use of "raw material"—the actual working forces of culture and society.[5] In this regard, the failure to recognize Baldwin within literary journalism largely stems from undervaluing this narrative form in relation to Baldwin's political advocacy. While signalling how Baldwin's eyewitness reporting seeks to explain hidden racial truths about actual people and events, this advocacy insists on "understand[ing] other subjectivities" (Hartsock 167), particularly subjectivities inseparable from racial crisis and transformation.

Tellingly, most of Baldwin's literary-journalistic essays seem to have as much "fiction" in them as his fiction does,[6] but, at the same time, their aims are different: the mediation between the reader and writer is sharper and closer in his first-person essays. This is the case even when the issues and events described are chronologically distant and overtly topical. Clearly, it is Baldwin's "I" that conflates the subjectivity of the personal essay and the objectivity of the public essay, the intelligence of the personal witness with the atemporal political prognostics that make his first-person accounts so powerful and compelling. Baldwin's first-person narratives will serve as a kind of template for what I suggest in this chapter. My argument presents an exploratory poetics of Baldwin's literary-journalistic forms, then focuses on *The Evidence of Things Not Seen* (1985) to further illustrate and add to this poetics, and ends with a discussion of what I call a "literary-journalistic reading pact," widely transferable to the variety of Baldwin's first-person forms.[7]

Baldwin's autobiographical selves

I start by sketching out a poetics appropriate to reading Baldwin's first-person nonfiction narratives. First, though, as conventional narrative categories go, the most substantial difference between a first-person nonfictional narrator and that of its counterpart in fiction is that the writer is not the same person as the narrator. In works of nonfiction, the writer and the narrator are almost always the same (see Heinze). To a certain extent, Baldwin's work can be productively conceptualized through such a division.[8] His first-person accounts generally give special attention to the relations among the narrator, the audience, and the something that has happened or perhaps might or will happen. Baldwin, the biographical author, turns himself into a narrator who reports directly to us on persons and events: either on his own experience, when the highly personal, autobiographical dimension prevails, or on others' when a more impersonal journalistic "story" is involved. Baldwin's first-person literary-journalistic pieces may be narrative, dramatic, or poetic—depending on which configuration dominates—or they may be all three. His literary journalism can be stretched in almost any direction, which can well explain the neglect of this genre in relation to Baldwin studies.[9]

Although for Baldwin the first person might be "the most terrifying point of view" ("Art of Fiction"), it is arguably his *preferred* point of view.[10] Baldwin will most often clearly identify his autobiographical self as the author of the text. For instance, the "Jimmy Baldwin" in the profile "Sidney Poitier" (1968) is the actual James Baldwin described in the text (223) as is the friend "Jimmy" to Lorraine Hansberry in the portrait "Sweet Lorraine" (1969) (757, 761). So, too, the obvious but unnamed young James Baldwin is the real-life protégé of Beauford Delaney, the African American visual artist, in "The Price of the Ticket" (1985). In this regard, Baldwin's narrative reflections in his essays commonly begin with an identification and an inquiry into the specific nature of the autobiographical self and then work outward toward social and racial realities as they affect this self. Similarly, Baldwin's narrative reflections in *Evidence* begin with this same process before expanding outward—to Atlanta, the United States, and beyond.

Congruently, Baldwin's autobiographical selves, which readily conduce to pronouncing his views on racial or ethnic communities *and* on his own writerly state, are usually explanatory in nature. "What the writer is always trying to do," Baldwin asserts in "As Much Truth as One Can Bear" (1962), "is [to] utilize the particular in order to reveal something much larger and heavier than any particular can be" (41). In a like manner, Baldwin goes from individualized to broader racial and cultural concerns in "The Discovery of What It Means to Be an American" (1961) when he gives his reasons for leaving America: "I left America because I doubted my ability to survive the fury of the color problem here. (Sometimes I still do.) I wanted to prevent myself from becoming merely a Negro; or, even merely a Negro writer" (137). Baldwin's literary journalism is more "tellable" (Schmitt, *Phenomenology* 72) than his fiction because its purpose is to *explain* the chaotic narrative of his experience. "Experientiality in narrative of personal experience," as Monika Fludernik argues, "consists in the dynamic interrelation between the description of personal experience on the one hand ... and the evaluative and rememorative transformation of this experience in the storytelling process: tellability and point of the story dialectically constitute each other" (70). For Baldwin, this dialectic results in an attempt to create a permanence for his writing self that the dangers of his social conditions cannot usurp. Although he certainly used his personal experiences as a template for understanding the larger world (Pinckney, "Magic" 367), he needed to find the most appropriate narrative forms for doing so.

This is why Baldwin, in such rarely examined profiles as "The Fight: Patterson vs. Liston" (1963), wished to provide the reader with a sensation of referential directness and clarity, while at the same time being about Baldwin's "self-story," rather than a conventional autobiographical "life story" (Schmitt, "Making" 130), and producing his conception of an essayistic literary style.[11] In "The Fight," first published in *Nugget* in 1963, Baldwin identifies himself as a "journalist,"[12] though a rather hapless one, suffering the press conferences, and freely admitting that he's not "an aficionado of the ring" (210). As Baldwin stated in a questionnaire in 1959, "the private life, his own and that of others, is the writer's subject" (Tóibín 62), a maxim teased out in "The Fight." That is, at crucial times in the essay, Baldwin focuses, both referentially and subjectively, on his real-life subjects' privacy (e.g., Patterson's "will to privacy") and on the narrator's own ("I had had a pretty definitive fight with someone with whom I had hoped to be friends") (183–84).[13]

And yet, unlike other writers traditionally considered as nonfictional writers or essayists, Baldwin does not insist on the unassailable verisimilitude of his writing. He recognizes that he does not have an unlimited authority over the life stories of his subjects, as a novelist would. Instead, Baldwin follows his emotions and intellectual logic while fusing his truth claims with the creation of himself as a symbolic cultural and racial figure who, with his journey of the "I" at the center (and not infrequently eliding into his various incarnations of "we"), freely imagines experiences and makes readers virtually *feel* his beliefs. In this way, for example, the dramatized "I" in such essays as "The Harlem Ghetto" (1955), "Equal in Paris" (1955), and "Stranger in the Village" becomes the persona of an alienated outsider who at the same time wishes to upset the comforting shibboleths of Western institutions. More precisely, the creation of this persona is yet another facet of Baldwin's autobiographical selves. As I later show, the importance of such a persona and the nature of Baldwin's literary-journalistic texts are in part determined by the position of the reader. That is, Baldwin's first-person literary-journalistic forms establish an affective model of aesthetic response that stresses the reader's activity. Although the act of reading is not an act of understanding something necessarily contained and given in advance by the text, it is, however, never separate from historical process and referent. With its interest in describing individual consciousness or experience, the first person lays its emphasis on the singularity of each reading encounter.

Furthermore, Baldwin's first-person literary journalism makes us think about what it means to read ourselves into history. Tracking the conditions of his first-person journeys constitutes a certain historical enterprise, "one that does not mitigate historical fact but persuades us of its inextricability from aesthetic articulateness" (Singer 59). *Notes of a Native Son* (1955), *Nobody Knows My Name* (1961), *The Fire Next Time* (1963), *No Name in the Street* (1972), *The Devil Finds Work* (1976)—all insist on the importance of their first-person historicity. Taken together, these collections reveal Baldwin's "preoccupation with history," which, as Kevin Birmingham contends, easily elides into his focus on "collective memory" and consciousness (226).

But, as Baldwin argues in "Autobiographical Notes" (1955), this historicity is impossible without an honest confrontation with one's past: "I think that the past is all that makes the present coherent, and further, that the past will remain horrible for exactly as long as we refuse to assess it honestly" (7). Baldwin's personal past is a constant presence in such literary-journalistic pieces as "Journey to Atlanta" (1955), "Equal in Paris," "Stranger in the Village," "Princes and Powers" (1961), "The Male Prison" (1961), and "The Harlem Ghetto": "All over Harlem now there is felt the same bitter experience with which, in my childhood, we awaited winter. It is coming and it will be hard; there is nothing anyone can do about it" ("Harlem" 42).

In his first-person forms, Baldwin constantly proclaims the necessity of his readers to understand the historical forces at work behind the racial conflicts he exposes:

> At the root of the American Negro problem is the necessity of the American white man to find a way of living with the Negro in order to be able to live with himself. And the history of this problem can be reduced to the means used by Americans—lynch law and law, segregation and legal acceptance, terrorization and concession. ("Stranger" 127)

"People are trapped in history as history is trapped in them" (119), the narrator of "Stranger in the Village" proclaims. For Baldwin, the reader must never forget this fact—and especially the responsibilities and dangers it entails.

Using such well-defined historical frames, Baldwin's first-person narratives maintain the literary as a structure of knowledge. It must be noted, though, that what one finds in his fiction—in the elements of figurative language, imagery, conflict, voice, and characterization—his first-person literary-journalistic pieces transform into an arguably closer polemical-emotional bond with the reader than his fiction allows. In this sense, it is symptomatic that Baldwin, like Joan Didion, tends to work in a smaller, more intimate range, creating sketches rather than large, synthetic narratives. As opposed to journalists who "routinely construct facts as existing independent from themselves" (Van Hout and Burger), Baldwin's literary-journalistic essays, by demonstrating how verifiable facts are not separate from his narrating self,[14] and by drawing on a visceral, experiential, and affective language to do so, produce this closer emotional-polemical bond. While often suggesting in his essays "the shape that a more effective form of [a] liberated being might take" (Murray 14), he provides a more forceful repertoire than any source-based reporting of facts.

At the same time, Baldwin's first-person essays can offer a precise sort of knowledge not available through other narrative genres and points of view.[15] Indeed, these first-person forms, which heavily rely on the literary, claim cognitive knowledge and value as an alternative to those features of writing commonly taken to be essential to the pursuit of truth: a reasoned argument, the offering of evidence, the proffering of facts and premises, and so on. "Literature standardly constructs *fictional* narratives that have *dramatic* structures," as John Gibson has argued, while "works of inquiry standardly attempt to construct *factual* narratives that have *argumentative* (or evidentiary) structures" (Gibson). Baldwin's particular first-person manner of engaging with reality produces its own "cognitive achievements intimately bound up with its aesthetic achievements" (Gibson).

Like many of Baldwin's lyric essays, "A Fly in the Buttermilk" (1961), which originated as a *Harper's* essay chronicling Baldwin's 1957 trip to the South (Leeming 137), has it both ways.[16] Based on dialogue, and literary devices and descriptions combined with expository/polemical forms and strategies, it presents Baldwin's unapologetic first-person point of view. Here is Baldwin's description of "G., one of the 'integrated' children, a boy of about fifteen" (188):

> He was tall for his age and, typically, seemed to be constructed mainly of sharp angles, such as elbows and knees. Dark gingerbread sort of coloring, with ordinary hair, and a face disquietingly impassive, save for his very dark, very large eyes. (188)

Baldwin's intense emotional connection to G. focuses on sensory intimacy and personal feeling that converge with his interrogation of black historical memory and experience. Indeed, an evidentiary purpose underlies the piece. "Segregation," the narrator affirms, "has worked brilliantly in the South, and, in fact, in the nation, to this extent: it has allowed white people, with scarcely any pangs of conscience whatever, to *create*, in every generation, only the Negro they wished to see" (195). As in so many of his essays, here Baldwin accounts for the value of such representations in cognitive terms, terms that constitute their own forms of cognitive insight.

Originally published in *The New Yorker*, Baldwin's "Down at the Cross" (1963) follows a similar narrative trajectory, inventiveness, and purpose. As in "A Fly in the Buttermilk," Baldwin begins by recounting something from his past life: the "religious crisis" he experienced when he was fourteen, his escape *into* the church (296, 298–99), and a self-inflicted, "merciless" judgement of himself (301). He goes on to describe his encounter with Elijah Muhammed, the leader of the Nation of Islam (NOI) from 1934 to 1975, whose "message did not strike [Baldwin] as being very original" (314). Nevertheless, while rejecting the NOI's ideological demands and political prescriptions, Baldwin sympathizes with the spirit of Muhammed's "history" and anger: "Who, then, is to say with authority where the root of so much anguish and evil lies? Why, then, is it not possible that all things began with the black man and that he was perfect—especially since this is precisely the claim that white people have put forward for themselves all these years?" (326). Baldwin then proceeds to "posit his own model of liberated subjectivity" (Murray 16) that eventually becomes the focus of the text. As D. Quentin Miller observes, the ideas expressed in this essay "were a virtual blueprint of the late 1960s, marked by assassinations, race riots, and the rise of radical militants such as the Black Panther Party as well as by the nonviolent protests led by Martin Luther King, Jr" (100).

But it can be argued that the main power of this piece is most revealing in the rhetorical force that Baldwin expresses in his dissent to the NOI philosophy, a dissent that takes distinctly figurative, psychological, and mythical forms. As soon as he enters Muhammed's spacious Chicago mansion, Baldwin begins to create the seductive aura of Muhammed's eventual "royal presence" (321) by describing, in a nostalgically lyrical way, the "large room" (322) where the meeting will take place:

> The sunlight came into the room with the peacefulness one remembers from rooms in one's early childhood—a sunlight encountered later only in one's dreams. I remember being astounded by the quietness, the ease, the peace, the taste. (322)

When Muhammed enters the room, Baldwin is immediately struck by how he teased the women "like a father" and his place among "the others" as if they were "his children" (323). Baldwin then observes, "He made me think of my father and me as we might have been if we had been friends" (323). The encounter, as Baldwin tells us, makes him feel as if he were "back in his father's house—as, indeed, in a way I was—and I told Elijah that *I* did not care if white and black people married, and that I had many white friends" (327). Then gently, kindly, pitifully remonstrated for these beliefs, Baldwin realizes that he has no "evidence to give [Muhammed's followers] that would outweigh Elijah's authority or the evidence of their own lives or the reality of the streets outside" (328). Significantly, when Muhammed announces to his members that "I've come … to give you something which can never be taken from you" (330), a different kind of light takes over:

> How solemn the table became then, and how great a light rose in the dark faces! This is the message that has spread through streets and tenements and prisons, through the narcotics wards, and past the filth and sadism of mental hospitals to a people from whom everything has been taken away, including, most critically, their sense of their own worth. People cannot live without this sense; they will do anything whatever to regain it. (330)

Baldwin concludes his description by dramatizing his departure from Muhammed in mythical terms. As the younger Baldwin had left his father's house and religious/racial belief systems in Harlem, so too he leaves Muhammed's doctrinal Chicago mansion:

> I felt very close to him, and really wished to be able to love and honor him as a witness, an ally, and a father. I felt that I knew something of his pain and his fury, and, yes, even his beauty. Yet precisely because of the reality and the nature of those streets—because of what he conceived as his responsibility and what I took to be mine—we would always be strangers, and possibly one day enemies ... He walked into his mansion and shut the door. (231–32)

Confirming the ideological schism that the encounter had led to, the prodigal son is cast from his father's world and dropped off at the symbolic "enemy's door" (333). As with "A Fly in the Buttermilk," Baldwin, constantly alternating between the personal and the social, returns to his place in a fractured 1960s nation.

As "A Fly in the Buttermilk" and "Down at the Cross" attest, Baldwin's first-person literary-journalistic essays tend to be diachronic rather than synchronic: these essays are and are not literature; they are and are not journalism; or rather they are not yet literature; or rather they are not yet journalism but could evolve or dissolve into either narrative form. This speaks to Baldwin's inclination, in his first-person narratives, toward a "free improvisation," which, as Carter Mathes argues, "begins to capture part of the critical and formal interplay between vernacular tradition and formal innovation that Baldwin executes in his texts" (591). In the case of these two pieces, however, the fact that they are concerned with ideas ultimately addressed directly by an author to a reader, assigns the genre primarily to a category of didactic, expository, or critical writing. In "Down at the Cross," responding to Elijah Muhammed's dictum on the necessity of protecting black women, Baldwin proclaims:

> *Protect your women*: a difficult thing to do in a civilization sexually so pathetic that the white man's masculinity depends on a denial of the masculinity of the blacks. *Protect your women*: in a civilization that emasculates the male and abuses the female, and in which, moreover, the male is forced to depend on the female's bread-winning power. *Protect your women*: in the teeth of the white man's boast "We figure we're doing you folks a favour by pumping some white blood into your kids," and while facing the Southern shotgun and Northern billy. (330–31)

Insofar as the literary-journalistic account's essential quality is persuasion, insofar as in its purest form it is argument, the aesthetic organization of the material remains subordinated to the treatment of an event or situation that exists in time and space, of an idea or text that the writer is ultimately committed to telling the "truth" about, a truth that, while perhaps not necessarily unassailable, he is answerable for.[17]

The Evidence of Things Not Seen: "I'm not a very aggressive journalist"

Cast in the first person, *Evidence* is a revealing indicator of how, through a literary-journalistic filter, Baldwin's "I" prompts us to understand his function as a writer bringing together or *pairing* literature and journalism.[18] And yet, in *Evidence*, Baldwin's journalism questions Atlanta's image as a thriving industrial capital on its way to full racial integration: "in the present case, the Black people of Atlanta found themselves, today, and under the intolerably brutal and indifferent public light, living nothing less than the ancestral, daily, historical truth of Black life in this country" (49). In his *Playboy* article, "Atlanta: The Evidence of Things Not Seen" (1981), which he expanded four years later into the revised book-length *Evidence*, Baldwin "dismantles the myth of Atlanta's exceptionalism as the jewel of the New South, decrying this myth as a capitalist fantasy that screened out and thus betrayed the urgent demand for black political sovereignty in the United States" (Eburne 261). To this end, Baldwin argues that racial segregation, plaguing the daily operations of the city, obviates its exceptionalist claims to integration:

> And as of this moment, when the white folks have fled, Atlanta becomes a black enclave. The whites flee by way of the bristling system of freeways— known as the "ring around the Congo"—or by means of the rapid-transit system, MARTA, which translates as "moving Africans rapidly through Atlanta," another joke, which might have elicited a girlish giggle from Scarlett O'Hara and a resigned yuk-yuk-yuk from Mammy. ("Atlanta" 142)

Baldwin's first-person narration in the *Playboy* article stands as a recognizable illustration of a first-person journalistic critique. On the level of a realistic nonfictional account, Atlanta is castigated as a city at odds with its vision of innocence and racial progress.

Baldwin's use of the first person works on several levels in *Evidence*. In this "much maligned work" (Reid-Pharr 133), Baldwin analyzes the disappearance and murders of over twenty-eight young African Americans in Atlanta, which occurred from 1979 to 1981, and the trial of the man who was charged with two of the murders, Wayne Williams. Alternating between literary-journalistic renditions and historical meditations, Baldwin clearly identifies his autobiographical self as the author of the text in the preface to *Evidence*. As in "Sweet Lorraine" and "The Price of the Ticket," Baldwin's narrative reflections in *Evidence* begin with an identification and an inquiry into the specific nature of the autobiographical self. "And, after all, what I remembered," Baldwin writes "—or imagined myself to remember—of my life in America (before I left home!) was terror. And what I am trying to suggest by what *one imagines oneself to be able to remember* is that terror cannot be remembered" (xiii).

This personal reflection on terror vis-à-vis the autobiographical self expansively contributes to Baldwin's description of the horrors of the Atlanta murders and their effects on the black communities in Atlanta and the United States at large: "in the present case, the Black people of Atlanta found themselves, today, and under the intolerably brutal and indifferent public light, living nothing less than the ancestral, daily, historical truth of Black life in this country" (*Evidence* 49). In a wider sense, however, this is the terror, Baldwin goes on to evoke, that is caused by a society structured on the rigid hierarchies of capitalism, which he links to the larger problem of global colonialism: "The situation of the Black American 'minority' connects with the situation of the so-called 'emerging' or Third World Nations. These existed, until only yesterday, merely as a source of capital for the 'developed' nations" (27). Consistent with such pieces as "Journey to Atlanta" and "Fifth Avenue Uptown: A Letter from Harlem" (1961), Baldwin blends such political pronouncements with emotional appeals in *Evidence* to inform his readers of *his* understanding of racial history: "I am making a very deliberate effort to make you put two ordeals—the Black and the White—side by side. The real and unanswerable character of that history that calls itself White is that, first of all, in the world in which we live, there is no other history" (80).

Evidence insists on the importance of its first-person historicity. Baldwin was a major player in the American civil rights movement and makes this fact known in the narrative (see Scott). In this regard, he recounts his experiences with the "Black demand" (*Evidence* 24) for desegregation:

> I was living in Washington, for example, in 1955, when downtown Washington had been desegregated for about a year. Almost none of the people I knew had yet tested these waters. I was one of the first parties to go downtown to see what would happen … All of the energy of a powerful Republic had kept those doors locked in our faces for a very long time. Men had died, in order to break down those doors. (23–24)

More specifically, as this passage and much of the text suggests, it is the internal perspectives of this literary-journalistic text (e.g., "Yet, I will remember, until I die, the face of the father of Patrick Balthazar, and the afternoon I spent with him, and his eyes and his voice" [80]), achieved through first-person narration, that best promotes narrator identification and reader empathy.

This empathy is perhaps most strongly evoked in Baldwin's descriptions of poverty.[19] Baldwin highlights the importance of poverty—not only as a "critical category" (see G. Jones 148) but also as a literary-journalistic frame for organizing and analyzing race and culture. Much of what Baldwin does in *Evidence* centers on the sociological precept that "the problem is not race, but class" (*Evidence* 38). In this sense, the only "pattern" that Baldwin can detect in the murders is that all the victims were "living in ... the eternity ... of poverty" (64):

> For the children came, mainly, from Atlanta's lowest economic stratum. This means that they were strangers to safety, for, in the brutal generality, only the poor watch over the poor ... If I say that the poor are strangers to safety, it is not only because others look on the poor with such a defensive disdain, it is also because the poor cannot bear to see the condescension and pity they see in the eyes of others. (62, 63)

Baldwin's fictional/nonfictional and autobiographical engagements with poverty unsettle literary-historical and literary-journalistic categories. In this connection, he is perennially aware that "societal relations must change, that existing affairs are onerous, incompetent, or evidently soul-destroying" and that we "need to [re]organize our collective interactions" (Russ 1). As suggested in the above passage, Baldwin's emotive language has declarative power that *tells* us about the state and nature of our present world. At the same time, his radical imagination, with its multiple valences, can suggest a collective potentiality, grounded in present experience and therefore disassociated from any fanciful utopia.

This kind of socioracial consciousness, when conjoined with Baldwin's literary-journalistic intensity, is inseparable from his first-person self-exposure, which can politically critique racial and intercultural relations and serve as a self-evacuating mode of writing. For example, in his meeting with Ms. Bell, the mother of one of the murdered Atlanta children, Baldwin becomes a hapless "listening" journalist, feeling, as never before, like an "interloper" and "stranger," and cursing "the editor whose brainstorm this had been" (*Evidence* 54, 55). Needless to say, this sort of self-exposure is an essential feature of Baldwin's first-person poetics. It can be seen as well in "Notes of a Native Son" in which he recounts the personal effects of a violent racist incident: "I had been ready to commit murder. I saw nothing very clearly but I did see this: my life, my *real* life, was in danger, and not from anything other people might do but from the hatred I carried in my own heart" (72). Or in "Equal in Paris" when the narrator, financially strapped and suffering, reveals his melancholy and fear in an alienating Paris: "I was beginning to be frightened and I bent all my energies, therefore, to keeping my panic under control. I began to realize that I was in a country I knew nothing about, in the hands of a people I did not understand at all" (105–06). Used as a constant reference point and reminder, Baldwin's first-person self-exposure is essential to the creation of the narrating self:

> If I speak to you, I want you to hear me—to hear *me*—and to see me. Speech and language, however ceremonious, complex, and convoluted, are a way of revealing one's nakedness; and this revelation is, really, our only human hope. (*Evidence* 43)

This self in *Evidence*, however, does not necessarily constitute any one unified entity or totalized self but rather expresses "a reflexive guise" (Velleman 1) under which certain facets of the narrator seem to be presented to himself and to the reader at the same time.

A fragmented, unchronological, and literary-impressionistic narrative, *Evidence* intimately associates Baldwin's own existential alienation with the racial and social power struggles then taking place in the United States (e.g., Baldwin contravening the idea of "racial integration" as defined by the dominant white society). As Jonathan Eburne contends, "his target is not the singularity of a horrific state of crimes but the social structures and relations of power within which the crimes appear as both a symptom and an earth-shattering event" (263). But Baldwin needed to create narrative forms most compatible to condemning such structures and relations and to presenting his alternatives to them. He does so in part through the dramatic "I" of *Evidence*, which functions as a vehicle for both private and public thoughts, its compass widening throughout the work. This is also a digressive, elliptical "I" that seeks to define not only the present menace of the Atlanta murders but also the political and ideological inheritance of African Americans:

> In any case, we are all born into communities, whether we like it or not or know it or not and whether or not we get along with the community. And when I speak of doing one's first works over, I am referring to the movement of the human soul in crisis, which, then, is forced to re-examine the depths from which it comes in order to strike water from the rock of the inheritance. (123)

It can be a private, intimate "I" most meaningful in a public, transracial, transnational sense.

> [African Americans] knew, at a glance, what would become of them if they did *not* become White .... I say, to "become" White, for they had not been White before their arrival, any more than I, in Africa, had been Black. In Africa, I had been part of a tribe and a language. (30)

It can be a reflective, emotive "I," embodying aspects of human experience and circumstance, as in Baldwin's reminiscences of Buddy, a "sinful" boy Baldwin met when Baldwin was fourteen, just after joining the church:

> By speaking to Buddy, I risked a reprimand and might have been forced to undertake a purifying fast ... Yet, I spoke to him. We talked awhile. But he scarcely knew me—I was not one of the "older" boys. I still remember his face, lightless and lonely, unbelievably lonely, looking at something far away or deep within. (121)

And it can be a journalistic "I" devoted to gathering information, revealing how Baldwin obtained it, and providing details of the Wayne Williams case and trial:

> This is the lawyer [Ms. Welcome] Wayne Williams chose to defend him. I am told that Wayne Williams would probably have met her while she was city solicitor, and while Wayne was acting, in effect, as unofficial, unconnected (and apparently unwanted) police reporter. He was, I am told, in what was described to me as an "imitation" unmarked police car, and with his camera and tape-recording equipment, at the scene of every accident, every crime, even going so far as attempting to get a job in the morgue. (117)

Perhaps most revealingly, however, the "I" in *Evidence* adopts a *persona* as an outside prophetic viewer of Western culture and history:[20]

> This is the only nation in the world that can hope to liberate—to begin to liberate—mankind from the strangling idea of the national identity and the tyranny of the territorial dispute. I know this sounds remote now, and that I will not live to see anything resembling this hope come to pass. Yet, I know that I *have* seen it—in fire and blood and anguish, true, but I have seen it. I speak with the authority of the issue of the slave born in the country once believed to be: *the last best hope of earth*. (124–25)

Here Baldwin's persona gives an account of how he acknowledges what he knows and of how this knowledge could designate the knower as a certain kind of visionary. And for this, as opposed to the elaboration of a political program, a certain vision of human possibility is necessary. Clearly, Baldwin's first-person literary journalism is exemplary not so much for the wealth of his knowledge as for his *vision*, a vision that contributes to bringing the writer's racial-historical conceptions as a whole before us. Thus, because "the present social and political apparatus cannot serve human need" (124), *Evidence* constitutes Baldwin's efforts to confront racial terror with visionary alternatives. As Hortense Spillers has argued, "[Baldwin's] conception ... of a prophetic dimension would be borne out in the democratic process as the route to the achievement of 'our country': one that is no longer based on skin color, but rather on consciousness" (244–45). Emphasizing the problems of white supremacy and massive social alienation and dislocation, *Evidence* points to this consciousness: to recognize that the world of a racial injustice can and should be changed and to imagine accordingly what social relations and institutions might "otherwise be" (Haiven and Khasnabish 3).

Literary-journalistic reading pact

As part of his first-person strategies, Baldwin (ideally) creates, heightened by his profusion of personal data and references, what I call a *literary-journalistic pact* or tacit narrative understanding with the reader. For the pact to be effective, not only must "the author, the narrator, and the protagonist … be identical" (Lejeune 5) but the author must be convincing both on a referential level and on a story or discourse level. Implicit in this pact is the reader's attention to the world created by the referential world outside the text *and* by the text itself. For Baldwin, this world would include the immeasurable problems of race, racial exclusion, and poverty as well as the possibilities of a modern racial ideal and, as suggested in *Nobody Knows My Name*, a deracialization of the self as a precondition for being in society.[21]

Thus the literary-journalistic pact cannot be concluded (or conclusively analyzed) by taking into consideration the text alone. Nor can it be concluded by neglecting the author's purposes of enlivening, reiterating, or bringing attention to the referential level. This pact forms the basic relationship through which literary journalists bind themselves to their readers—that is, by warranting true statements that can be factually verified, by insisting on a verifiable autobiographical self, and by simultaneously employing a literary expressiveness that is as effective as the discourse of a literary text. In contrast, in a fictional text, the author is not necessarily identical to the narrator, and the protagonist and the contents of the text need not be verifiable.[22] This pact therefore suggests that the literary-journalistic text is as much a mode of reading as it is a genre of writing—which, in my view, most differentiates literary journalism from either literature or journalism.[23] For the pact to work, however, "the lure and the blur of the real" must effectively combine with an "overly literal tone, as if a reporter were viewing a strange culture" (Shields 5). As if this strange culture were being explained for the first time.

The reading of Baldwin's first-person narratives should be an attempt not only to look at literary-journalistic writing as a cultural or historical document but also to attend to what these narratives do as distinct from other language acts. More precisely, congruent to the pact, this position entails a phenomenology of reading in which experience is always related to narrative and new experiences will constantly affect our narrative interpretations. As Hanna Meretoja has argued in her discussion on the ontological significance of narratives: "narrative interpretations have a very real effect on our being in the world: they take part in the making of the intersubjective world … and affect the ways in which we act in the world with others" (101).[24] Reading Baldwin's use of the first-person singular—and of such forms in general—demands new formalistic tools based on such a pact, the value of which is inescapably linked to the experience of the reader and to the reader's willingness to be changed by his or her reading experience. With the aim of a reader's racial and cultural understanding at their center, Baldwin's literary-journalistic essays—particularly those in the first person—treat the world foremost as a subject of concern. They engage in a form of worldly investigation that is markedly different from either fiction or nonfiction.

Notes

1 I prefer the term literary journalism over nonfiction and other narrative classifications because the works by Baldwin that I assign to this narrative form are not merely editorials, essays, autobiographies, memoirs, or travel narratives, as conventionally defined. What I call literary journalism in relation to Baldwin involves artistic practices that are most often used to investigate social, racial, cultural, or political circumstances.

2 For an incisive overview of African American literary journalism, see Maguire.

3 I take my definition of the lyric essay from Deborah Tall and John D'Agata: "Given its genre mingling, the lyric essay often accretes by fragments, taking shape mosaically—its import visible only when one stands back and sees it whole. The stories it tells may be no more than metaphors. Or, storyless, it may spiral in on itself, circling the core of a single image or idea, without climax, without a paraphrasable theme. The lyric essay stalks its subject like quarry but is never content to merely explain or confess. It elucidates through the dance of its own delving." See also D'Agata; and Shields 26–27.

4 This critical neglect overlooks the essential functions of Baldwin's "I" narratives in relation to his racial politics, cultural commitments, and essayistic eloquence. Essentially ignoring Baldwin's fusions of narrative mediums, the artificial bifurcation has also resulted in a critical neglect of Baldwin's aesthetics—and specifically how his activism and writing have mutually influenced each other. For exceptions to this neglect, see Dekoven; Karrer 113–28; and Cunningham. For a formal analysis of Baldwin's poetry, see M. D. Jones.

5 This chapter is adapted from and expands on the ideas I presented in "Reading Otherwise: Literary Journalism as an Aesthetic Cosmopolitanism."

6 As John Henrik Clarke stated in his 1969 essay, "The Alienation of James Baldwin," "Baldwin, more than any other writer of our times, has succeeded in restoring the personal essay to its place as a form of creative literature" (351).

7   My argument is in the spirit of Douglas Field's recent advice on the future
    direction of Baldwin studies: "Scholars no longer need to write about
    [Baldwin's] critical neglect; the critical ground has been cleared, and it should
    make way for criticism that pays more attention to Baldwin's style—to his
    formal qualities as poet, playwright, novelist and essay writer" (Sinitiere).

8   But narrative theorists have complicated this conventional equation by
    questioning first-person narrative taxonomies. Paul John Eakin, for example,
    argues that all first-person narratives can be defined as "autobiographical
    narratives" since such narratives depend as much on a process of self-invention
    and imagination as on historical fact (330). In a different vein, J. David
    Velleman, objecting to equating "selves" to "actual persons," emphasizes the
    relationship of reflexivity to self-knowledge: "the self does not denote any
    one entity but rather expresses a reflexive guise under which parts or aspects
    of a person are presented in his own mind" (1). Narrative creation may be a
    significant feature of the self but does not necessarily compose a whole life
    narrative. The generic ambiguity of first-person narrations and taxonomies
    of the self aside, however, Baldwin imparts to his texts a fictional status while
    at the same time distilling within his texts autobiographical facts that can be
    authenticated as biographical data.

9   More generally, there is a lack of criticism devoted to interpreting works
    variously called literary journalism, narrative journalism, creative nonfiction,
    narrative reportage, the lyric essay, and more. On this matter, see Wilson.

10 For example, in *Notes of a Native Son* (1955), eight of the eleven pieces in the
    collection are cast in the first person; in *Nobody Knows My Name* (1961),
    only one out of the fourteen essays is not in the first person. In the majority of
    Baldwin's essays, the first-person can be seen to dominate.

11 For this distinction, see Schmitt, "Making" 130–33.

12 As with Zora Neale Hurston, Nella Larsen, Richard Wright, and Langston
    Hughes studies, this is a self-identification largely unexamined in Baldwin
    scholarship.

13 Baldwin is referring to Norman Mailer here. See Leeming 183–84.

14 For an astute discussion on how "Baldwin portrays his personal experience
    within a racial system," see Norman 87–115.

15 For the importance of the first-person singular and the phenomenology
    of reading, see my article "Reading Otherwise: Literary Journalism as an
    Aesthetic Cosmopolitanism."

16 As David Leeming has remarked, "Baldwin's perspective throughout the trip
    to the South was as much that of a novelist as of the reporter or social activist.
    What did racism do to the inner lives of people—black people and white
    people?—was always the question" (140).

17 In an ancillary way, we might ask if Baldwin's first-person literary journalism,
    besides being a narrative mode, might more productively be conceived as
    an analytical mode that—in evoking a certain authority to the referential—
    distinguishes itself from fiction and conventional journalistic texts, and
    whether we must adjust our reading practices accordingly.

18   "I'm not a very aggressive journalist" is Baldwin's self-description in "The
      Fight: Patterson vs. Liston" (211), an apt description of the journalist-narrator
      in *Evidence*.

19   For an assessment of the critically overlooked relationship between Baldwin
      and poverty, see Lyne.

20   Allowing the necessary latitude for him to discuss both his public and his private
      responsibilities, Baldwin's first-person visionary potential is everywhere in his
      essays. See, for example, in the *Collected Essays*, "Nobody Knows My Name"
      230; "They Can't Turn Back" 628; "Take Me to the Water" 385; "To Be Baptized"
      431–32; and especially "Down at the Cross": "Everything now, we must assume,
      is in our hands; we have no right to assume otherwise. If we—and now I mean
      the relatively conscious whites and the relatively conscious blacks, who must like
      lovers, insist on, or create, the consciousness of the others—do not falter in their
      duty now, we may be able, handful that we are, to end the racial nightmare, and
      achieve our country, and change the history of the world" (346–47).

21   As more explicitly expressed in Baldwin's later writings and interviews, this
      ideal would also include a "sexual maturity" dependent on a "racial maturity."
      As Baldwin stated in the 1984 interview with Richard Goldstein, "the sexual
      question and the racial question have always been entwined ... If Americans
      can mature on the level of racism, then they have to mature on the level of
      sexuality" (Baldwin, "'Go the Way'" 178).

22   My argument here is indebted to Philippe Lejeune's *On Autobiography* and
      Philippe Carrard's "Picturing Minds: Biography and the Representation of
      Consciousness."

23   How might the distinctiveness of reading literary-journalistic texts result in
      certain epistemological forms of interpretation? In a matter of degree vis-à-vis
      literary and "mainstream" journalistic works, does narrative journalism, in
      its reading demands, encourage more a cocreating or forging of links between
      things that were previously unconnected? Might the emphasis on reading
      such texts be on acts of making rather than unmaking, composing rather than
      critiquing, substantiating rather than subverting?

24   Randall Kenan raises a related point in his discussion of fictional and
      nonfictional forms: "It is telling that we are now at a time when the American
      literary establishment is reassessing nonfiction's relationship to fiction. Which
      is the superior form? Can a work of nonfiction compare to a great novel?"
      Kenan goes on to suggest that "James Baldwin's legacy seems tailor-made for
      this literary debate" (59). But Baldwin criticism has not adequately engaged in
      the debate, particularly as it concerns Baldwin's first-person forms.

Works Cited

Baldwin, James. "The Art of Fiction No. 78." Interview by Jordan Elgrably. *The
      Paris Review*, no. 91, Spring 1984, theparisreview.org/interviews/2994/the-art-
      of-fiction-no-78-james-baldwin. Accessed 23 Aug. 2018.

Baldwin, James. "As Much Truth as One Can Bear." Baldwin, *The Cross of Redemption*, pp. 34–42.

Baldwin, James. "Atlanta: The Evidence of Things Not Seen." *Playboy*, Dec. 1981.

Baldwin, James. "Autobiographical Notes." Baldwin, *Collected Essays*, pp. 5–9.

Baldwin, James. *Collected Essays*. Edited by Toni Morrison, Library of America, 1998.

Baldwin, James. *The Cross of Redemption: Uncollected Writings*. Edited by Randall Kenan, Vintage, 2011.

Baldwin, James. "The Discovery of What It Means to Be an American." Baldwin, *Collected Essays*, pp. 137–42.

Baldwin, James. "Down at the Cross." Baldwin, *Collected Essays*, pp. 296–348.

Baldwin, James. "Equal in Paris." Baldwin, *Collected Essays*, pp. 101–116.

Baldwin, James. *The Evidence of Things Not Seen*. Henry Holt, 1985.

Baldwin, James. "The Fight: Patterson vs. Liston." Baldwin, *The Cross of Redemption*, pp. 207–21.

Baldwin, James. "A Fly in the Buttermilk." Baldwin, *Collected Essays*, pp. 187–96.

Baldwin, James. "'Go the Way Your Blood Beats': An Interview with James Baldwin." Interview by Richard Goldstein. *James Baldwin: The Legacy*, edited by Quincy Troupe, Simon and Schuster, 1989, pp. 57–74.

Baldwin, James. "The Harlem Ghetto." Baldwin, *Collected Essays*, pp. 42–53.

Baldwin, James. *No Name in the Street*. Baldwin, *Collected Essays*, pp. 349–476.

Baldwin, James. "Notes of a Native Son." Baldwin, *Collected Essays*, pp. 63–84.

Baldwin, James. "Sidney Poitier." Baldwin, *The Cross of Redemption*, pp. 222–32.

Baldwin, James. "Stranger in the Village." Baldwin, *Collected Essays*, pp. 117–36.

Baldwin, James. "Sweet Lorraine." Baldwin, *Collected Essays*, pp. 757–61.

Birmingham, Kevin. "No Name in the South: James Baldwin and the Monuments of Identity." *African American Review*, vol. 4, no. 1–2, Spring/Summer 2011, pp. 221–34. doi: 10.1353/afa.2011.0014.

Carrard, Philippe. "Picturing Minds: Biography and the Representation of Consciousness." *Narrative*, vol. 5, no. 3, Oct. 1997, pp. 287–305. *JSTOR*, jstor. org/stable/20107125. Accessed 24 Aug. 2018.

Clarke, John Henrik. "The Alienation of James Baldwin." *Black Expression*, edited by Addison Gayle, Weybright and Talley, 1969, pp. 350–53.

Cunningham, James. "Public and Private Rhetorical Modes in the Essays of James Baldwin." *Essays on the Essay: Redefining the Genre*, edited by Alexander J. Butrym, U of Georgia P, 1989.

D'Agata, John. *The Next American Essay*. Graywolf Press, 2003.

Dekoven, Marianne, editor. *Feminist Locations: Global and Local, Theory and Practice*. Rutgers UP, 2001.

Dow, William. "Reading Otherwise: Literary Journalism as an Aesthetic Cosmopolitanism." *Literary Journalism Studies*, vol. 8, no. 2, Fall 2016, pp. 119–37.

Eakin, Paul John. *Fictions in Autobiography: Studies in the Art of Self-Invention*. Princeton UP, 1985.

Eburne, Jonathan. "The Terror of Being Destroyed." *Critical Philosophy of Race*, vol. 3, no. 2, 2015, pp. 259–83.

Fludernik, Monika. *Towards a "Natural" Narratology*. Routledge, 1996.

Gibson, John. "Literature and Knowledge." *The Oxford Handbook of Philosophy and Literature*, edited by Richard Eldridge, Oxford UP, 2009. *Oxford Handbooks Online*.

Haiven, Max, and Alex Khasnabish. *The Radical Imagination: Social Movement Research in the Age of Austerity*. Zed Books, 2014.

Hartsock, John C. *A History of American Literary Journalism: The Emergence of a Modern Narrative Form*. U of Massachusetts P, 2000.

Heinze, Ruediger. "Violations of Mimetic Epistemology in First-Person Narrative Fiction." *Narrative*, vol. 16, no. 3, Oct. 2006, pp. 279–97.

Jones, Gavin. *American Hungers: The Problems of Poverty in U.S. Literature, 1840–1945*. Princeton UP, 2008.

Jones, Meta Duewa. "Baldwin's Poetics." *The Cambridge Companion to James Baldwin*, edited by Michele Elam, Cambridge UP, 2015, pp. 41–55.

Kaplan, Cora, and Bill Schwarz, editors. *James Baldwin: America and Beyond*. U of Michigan P, 2011.

Karrer, Wolfgang. "Discursive Strategies in James Baldwin's Essays." *James Baldwin: His Place in American Literary History and His Reception in Europe*, edited by Jakob Köllhofer, Peter Lang, 1987, pp. 113–28.

Kenan, Randall. "James Baldwin, 1924–1987: A Brief Biography." *A Historical Guide to James Baldwin*, edited by Douglas Field, Oxford UP, 2009.

Leeming, David. *James Baldwin: A Biography*. Arcade Publishing, 1994.

Lejeune, Philippe. *On Autobiography*. Translated by Katherine Leary, U of Minnesota P, 1989.

Lyne, Bill. "God's Black Revolutionary Mouth: James Baldwin's Black Radicalism." *Science & Society*, vol. 74, no. 1, Jan. 2010, pp. 12–36. doi: 10.1521/siso.2010.74.1.12.

Maguire, Roberta, editor. *African American Literary Journalism*, special issue of *Literary Journalism Studies*, vol. 5, no. 2, Fall 2013.

Mathes, Carter. "'The Mind Is a Strange and Terrible Vehicle': Fractured Time and Multidimensional Sound in *No Name in the Street*." *African American Review*, vol. 46, no. 4, Winter 2013, pp. 587–604. doi: 10.1353/afa.2013.0090.

Meretoja, Hanna. "Narrative and Human Existence: Ontology, Epistemology, and Ethics." *New Literary History*, vol. 45, no. 1, Winter 2014, pp. 89–109. doi: 10.1353/nlh.2014.0001.

Miller, D. Quentin. "James Baldwin's Critical Reception." *Critical Insights: James Baldwin*, edited by Morris Dickstein, Salem Press, 2011, pp. 95–112.

Murray, Rolland. *Our Living Manhood*. U of Pennsylvania P, 2007.

Norman, Brian. *The American Protest Essay and National Belonging*. SUNY P, 2007.

Pinckney, Darryl. "The Magic of James Baldwin." *Critical Insights: James Baldwin*, edited by Morris Dickstein, Salem Press, 2011, pp. 365–99.

Pinckney, Darryl. "On James Baldwin." *The New York Review of Books*, 4 Apr. 2013, nybooks.com/articles/2013/04/04/james-baldwin/. Accessed 24 Aug. 2018.

Reid-Pharr, Robert. "Rendezvous with Life: Reading Early and Late Baldwin." Kaplan and Schwarz, pp. 126–40.

Russ, Andrew R. *The Illusion of History: Time and the Radical Political Imagination*. Catholic U of America P, 2013.

Schmitt, Arnaud. "Making the Case for Self-Narration against Autofiction." *Auto/Biography Studies*, vol. 25, no. 1, Summer 2010, pp. 122–37. doi: 10.1353/abs.2010.0012.

Schmitt, Arnaud. *The Phenomenology of Autobiography: Making It Real.* Routledge, 2017.

Scott, Lynn Orilla. "Challenging the American Conscience, Re-Imagining American Identity: James Baldwin and the Civil Rights Movement." *A Historical Guide to James Baldwin*, edited by Douglas Field, Oxford UP, 2009, pp. 141–76.

Shields, David. *Reality Hunger: A Manifesto*. Vintage, 2011.

Singer, Alain. "Literature *Is* History: Aesthetic Time and the Ethics of Literary Will." *The Values of Literary Studies: Critical Institutions, Scholarly Agendas*, edited by Rónán McDonald, Cambridge UP, pp. 59–64.

Sinitiere, Phillip Luke. "The Art and Lives of James Baldwin: An Interview with Douglas Field." *Black Perspectives*, African American Intellectual History Society, 15 Jan. 2017, aaihs.org/the-art-and-lives-of-james-baldwin-an-interview-with-douglas-field/. Accessed 24 Aug. 2018.

Spillers, Hortense. Afterword. Kaplan and Schwarz, pp. 241–46.

Tall, Deborah, and John D'Agata. "The Lyric Essay." *Seneca Review*, vol. 27, no. 2, Fall 1997, www.hws.edu/senecareview/lyricessay.aspx. Accessed 24 Aug. 2018.

Tóibín, Colm. "Baldwin and 'the American Confusion.'" Kaplan and Schwarz, pp. 53–68.

Van Hout, Tom, and Peter Burger. "Mediatization and the Language of Journalism." *The Oxford Handbook of Language and Society*, edited by Ofelia García, Nelson Flores, and Massimiliano Spotti, Oxford UP, 2016. *Oxford Handbooks Online*.

Velleman, J. David. *Self to Self: Selected Essays*. Cambridge UP, 2006.

Wilson, Christopher. "The Chronicler: George Packer's *The Unwinding*." *Post45*, 5 May 2017, post45.research.yale.edu/2017/05/the-chronicler-george-packers-the-unwinding-2013/. Accessed 24 Aug. 2018.

PART THREE

Baldwin Re-Sighted Transnationally

7

French Baldwin (on Screen): *"le criminel artiste"*

Claudine Raynaud

James Baldwin moved to France in 1948, and after that time he was often solicited for interviews and appeared on French television on various occasions in the late 1950s and in the 1970s (i.e., at the time of his 1957 involvement in the civil rights movement and after he had achieved celebrity status in the United States with the publication of his essays and novels). In these interviews with famous French journalists—such as Pierre Desgraupes and Pierre Dumayet (*Lectures pour tous*); Michel Polac (*Post-scriptum*); and Danièle Guilbert (*Italiques*)—Baldwin speaks French. From the first interview in 1957 to the *Italiques* show in 1972, one can trace how much more proficient in the language he became as the years went by.[1] Harlem Renaissance poet Countée Cullen had taught Baldwin French at Frederick Douglass Junior High (Leeming 22). It is thus a French Baldwin that the viewer discovers expressing himself in Molière's language with a strong American accent. Yet the difficulty of the foreign tongue does not deter him from engaging in heated exchanges and expressing the complexity of his thoughts.

Baldwin, his biographer James Campbell explains, gave hundreds of interviews in the 1960s at a time when "his confessor was the interviewer" (179). However, the author of *The Critical Reception of James Baldwin in France*, Rosa Bobia, writes: "When Baldwin, his biographers, and many of his American critics discuss Baldwin's nearly forty-year relationship with France, they tell only half of the story" (*"If Beale Street"*). The other half of Baldwin's story in France is examined in her study that documents the French critical response to Baldwin's writings.[2] Quite humbly, I add an analysis of his on-screen presence in France throughout the period of the late 1950s, the Vietnam War, May 1968, and the early 1970s when France's left-wing anti-Americanism was at its height. It is my contention that Baldwin used his television appearances in France to explain to the French their misperceptions of American blackness, particularly to demystify Hollywood stereotypes of black men and women, and to teach them about black history and the current unfolding of the civil rights movement. His aim was to culturally translate for them what being black in America means.[3] Early American television literary talk shows, such as *Author Meets the Critics* broadcast by NBC, ABC, and DuMont Television Network, ended in 1954, while other formats devoted generally to celebrities from the world of entertainment and politics took over. *The Dick Cavett Show*, however, featured Baldwin in a heated debate with Yale professor Paul Weiss, among other guests, in 1968.[4] French literary shows focused on Baldwin the writer, on his creative output, even as they obsessively returned to the autobiographical dimension and the societal context of the experience of race in America.

By seeking to understand the French Baldwin better, American appreciations of Baldwin's radical foresight with respect to the perception of American blacks would be more justly reappraised. For instance, the centrality of the black child's response to race as both constitutive *and* destructive of the psyche vividly comes across. Reassessing Baldwin's presence on French television also means understanding how the creative writer—"Baldwin the author"—was more readily apprehended in France as opposed to in the United States, due to his being an "other" of French culture, a *foreign* novelist. It explains Baldwin's international appeal and conversely his own pressing need for a worldwide forum. It operates a transnational re-sighting of the writer. These television programs are also the public image of Baldwin's presence in France, a country where he wrote his major works and which de facto provided the solace needed for artistic creation.[5] Consequently, in the same way as his stay in Turkey throws light on his literary output, as Magdalena Zaborowska has shown, the Algerian War, the Arab presence in France, and the companionship of other black expatriates or visitors cannot be separated from his literary and political production while he made his home in that country. His presence on these shows helps negotiate his statement about the beginning of his sojourn ("The French [...] didn't see me: on the other hand, they watched me" [Gates 264]) and his being awarded the Légion d'Honneur in 1986 by François Mitterrand. As he stated, "The French did not and don't know what a black man is" (Gates 268).

Baldwin's first televised appearance took place when French television at the time, the ORTF (Office de Radiodiffusion-Télévision Française), was state owned. Whereas Michel Polac was a polemicist whose shows were eventually censored, Desgraupes and Dumayet's intellectual literary program had a consensual character, in the line of famous radio shows that promoted renowned talented writers.[6] Indeed, Baldwin was not the only foreign writer invited alongside journalists and art critics: Henry Miller, another American exile to France in the 1930s, who spoke French, was also a guest of Desgraupes's. On May 6, 1959, in his first-ever television interview, Miller promoted the French translation of his autobiographical *Big Sur and the Oranges of Hieronymus Bosch* (1957). Desgraupes also interviewed, among others, Paul Claudel (May 27, 1954) and Françoise Sagan in her garden (June 5, 1959) in *Cinq colonnes à la une*, while Dumayet conversed with Louis-Ferdinand Céline (July 17, 1957) and Raymond Queneau (February 4, 1959). Baldwin's presence on that show must thus be placed within that lineage and in that context; the writers interviewed could be the authors of provocative works as the programs featuring Miller and Céline attest, and not all interviewees were French. In 1962, the show addressed Jean Lacouture's latest essay on the United Nations as well as an album by the cartoonist Sempé. The appeal of the show went beyond the strictly literary to embrace political analyses and popular publications.

Baldwin lived in France on and off throughout the 1950s and 1960s, when he also spent time in Turkey. He eventually bought a home in Saint-Paul-de-Vence, where he died in 1987. Michel Fabre's section on Baldwin in his *From Harlem to Paris* explains that the writer was aware of French racism—the Algerian War[7] was raging when he arrived—but, as Baldwin repeatedly asserted, "the French left him alone" (Gates 264).[8] The television shows bear witness to how the French responded to him after he had gained fame in his home country as an outspoken political activist and the celebrated author of the bestselling *The Fire Next Time* (1963). Depending on the program, what was set forward was either Baldwin the author, Baldwin the representative of black America, or Baldwin the essayist, the format of the show obviously influencing the way in which he came across and what he could say, or not say. One should bear in mind that Baldwin, between his appearances on *Lectures pour tous* and *Post-scriptum*, was featured on the cover of *Time* magazine (May 24, 1963). He also participated with Harry Belafonte, Sidney Poitier, Marlon Brando, Charlton Heston, and Joseph Mankiewicz in a much-publicized roundtable on August 28, 1963, the day of the March on Washington. He debated Malcolm X on March 5, 1963, and two years later William Buckley at Cambridge University (the latter was broadcast in the United States on NET). At the height of his fame, his personal life underwent deep changes since he separated from his lover Lucien Happersberger. Moreover, Malcolm X's death in 1965 was earth shattering to him. He progressively radicalized himself.

April 3, 1957: *Les élus du Seigneur* (1957), Editions de la table ronde (*Go Tell It on the Mountain*, 1953)

The first program is an episode of *Lectures pour tous*, the famed French television program on literature that purported to advertise a recently published novel for the general public. The level of analysis was quite demanding, and the format was that of questions and answers with the author present in the studio. Cultural critics have seen this show as framed by the ideology of "schoolteachers' television," an attempt to bring a veneer of general culture to an audience that did not necessarily read much. Television had a cultural (i.e., pedagogical) mission alongside its obvious use as a means for promoting recently published works.[9] Vincent Casanova, for instance, analyzes Desgraupes's method in his interview of Nathalie Sarraute for the promotion of *Tropismes* (1957) as follows:

> As if the TV host were taking a case to court, the interview thus attempts as faithfully as possible to reconstruct the author's intention. With close-ups of the guest's face, the idea was that by stripping the individual bare, one would understand the work, pierce the mystery of literary creation. The structure and the style of the show laid the foundation of the "talk show": it accompanied the revolution that book publishing went through; those were indeed the years of paperback editions and bestseller lists. Little by little, for authors and publishers, an appearance on *Lectures pour tous* became a must in the literary world. (my trans.[10])

Of course, the interview with James Baldwin led Desgraupes away from literary analysis into questions on his own life story and the conditions of blacks in America, but the focus and the framework was on the literary dimension of the work.

Go Tell It on the Mountain appeared in France in 1957, four years after its publication in the United States. According to Baldwin, the French press received his first novel with, in his words,

> A certain amount of accuracy, that is they did not take it as a *petit nègre* folklore exercise. It was taken as a serious attempt to present a universal religious experience. In a sense, it afforded the French some clue to the Black American personality. Until the Second World War, the image of Black Americans held by the French was one disseminated by Hollywood. They knew Josephine Baker and Louis Armstrong. They didn't understand Richard [Wright] at all. That is not an overstatement. The American G.I. changed that image. In that context, *Mountain* was

very useful to the French. What was happening in the United States in the fifties was very mysterious to the French. (qtd. in Bobia, "*If Beale Street*")

Desgraupes introduces the theme of the book, "a very, very beautiful book," as a young black man's attempt to be accepted/integrated into the white world, but he also refers to Richard Wright, placing Baldwin in the master's shadow. Baldwin had attended in September 1956 the first Congress of Black Writers and Artists at the Sorbonne at which Richard Wright had spoken. The article Baldwin had written for that event, "Princes and Powers," came out in 1957. Baldwin politely corrects Desgraupes on his analysis of the novel's main character: "sauf ..." (except ...). He continues:

le drame, pour John, dans le livre, n'est-ce pas, c'était que, à moment donné, il s'est rendu compte qu'il y avait deux mondes. Il était né dans le monde noir et il y avait le monde blanc autour. Il avait envie de entrer là dedans, mais le livre ... , le drame pour lui, et la résolution de ce drame, dans un certain sens; il s'est rendu compte qu'il ne pouvait rien faire jusqu'il a accepté son identité, son vrai identité, c'est-à-dire, le passé, très [*garbled*] et dur et, dans un certain sens, humiliant, mais jusqu'il est arrivé d'accepter qu'il était le fils d'un esclave, dans un certain sens, et un noir, il ne pouvait pas devenir un homme.[11]

Desgraupes is straight away interested in the autobiographical dimension of the work.[12] Baldwin acquiesces and makes plain that if the *milieu* is the same as his own, the situations are "almost" similar. He stresses the importance of the black church. In that context, Desgraupes's use of the word "mystical," his attempt to translate the specificity of evangelical Protestantism to a French audience, fails to grasp the true features of the type of Pentecostal faith in which Baldwin was raised. His later qualification of that mysticism as "enthusiastic" comes closer to the mark. The literary show also becomes a means of questioning Baldwin himself on his views of black America. The novel's literary dimensions are not directly tackled; rather, the text is seen as the repository of answers on the links between the black church and African Americans, the current state of America, and the plight of black Americans ("le problème noir" or the "Negro problem," as Baldwin would himself put it, while undermining the very terms of the expression).[13] In answer to his host's query, he describes the experience of racial prejudice: the black child understands there is a problem at age five or six.

In the course of the interview, Baldwin explains the Great Migration ("l'exode") that saw his father move north after the First World War in 1919, with thousands of black men and women, fleeing riots and lynchings. He differentiates between his father and himself in terms of generations.

He was not born in the South, unlike his father, and was called "Mister" where he grew up.[14] He describes his relationship to his father in terms of a kind of struggle ("une espèce de lutte"). His father was promised less than he was. If he had more than his father, he was promised more than he was given. Desgraupes wants to know if it is still the case today. Baldwin explains that there is a drama for each generation of black men, as they have to confront the impossibility of their dreams of conquest due to racism. He also stresses how the past—the past of slavery and its memory kept alive in the Negro spirituals and the music of Louis Armstrong—is being erased: the churches are starting to disappear and with them a certain sense of identity. Desgraupes equates race and religion in African American identity as it comes across in the expression "God's Chosen people": "Il y a une certaine adéquation entre la croyance d'être l'élu du Seigneur et la race noire américaine [...] Quel rôle joue cette foi dans l'histoire noire américaine?"[15] The conversation turns toward Christianity and slavery when the black man was placed in the position of accepting the Bible and the white man to whom he belonged, whose property he was. "We were on the good side from the moral point of view," Baldwin acknowledges. He adds that there is an ironic side to the French title "God's Chosen People," the literal translation of *Les élus du Seigneur*. The book was later republished as *La conversion*.

The last comment is Desgraupes's review of Faulkner's vision of the black man. His suffering is necessary, like Christ's sacrifice, for the redemption of mankind. Baldwin retorts that it is too easy for Faulkner to wash his conscience clean with the sufferings of black people:

> BALDWIN. C'est trop facile, d'abord; c'est trop facile, je ne l'accepte pas moi-même [...] c'est trop facile pour Monsieur Faulkner de laver sa conscience avec la souffrance des autres et lorsque Faulkner parle de cela, vraiment, il parle aussi de [son] passé, n'est-ce pas, de guerre civile, puisque qu'il est du Sud, n'est-ce pas, et, ah, enfin, on peut pas, on peut pas regarder quelqu'un d'autre souffrir, n'est-ce pas, en disant qu'il faut qu'il souffre, n'est-ce pas, pour sa rédemption, pour son salut, surtout pour le votre. Parce que la vraie idée, c'est que Faulkner ne veut pas appeler un Noir « Monsieur », lorsqu'il pense au Noir, il pense toujours à la guerre civile.
>
> DESGRAUPES. Il pense qu'il souffre pour lui.
>
> BALDWIN. Ce qui était vrai, mais, dans un certain sens aussi, c'est pour ça que Faulkner est un bon écrivain, mais, dans la vie actuelle, dans la vie sociale, dans la vie pratique, cela ne marche pas du tout, évidemment.[16]

Baldwin had just written "Faulkner and Desegregation" in 1956 in answer to Faulkner's statement that he had to support Mississippians in the struggle over desegregation "even if it meant going out in the streets and shooting Negroes" (qtd. in Leeming 117).[17] Baldwin would later comment on Faulkner's work in a BBC television show hosted by Peter Duval Smith (1963). Faulkner, one must remember, was highly regarded in French literary circles, his fame in France having preceded his positive reception in the United States. Desgraupes concludes by stating that "this is a very, very beautiful novel" and that "it can take its place among the black novels that we already know." Desgraupes's use of black ("noir") to qualify Wright and Baldwin, who are each "un écrivain américain noir" rather than "un écrivain noir américain," highlights the fact that they are American writers first and foremost who are black, and not black American writers. In sum, Baldwin's work is assessed vis-à-vis Wright's and Faulkner's while his novel is qualified as "un roman noir," a black novel.

In 1968, a strike at the ORTF (May 17–June 23) resulted in the firing of sixty journalists. Whereas there were only two channels, both of them state owned, post-1968 television saw the emergence of independent channels when the ORTF collapsed in 1974. Cultural historian Frédéric Delarue analyzes the literary show, or book show, in 1970 as full of paradoxes:

> The increasingly heavy echo of publishing events cohabits with the cultural ambition of the television of schoolteachers, and then of more confidential heirs. The writer appears as an "intellectual hero" but also as a social figure, as a significant proportion of Frenchmen (30% in 1973, 26% in 1981) declare that they have not read a book over the last twelve months … Counterculture tries to find a forum on television, but Michel Polac becomes marginalized in his attempts to translate it on screen. (485)[18]

Between 1968 and 1975, the book show focuses on societal issues. The host becomes a master of ceremony at the expense of the author and of literature itself.

October 21, 1970: James Baldwin in Michel Polac's *Post-scriptum*, produced by Maurice Dugowson

The second excerpt I wish to discuss is Baldwin's presence in one of the first literary television shows that tried to single itself out from the rather professorial, dusty, and mainstream *Lectures pour tous*. It was aired every Tuesday at 10:30 p.m. Michel Polac, known to French radio audiences for his *Le masque et la plume*, decided to create a literary talk show that would translate the counterculture of the times. The guests are in a bistrot (café), they drink and smoke, and a selected novel is debated. The first show had,

James Baldwin et Jean-François Revel, Post-scriptum, October 21, 1970, hosted by Michel Polac and produced by Maurice Dugowson for ORTF, INA video archive, http://www.ina.fr/video/I00017698

James Baldwin sur la situation des Noirs américains, Post-scriptum, October 21, 1970, hosted by Michel Polac and produced by Maurice Dugowson for ORTF, INA video archive, http://www.ina.fr/video/I00017702 5

for instance, François Truffaut among its many guests (writers, literary critics) and promoted the recently published *Le gai ghetto* (*Gay Ghetto*) by Patricia Finaly.[19] It was avowedly irreverent, controversial, and preferred the avant-garde to the establishment. At the beginning of the show, addressing the audience, Polac calls on librarians, literary critics, and nonspecialists to write to him and Pierre Lattès: people should talk about why they loved, or did not like, a given book.

In the case of Baldwin's *Tell Me How Long the Train's Been Gone* (1968) (*L'homme qui meurt*, Gallimard, 1970), the writer, essayist, and political analyst Jean-François Revel is Baldwin's debater.[20] Revel explains that the book is the story of a childhood. The acute sensitivity of the child who realizes that he is considered inferior because of the color of his skin is understood as necessarily playing a large part in the novel's makeup. The second theme according to him is the way in which the black hero (who is an actor) must compromise with white society once he has become famous, such as his relationship to commercial networks. Revel, who had been in New York the previous winter, explains how students are now demanding a black curriculum. In the same way, a black theater catering to a black audience with black actors is a pressing demand of black people now. He argues that black people wish to conquer a new cultural autonomy or create their own cultural autonomy. One understands that he refers to the creation of black studies and to the Black Arts movement.

Baldwin explains that his hero (Leo Proudhammer) climbs up the American ladder (following the pattern of the rags-to-riches storyline or Horatio Alger's young adult narratives) and at thirty-nine realizes that this effort has not changed much, has not changed his past. It is a question of saving the lives of others, the youngest, and also of saving a history, a cultural history. Baldwin states that one must uproot the past to save the future ("arracher le passé pour sauver l'avenir"). The truth about yourself, about your ancestors, and above all about your sons, must be uprooted from far back, extremely far back in the past. He makes plain that things are not limited to "la question noire" (the black problem); what is at stake is the salvation of a whole country ("sauver un pays").

At one point in the program, Baldwin addresses the presence of white students in the organization SDS (Students for a Democratic Society) and stresses how whites understand far less than blacks the plight of blacks in America. He insists that one is "mistaken about this so-called revolution that started in 1964, or even in 1960." It started in Montgomery, Alabama, in 1956. Baldwin refers to Rosa Parks's refusal to give up her seat, an event that actually took place in late 1955. According to him, to this day, neither America nor the Western world can understand the seriousness of all these events. He fears being interrupted and asks to finish what he has to say:

> SDS, c'est un … , moi, je parle comme un Noir américain, n'est-ce pas. SDS, c'est une organisation mondiale, une réaction; on met quelques étudiants blancs qui, et j'ai rien contre eux, mais qui comprend beaucoup moins bien que Rap Brown[21] par exemple, beaucoup moins bien que n'importe quel Noir, la vérité sur la vie noire américaine … et c'est pour ça que nous sommes un peu, les Noirs—pas parce qu'on est racistes—il faut qu'on se méfie un peu; on a déjà vu les révolutionnaires blancs en Amérique depuis la dernière guerre mondiale. Il peut toujours changer de vie et rentrer chez eux. C'est pas Sacramento,[22] c'est pas Washington,[23] c'est pas fini; ce que je veux dire, c'est ceci, il me semble qu'on se trompe sur cette soi-disant révolution qui a commencé en 1964 ou en 1960. Ça a commencé pour notre époque à Montgomery, Alabama, en 1956, avec une Noire, une Noire, n'est-ce pas, qui a refusé ce jour-là de céder son siège à un Blanc, et tout a été déclenché de ce moment-là, jusqu'au … aujourd'hui, et je finis, ni l'Amérique, ni le monde occidental n'est capable de comprendre la gravité de tous ces événements.[24]

The show is thus a rare moment when Baldwin can set the record straight and explain the origins of the civil rights movement to a French television audience, counter a certain amount of misinformation—in short, correct official history. In a way, one could say that the format of the show and the freedom it gave its guests serve Baldwin, who was not, as he was in the interview with Desgraupes, limited to the promotion of his novel or to providing information about his own life. The questions were given beforehand to the writer in that type of talk show. Polac grants indeed more freedom to his guest, who does not have to follow any preestablished script. The format of the debate is a kind of public engagement that Baldwin excelled in and did not shun. For example, the transcript of the fiery televised exchange on Thames Television with Peregrine Worsthorne, chaired by Bryan Magee, on the program *Something to Say*, shows how Baldwin's "I" is that of all black men who, he contends, are all "slaves" (Magee 113–26).

July 20, 1972: "James Baldwin on his Harlem Childhood" (*Italiques* with Danièle Guilbert)

The third piece is entitled "James Baldwin on his Harlem Childhood" ("James Baldwin à propos de son enfance à Harlem"). It is the July 20 program that was aired in 1972 as part of the literary show called *Italiques*. Directed by Gérard Poitou and produced by Marc Gilbert and Jacques Legris, it lasts over fifteen minutes. *Italiques* was a political and cultural television show produced and presented by Marc Gilbert from 1971 to 1974.[25] In 1972, programs dedicated to Norman Mailer and Kate Millett followed Baldwin's interview. Mailer is seen walking through New York City, while Millett is interviewed on her feminist engagement. A short five-minute interview with the editor of *The New York Times Review of Books*, Robert B. Silvers, in 1972 (July 27) points to the ways in which American writers such as Philip Roth, William Styron, Saul Bellow, and even John Updike then dealt with societal subjects and the war when they were not writing on political issues (e.g., *The Confessions of Nat Turner* by Styron). Moral questions are now an obsession for intellectuals and writers. Unlike what happened in the 1920s, writers do not choose exile but prefer to stay in the United States despite their rebellion against the system, the viewers are told. One wonders what this statement means for Baldwin, who chose expatriation.

This 1972 interview shows Baldwin in his garden in his home in Saint-Paul, seated on a bench: the outline of the fortified Provençal village, with its church spire, can be made out in the background. His interviewer is Danièle Guilbert, but, unlike Desgraupes in the 1957 show, she does not appear on the screen. The author is clearly at the center of the interview, while the host disappears. Guilbert's soft feminine voice is heard in the questions that start with an invitation to testify: "Qu'est-ce que c'était la vie d'un petit garçon noir à Harlem?" The journalist goes over Baldwin's life with him: his childhood, his father, the church. An excerpt from *Tell Me How Long the Train's Been Gone* is read in which the ten-year-old Leo and his brother are arrested and frisked by two white policemen at night. The excerpt is reworked so that the audience does not get lost. The references to the film Leo has just seen and that Caleb must remember in order to cover up for the time spent with his girlfriend Dolores are cut out. What remains is the dialogue with the policemen and the stream of consciousness of the ten-year-old: "'Turn around ... And keep your hands in the air.' ... We did as we were told. I felt the grainy brick beneath my fingers. A hand patted me all over my body, front and back, every touch humiliating, every touch obscene" (*Tell Me* 57). The reading ends dramatically with Leo looking at his brother's trembling hands: "I watched the white faces. I memorized each mole, scar, pimple, nostril hair; I memorized the eyes, the contemptuous eyes. I wished that I were God and then I hated God" (58). These last words are superimposed on the shot of Baldwin seated, looking at children playing around him in Saint-Paul-de-Vence. He is beaming. Without any transition, we are back to the interview. Baldwin carries on unveiling the autobiographical dimension of the episode, a faithful rendering of what happened to him:

> J'avais dix ans; c'était évident que j'avais dix ans. Je ne sais pas ce que j'ai dit, mais je me souviens toujours que, à un moment donné, un des flics me poussait, et avec le réflexe d'un garçon, le réflexe d'un gosse, je n'avais pas encore eu le temps d'avoir peur, j'ai réagi de façon hostile, je l'ai poussé. Enfin, je ne sais pas qu'est-ce que j'ai fait, mais je me souviens qu'ils m'ont battu, tous les deux, un garçon de dix ans, Et ça m'avait frappé énormément plus tard, pas uniquement, pas parce que c'était moi. Evidemment, au début, c'était parce que c'était moi, mais quand j'ai compris que c'est parce que j'étais noir, il y avait quelque chose d'autre qui est arrivé dans l'esprit. Maintenant, ça va pour moi, parce que j'ai presque 50 ans. On ne peut pas, on n'a pas le droit de laisser les autres faire la même chose avec un garçon de dix ans, un garçon noir de dix ans, maintenant.[26]

Archival shorts about Harlem children are shown. They melt into images where the camera follows James Baldwin as he walks the streets of Saint-Paul and sits leisurely with French children, seemingly happy. Once again, the trauma of the childhood experience is at the heart of the sequence, and here it is highly dramatized by the montage.[27]

Along with the carefully chosen excerpt from *L'homme qui meurt*, several choice excerpts from Bessie Smith's recordings are heard in the soundtrack that link the 1930s of Baldwin's childhood and the man on the screen whose voice we are hearing and whose body we are seeing, creating a continuum of suffering and creation, creation out of suffering. The first one is the opening stanza of "In the House Blues":

> Settin' in the house with everything on my mind
>
> Settin' in the house with everything on my mind
>
> Lookin' at the clock and can't even tell the time.

The second one, "Moan, You Moaners," illustrates how immersed in the black church Baldwin was since his father, the Reverend David Baldwin, was a Sunday preacher:

Sisters and brothers, we met here on some serious business!

There's been some back-bitin' goin' on,

And the thing I wants to know

Is who's been doin' it?

It's a shame, it's a shame, it's a shame!

The thing I wants to know

Is what bit me on my, I mean who bit me on my back?

The blues song "Long Road" is heard toward the end as a police car appears on the screen, heading to Harlem:

It's a long road but I'm gonna find the end

It's a long road but I'm gonna find the end

And when I get there, I'm gonna shake hands with a friend.

One recalls that Baldwin was playing Smith's records when he was finishing writing *Go Tell It on the Mountain* in Switzerland.[28] In "The Uses of the Blues," he explains that the blues contain the "toughness that manages to make this experience of life articulate" (70). The correspondences between the lyrics of Bessie Smith's songs, Baldwin's words about his father going crazy, and his own narrow escape from death create a close and dense network that highlights the link between artistic creation and the possibility of survival:

> QUESTION: Quand tu avais quatorze ans, tu découvrais l'amour et la révolte en même temps. Comment cette double découverte s'est-elle poursuivie après dans ta vie?
>
> BALDWIN. Ca, c'est tellement difficile à exprimer ça, parce que … Il a fallu d'abord que je regarde de très près, les Blancs, parce que je me suis rendu compte que je risquais de sombrer dans une espèce de haine, une espèce d'amertume qui tuerait personne que moi. Donc, il a fallu que je commence à regarder les gens d'une autre manière, [à] décider pour moi-même qui était blanc, qui était … , qui était qui, parce ce qu'on ne pouvait pas décider selon la couleur de la peau. Ça m'a sauvé, d'une certaine manière, de mourir. Parce que ça, c'est le grand risque: mourir ou devenir fou. Mon père était mort dans un asile; j'ai bien compris pourquoi.[29]

Going over material already addressed in the first interview, the intimacy created between the journalist and James Baldwin, whom she addresses as "tu," comes across to the viewer. The nostalgia effect—the shorts being used as if they were visual images in Baldwin's mind—is countered by the writer's broad smile as he watches the children in the Provençal village. Police violence, made plain in the excerpt, is underlined by footage of police presence in the streets of Harlem, the shorts "illustrating" the writer's words, echoing in real life what the fiction brought home. The fiction is, however, robbed of its imaginary dimension since the writer's on-screen presence helps the viewer equate Leo and James Baldwin.[30]

Conclusion

The three programs devote time to the moment when the black child becomes conscious of his or her color. They all try to probe the question of the emergence of racial consciousness and put forward the desecration of a child's innocence. An attempt is made in order to understand the historical and societal causes of racism and to show racism as a systemic collective production rooted in history yet autobiographical grounding and personal experience are the privileged points of entry into Baldwin's thought and creative writing. The pathos of the primal encounter and the destructive violence of racial prejudice are brought to the fore in a double gesture of witnessing and consciousness raising. In the first book show, Baldwin tells of that moment when the child plays with white children and somebody intervenes (perhaps his parents), telling him not to play with so and so. The French word "nègre" comes to his lips; "sale nègre" is how he also words this racial slur in the 1972 piece, an echo of Fanon's insult uttered by the small child in his chapter "L'expérience vécue du Noir" from *Black Skin, White Masks* (19), flatly and mistakenly translated as "The Fact of Blackness." In the *Post-scriptum* interview, he insists that this hatred, this loathing is not specific to black people: Jews and Arabs also share this experience of racism. One recalls his words to writer and publisher Christian de Bartillat in an unpublished 1974 interview: "Je n'ai eu jamais d'enfance." "I never had a childhood" or rather "I had never a childhood" (Campbell 3). Baldwin's "incorrect" French increases the poignancy of the statement since he coins the expression "never a childhood," a more psychologically accurate insight into his psychic makeup. He adds bluntly: "Je suis né mort" (Campbell 3; "I was born dead"). These French words start Campbell's biographical narrative: childhood and racism, death as his (the black man's) experience of life. Powerful as they are, the interviews necessarily put forward individual experiences and the potential force of the creative artist. Baldwin grounding his work and thinking in autobiographical material thus runs the risk of having the viewer isolate his testimony from the broader issue of racial violence and police brutality, whose repeated upsurge and stubborn persistence is with us today. Conversely, they elevate the autobiographical to the means of achieving in the creative process knowledge and power about the racial question. These French words, uttered by Baldwin, also help us accede to an otherness in a different language that is part and parcel of Baldwin's transnational being, as they both translate (i.e., displace) *and* transcend what it is to be a black American man.

Notes

1   Within the limits of this essay and since this research is in progress, I do not address the television show hosted by Dumayet on May 12, 1972, *Le temps de lire*, where Baldwin promotes *Chassés de la lumière (No Name in the Street)*, published in France in 1972 by Stock and translated by Magali Berger, and his collaboration with Margaret Mead, *Le racisme en question (A Rap on Race)* (Calmann-Lévy, 1972). I am also leaving out the analysis of the September 8, 1985, interview on Antenne 2 (*Antenne 2 midi*) with Bernard Pardinaud on *Meurtres à Atlanta (The Evidence of Things Not Seen*, Stock, 1985). Neither do I tackle the interviews in French given to Canadian television (*Le sel de la semaine*, interview with Fernand Seguin, September 4, 1967) or to Swiss television (*La voix au chapitre*, interview with Catherine Charbon, November 16, 1972). There are no radio interviews in the INA (Institut National de l'Audiovisuel) archives. Also of note is a short film "Un étranger dans le village" (28 minutes) produced for Swiss television in 1962 by Pierre Koralnik, in which Baldwin explains in French his experience of the racial encounter in the village of Loèche-les-Bains, where he wrote *Go Tell It on the Mountain* while perambulating surrounded by children.

2   For the American critical response to Baldwin's work, see Francis.

3   For a better understanding of the opposition between the "French" Baldwin and the way Baldwin appeared on American, English, Turkish, Canadian, and Swiss television, a more thorough comparative analysis is required that would list the common points and the differences. Baldwin becomes a witness on an international scale and tests visions and insights afforded by these countries' perspectives on the United States. Abroad, the freedom that Baldwin underlined in the French context could be exercised, while at home the activist surely takes over, or at least per force comes forward, as national perceptions of black Americans apply.

4   Another appearance on that same show took place in 1973.

5   For his life in Saint-Paul-de-Vence, see Farber.

6   Michel Polac also created with François-Régis Bastide *Le masque et la plume (The Mask and the Pen)*, a radio show dedicated to literature, to the theater, and, later, to film reviews, on November 13, 1955. The show was suspended for six months in 1960 to censure the signatories of the Manifesto

of the 121, who opposed French intervention in Algeria and supported the FLN (Front de Libération Nationale, founded in 1954 to obtain the independence of Algeria from France). Polac left the show in 1970. The show is still aired to this day. Delarue analyzes *Post-scriptum* as follows: "The choice of live television, of over-the-shoulder shots, directly borrowed from the 'New Vague' by Maurice Dugowson, and of a single theme aims at revamping the formula halfway between the 'café-bistrot' dedicated to as broad a coverage as possible of present-day challenges (each guest is offered a drink, conversation topics fuse while the exchange of contradictory views and the speed of the conversation contrast with the rhythm and the 'regimes of truth,' dear to Pierre Desgraupes and Pierre Dumayet's confession-interviews)" (491).

7   On black expatriates to France and the Algerian War, see Stovall.

8   Rosa Bobia concurs with this statement and contrasts France's reception of Richard Wright to the indifference with which Baldwin was welcome: "Baldwin was left alone to create his space, which he admits was one of his reasons for leaving the United States" ("*If Beale Street*").

9   "The literary vigil that *Lectures pour tous* (aired each week in the third part of the evening) incarnated rested on a clever balance between Pierre Desgraupes and Pierre Dumayet's confessions-interviews (where the author, 'the case to build,' was subjected to the two producers' carefully prepared questions) and Max-Pol Fouchet and Nicole Vedrès's chronicles" (Delarue 486).

10 Unless otherwise indicated, all translations from the French are mine.

11 "The drama, for John, in the book, was that, at a certain point, he realized that there were two worlds. He was born into the black world and there was the white world around it. He felt like entering it, but the book … , the drama for him, and the resolution of this drama in a certain sense, he realized that he couldn't do anything until he accepted his identity, his true identity, that is, the past, very [*garbled*] and hard and, in a certain sense, humiliating, but until he managed to accept that he was the son of a slave, in a certain sense, and black, he couldn't become a man." Translated by Mark Ennis.

12 It was precisely this autobiographical dimension that for some critics came in the way of artistic excellence, as Conseula Francis explains, commenting on Harvey Breit's response to his work: "Because Baldwin writes so publicly and so honestly about his experiences as an American black man and because he is called upon so often to speak on this topic (and seems to be so willing to), it seems a futile effort to consider his work in anything other than in this context" (25).

13 See his conversation with François Bondy in *Transition* in which he rejects that expression (Baldwin, "James Baldwin, as Interviewed by François Bondy").

14 Desgraupes does not understand Baldwin's sentence "Je n'ai jamais subi cette étiquette" because of the use of the French word "etiquette." So Baldwin explains that he did not have to behave in the same way as his father who was subjected to Southern etiquette; he was freer, which his father did not understand.

15 "There is a certain *congruence* between the belief in being chosen by God and
the black American race [...]. What role does faith play in black American
history?" Translated by Mark Ennis. All ellipses in brackets in this chapter are
mine.

16 "BALDWIN. It's too easy, first of all, it's too easy, I can't accept it myself [...]
it's too easy for Mr. Faulkner to cleanse his guilty conscience with the suffering
of others, and when Faulkner talks about this, really, he is also talking about
his past, the Civil War, and, uh, you can't watch someone else suffer and say
that he has to suffer for his redemption, for his salvation, above all, for your
own. Because the real idea is that Faulkner does not want to call a black man
'Sir' because when he thinks of him, he still thinks of the Civil War.

DESGRAUPES. He thinks that he suffers for him.

BALDWIN. Which was true, but also in a certain sense, that's why Faulkner
is a good writer, but, in life today, in social life, in everyday life, that doesn't
work at all, obviously." Translated by Mark Ennis.

17 Faulkner gave this interview to *Reporter* in March 1956. Baldwin states:
"What is the evidence of the struggle he has been carrying on there on behalf
of the Negro? ... Why and how does one move from the middle of the road
where one was aiding Negroes into the streets to shoot them?" (qtd. in
Leeming 117).

18 The expression "intellectual hero" is Clark's (159).

19 The other guests were Lucien Bodard, Michel Cournot, Nella Bielski,
Jacqueline Barde, and Pierre Bourgeade. They are linked to *Actuel*, a left-
wing magazine, founded in 1967, dedicated to free jazz that underwent a
refoundation in 1970.

20 Jean-François Revel (1924–2006) was a philosopher, writer, and journalist
who in 1970 headed the French magazine *L'express*, a position he held until
1981. He is the author of the bestselling essay *Ni Marx, ni Jésus: De la seconde
révolution américaine à la seconde révolution mondiale* (1971) (*Without
Marx or Jesus: The New American Revolution Has Begun*, Delacorte, 1972)
and *L'obsession anti-américaine* (Plon, 2002), translated as *Anti-Americanism*
(Encounter Books, 2004). He opposed communism and supported a positive
image of the United States, its free enterprise ethos, and its social progress.

21 Hubert Gerold Brown, also known as H. Rap Brown (1943–), headed the
Student Nonviolent Coordinating Committee (SNCC) in the 1960s. He
also served as minister of justice of the Black Panther Party (BPP) when the
SNCC and the BPP were allied. He is currently serving a life sentence for
murder.

22 Sacramento was the city that saw the 1966 Farmers' March under the
leadership of Cesar Chavez and the creation of the United Farm Workers
Organizing Committee (UFWOC).

23 Baldwin must be referring here to the March on Washington on August 28, 1963.

24 "SDS, it's a ... , me—I say this as a black American. SDS is a world
organization, a reaction; you bring together a few white students who, and
I've got nothing against them, but who don't understand as well as Rap

Brown, for example, much less than any black man, the truth about the lives of black Americans ... and this is why we are a little, we blacks—and not because we are racists—you have to be a little careful; we've already seen white revolutionaries in America since the Second World War. They can always start a new life and go back home. It's not Sacramento, it's not Washington, it's not over; what I mean is that it seems to me that you're mistaken about this so-called revolution which, I suppose, started in 1964 or in 1960. It all started in Montgomery, Alabama, in 1956, with a black woman—it was a black woman—who refused to give up her seat to a white man, and it all began at that moment, until ... today, and let me finish with this, neither America, nor the western world is capable of understanding the gravity of all these events." Translated by Mark Ennis.

25 When the ORTF broke up in January 1975, Marc Gilbert had to leave. President Giscard's government issued orders: considered a left-winger—he had founded the Union of Television Producers—Gilbert's on-screen presence was no longer desired.

26 "I was ten years old; it was obvious that I was ten years old. I don't know what it was I said, but I still remember that, at a certain point, one of the cops pushed me, and, reacting like a boy, like a kid, I hadn't yet had the time to be afraid, I had a hostile reaction, I pushed him back. Well, I don't know what I did, but I remember that they beat me, the two of them, a ten-year-old boy. And that really impressed me tremendously later on, not only, not because it was me. Obviously, at the beginning, it was because it was me, but when I understood that it was because I was black, something else happened in my mind. Now, I'm okay, because I'm almost 50. You can't, you don't have the right, to let others do the same thing with a ten-year-old boy, a black ten-year-old boy, now." Translated by Mark Ennis.

27 A comparison and contrast could be made between this film and an earlier American documentary of a visit to San Francisco, *Take This Hammer*, originally produced by KQED for National Educational Television (NET), first aired on February 4, 1964, at 7:30 p.m. on KQED channel 9 in the Bay Area.

28 See the 1961 interview with Terkel 3–4.

29 "QUESTION: When you were fourteen, you discovered love and revolt at the same time. How has this double discovery played out since then in your life?

BALDWIN. That's so hard to express, because ... first I had to look very closely at white people, because I realized that I could very well have sunk into a kind of hatred, a kind of bitterness which wouldn't kill anyone but me. So, I had to start looking at people in another way, [to] decide for myself who was white, who was ... , who was who, because you couldn't decide based on skin color. That saved me, in a certain way, from dying. Because that, that's the real danger: to die or go crazy. My father died in an asylum; I understand why." Translated by Mark Ennis.

30 Leeming stresses that Leo Proudhammer *is* Baldwin yet at the end of his analysis asks the reader to read the novel as a parable (280).

Works Cited

Baldwin, James. "Faulkner and Desegregation." *Partisan Review*, vol. 23, no. 4, Fall 1956, pp. 568–73.

Baldwin, James. "James Baldwin, as Interviewed by François Bondy." *Transition*, no. 12, Jan.–Feb. 1964, pp. 12–19. doi: 10.2307/2934484.

Baldwin, James. "James Baldwin et Jean-François Revel." *Post-scriptum*, directed by Maurice Dugowson, Office National de Radiodiffusion Télévision Française, 21 Oct. 1970. Institut National de l'Audiovisuel, ina.fr/video/I00017698/jamesbaldwin-et-jean-francois-revel-video.html.

Baldwin, James. "James Baldwin à propos de son enfance à Harlem." Interview by Danièle Guilbert. *Italiques*, directed by Gérard Poitou, produced by Marc Gilbert and Jacques Legris, Office National de Radiodiffusion Télévision Française, 20 July 1972. Institut National de l'Audiovisuel, ina.fr/video/I09211837.

Baldwin, James. "James Baldwin à propos de son livre 'Les élus du Seigneur.'" Interview by Pierre Desgraupes. *Lectures pour tous*, directed by Jean Prat, Office National de Radiodiffusion Télévision Française, 3 Apr. 1957. Institut National de l'Audiovisuel, ina.fr/video/I00016118/james-baldwin-a-propos-de-son-livre-les-elus-du-seigneur-video.html.

Baldwin, James. *Tell Me How Long the Train's Been Gone*. Dial Press, 1968.

Baldwin, James. "The Uses of the Blues." *The Cross of Redemption: Uncollected Writings*, edited by Randall Kenan, Random House, 2011, pp. 70–81.

Baldwin, James. "Writers and Writing: Wonder and Terror." Interview by Peter Duval Smith. *Bookstand*, produced by Christopher Burstall, BBC Television, 16 April 1963. https://www.youtube.com/watch?v=dNd1xh-BNbE.

Bobia, Rosa. "*If Beale Street Could Talk*: The French and American Criticism of James Baldwin's 'Prison Parable.'" *Revue LISA/LISA e-journal*, 1 Jan. 2005. journals.openedition.org/lisa/609.

Campbell, James. *Talking at the Gates: A Life of James Baldwin*. U of California P, 1991.

Casanova, Vincent. Note on the interview "Le nouveau roman et Nathalie Sarraute." *Jalons version découverte*, fresques.ina.fr/jalons/fiche-media/InaEdu01229/le-nouveau-roman-et-nathalie-sarraute. Accessed 6 Sept. 2017.

Clark, Priscilla Parkhurst. *Literary France: The Making of a Culture*. U of California P, 1987.

Delarue, Frédéric. "Les années 1970 en France au prisme de la médiation littéraire au petit écran." *Enthymema*, no. 7, 2012, pp. 484–512. doi: 10.13130/2037-2426/2709.

Fabre, Michel. *From Harlem to Paris: Black American Writers in France, 1840–1980*. U of Illinois P, 1991.

Fanon, Frantz. *Black Skin, White Masks*. Translated by Richard Wilcox, Grove Press, 2008.

Fanon, Frantz. *Peau noire, masques blancs*. Seuil, 1952.

Farber, Jules B. *James Baldwin: Escape from America, Exile in Provence*. Pelican, 2016.

Francis, Conseula. *The Critical Reception of James Baldwin, 1963–2010: "An Honest Man and a Good Writer."* Camden House, 2014.

Gates, Henry Louis, Jr. "An Interview with Josephine Baker and James Baldwin."
    Standley and Pratt, pp. 260–69.

Leeming, David. *James Baldwin. A Biography*. Arcade Publishing, 1994.

Magee, Bryan. "A Television Conversation: James Baldwin, Peregrine Worsthorne,
    Bryan Magee." Standley and Pratt, pp. 113–26.

Mead, Margaret, and James Baldwin. *Le racisme en question*. Calmann-Lévy, 1972.
    Originally published as *A Rap on Race* (Lippincott, 1971).

Smith, Bessie. "In the House Blues." Columbia Records, 1931.

Smith, Bessie. "Long Road." Columbia Records, 1931.

Smith, Bessie. "Moan, You Moaners." Columbia Records, 1930.

Standley, Fred L., and Louis H. Pratt. *Conversations with James Baldwin*. UP of
    Mississippi, 1989.

Stovall, Tyler. "The Fire This Time: Black American Expatriates and the Algerian
    War." *Yale French Studies*, no. 98, 2000, pp. 182–200. doi: 10.2307/2903235.

Terkel, Studs. "An Interview with James Baldwin." Standley and Pratt, pp. 3–23.

Zaborowska, Magdalena J. *James Baldwin's Turkish Decade: Erotics of Exile*.
    Duke UP, 2009.

8

The Terror Within: *Giovanni's Room*, *L'Étranger*, and the Possibility of an Absurd Heroism

Timothy McGinnis

I

Giovanni, like Maman, dies today. Such is the case every day a reader picks up a copy of James Baldwin's *Giovanni's Room* (1956) or Albert Camus's *L'Étranger* (1942). Each reading is its own movement through time, each rereading its own experiment in memory. Both texts center on a murder—*L'Étranger* textually locates a murder at its core; *Giovanni's Room* spirals around, while slouching toward, a violent death—and both narrators embrace memory as a means of redemption. They do so quite differently. Whether either succeeds is part of my question here. What draws my attention, and what I would like to share if you read with me, is the way Baldwin crafted *Giovanni's Room* and how its shape, style, and content speak to the efforts of both Meursault and David, Camus's and Baldwin's respective protagonists. I call them both heroes for that is what their authors took them to be or, in David's case, the narrators hint at themselves. For Camus and Meursault, the heroism hearkens to the pre-Christian tradition of tragedy; David, trapped in the awareness that the man he most powerfully loves will soon die, is similarly destined to bear grief.[1] Where Meursault is assaulted by the sunlight tearing at his eyes, David keeps looking. He finds a mystery in the mirror, rather than a self capable of mastery, and the terror of such a discovery shakes him. It is similar to yet powerfully different from Meursault's imprisoned embrace of the "gentle indifference of the world" (Camus 122).

Though Baldwin was no saint and Camus was no charlatan of the existentialist cause,[2] the differences between *Giovanni's Room* and *L'Étranger* are significant both for the stakes of the heroism and the texture of interrelationship they create on the page. I am partial to Baldwin's text, with its pirouettes of flashback sifting through reflection driven onward toward dawn. And I show how this partiality is of worth for those readers, like so many of us, who come to more expansive forms of consciousness and life through reading. If one were to know Meursault without David, something precious would be missing. When the literary field's boundaries of respectability are so thoroughly shaped by contours of power that privilege whiteness, it is safe to say much was and often is missing from the texts. Nonetheless, Camus and Baldwin contributed to those contours in their own ways, and my focus is not on the scale of their impact but rather on that space where the two works speak to one another and the second, *Giovanni's Room*, reworks the prior. In this more intimate space, I hope to show how *Giovanni's Room* inverts, recycles, and eclipses *L'Étranger* and the "absurd" heroism depicted therein.

Moving between the two texts, I offer a reading of *Giovanni's Room* that contributes to the growing body of scholarship attending to marginality, memory, and otherness in Baldwin's concern with American identity. Where others have explicated the intricacies of race in a seemingly "race-less" novel and still more have examined the force of sexuality in the text,[3] reading David as a reenvisioning of the Meursault of the 1940s evinces how Baldwin's authorship reframed the project of confronting the absurdity and pain of life in the twentieth century.

Both Camus and Baldwin wrestled with social worlds in which an extant morality, or God, had become elusive, yet both authors wrote with an impassioned commitment to the possibility of ameliorative change. Camus contended with the violence of the Second World War on one hand and Jean-Paul Sartre's existentialism on the other, orienting his work toward a concept of absurdity that he believed defined a Europe unfettered by a belief in God. Absurdity, for Camus, "arises from the clash between reasoning, finite man ... and the silent, unreasonable world"; absurdity defines a condition "of conscious man fully aware of death and nothingness; lucid reason pitted against chaos" (McMurray 31). Baldwin takes absurdity further, or I have him do so in making the comparison between David and Meursault. We, individuals and collectives alike, are neither so reasonable nor finite (definable) as that fantasy of liberal selfhood.[4] In Camus's world, it is possible that "the sun" prompted Meursault's murder of an Arab man; he searches and knows his mind, finding no motive for murder.[5] Meursault's task, ultimately, is to embrace the contingency of his mortality. How neat.

He, like Sisyphus, may go to the guillotine happy, while the lovers and families he marred have faded from his memory.

With David, Baldwin pushes the absurdist hero found in Meursault past the point of accepting the indifference of the universe. Although the Nobel Committee awarded Camus the 1957 prize in literature for his "clearsighted earnestness [that] illuminates the problems of the human conscience in our times," in 1956 Baldwin gave that literary scene a glimpse of a kind of absurdity and heroism unexplored by the "human conscience" Camus manifested in his text. As Louise Horowitz contends, Camus's "discovery of the Absurd ... is a restrictive experience, whose universality exists solely in the minds of those able and willing to participate in the unspoken, but nonetheless screamingly apparent, premises of [his] works" that absolve Meursault of guilt for the murder of an Arab man (57).

Baldwin undeniably was wont to make "pronouncements of a highly universal nature result[ing] from highly *specific* experiences" as well (Horowitz 57). His success with David, however, is in premising one such universal pronouncement on the unknown: the mysteries we remain to ourselves. Absurdity may define something of the relationship between a person and the world (what a grandiose dichotomy!), yet far more absurd is the belief that one's self is within reach of mastery. David may be but a ventriloquist's puppet for Baldwin when he observes that "People who believe that they are strong-willed and the masters of their destiny can only continue to believe this by becoming specialists in self-deception" (*Giovanni's Room* 30). Baldwin was no stranger to existential questions: he so often asked of himself and others "who am I, who are we, who can we become together?" He surely regarded "the world's [lack of interest] in anyone's identity" (*Nobody Knows My Name* 279). Yet David exemplifies the consequences of mistaking oneself for a will in the world. "To *choose*!" Giovanni exclaims when David makes such a mistake, "Ah, you are really an American" (49). What David (and Baldwin) offers in the wake of such an error amounts to the significant difference of one man's heroism compared to that of another.

In reading *Giovanni's Room* alongside *L'Étranger*, I, like Radiclani Clytus and Bruce Lapenson before me, run the risk of suggesting that Baldwin took on and advanced the cause of existentialism. As "there is no material evidence that Baldwin was a disciple of Sartrean existentialism," I certainly do not intend to disciple Baldwin to Camus. It goes too far even to describe parallels and aligned arguments as "display[ing an] awareness and application of Sartre's vision for a more radical view of identity" (Clytus 74). I do not know what necessitates the leap from "no material evidence" to a displayed "awareness and application" of *Sartre's* vision, especially when one may argue that many a philosopher recreates Judeo-Christian praxes in secular form.[6] At the very least one may find a few of Baldwin's thoughts on Camus in *Nobody Knows My Name* (he did not think too highly of the man).

Setting aside issues of who has what claims to which existential primacy, it is more fun and, I hope, edifying to imagine Baldwin vigorously and playfully reworking the given forms of his day. Regarding Camus, for one, I like to imagine Baldwin winking at us.[7] Baldwin's "our" was surely big enough to include that civilization to which Camus referred when he quipped that "Meursault is the only Christ that modern civilisation deserves" (Maher). It is with a wink to Camus that I imagine Baldwin may have penned David's grim observation of his role in Giovanni's death, as David stands over his emotionally broken lover to comfort him one last time. Putting his hands on Giovanni's shoulders, forcing himself to look the other in the eye, David smiled—"and I really felt at that moment that Judas and the Savior had met in me" (*Giovanni's Room* 147). This is serious play. Hero, antihero, both and neither, Baldwin cloaked his protagonist in whiteness, delivering an image of a white American man with the conviction that doing so might free us all a little bit more. David is not so much a stranger to society as he is the embodiment of an estranged society's torturous values. Memory, though it threatens madness, is David's only hope through a world worn not so much by indifference as it is marred by the sorrow his estrangement has wrought. In this heroism dependent on both memory and forgetting, we may find the project Baldwin envisioned for America. That is, in *Giovanni's Room*, Baldwin compels us to witness the violence wrought by ignoring the forces of past and present mystery that make us who we are. Were David and Meursault to meet, beyond the fleeting relief won in accepting the world's indifference, David could enlighten Meursault as to the violence that comes of ignoring the terror within and refusing love.

II

To read David with and against Meursault, to regard how Baldwin's craft refashions the work of Camus, it is helpful to consider the works' respective structures. Where *Giovanni's Room* loops through time, *L'Étranger* moves methodically, linearly, through two parts. The first, Camus admits, was modeled on what he called "an American method": short declarative statements with little to no space devoted to reflection (Ward v). Part 1 unfolds much like its opening lines: "Maman died today. Or yesterday maybe, I don't know. I got a telegram from the home: 'Mother deceased. Funeral tomorrow. Faithfully yours.' That doesn't mean anything" (Camus 3). Sentence by sentence, Meursault moves along from work as a clerk to sexual ventures with his lover Marie until, briefly, "Camus suddenly resorts to poetry" in describing how the heat, the blurring light, and a pounding headache drive Meursault to squeeze the trigger of a gun pointed at an unnamed Arab man whom Meursault's pimp of a friend had assaulted earlier in the day (Viggiani 882). In this moment of poetry, Meursault is held fast by forces in the blazing heat that extend beyond his awareness. Time itself seems immobilizing, mounting the pressure that leads to murder by the seaside: "The sound of the waves was even lazier, more drawn out than at noon. It was the same sun, the same light still shining on the same sand as before. For two hours the day had stood still; for two hours it had been anchored in a sea of molten lead" (Camus 58). As if on a whim, Meursault observes a similarity between this stasis and one he had felt before.

> The sun was the same as it had been the day I buried Maman, and like then, my forehead especially was hurting me, all the veins in it throbbing under the skin. It was this burning ... that made me move forward. I knew that it was stupid, that I wouldn't get the sun off me by stepping forward. But I took a step, one step, forward. (59)

And as Meursault steps, the other man holds his knife steady. Yet, with the sun being the force it is,

> The light shot off the steel and it was like a long flashing blade cutting at my forehead. At the same instant the sweat in my eyebrows dripped over my eyelids all at once and covered them with a warm, thick film. My eyes were blinded behind the curtain of tears and salt ... That's when everything began to reel. The sea carried up a thick, fiery breath. It seemed to me as if the sky split open from one end to the other to rain down fire. My whole being tensed and I squeezed my hand around the revolver. The trigger gave; I felt the smooth underside of the butt; and there, in that noise, sharp and deafening at the same time, is where it all started. I shook off the sweat and sun. I knew that I had shattered the harmony of the day, the exceptional silence of a beach where I'd been happy. Then I fired four more times at the motionless body where the bullets lodged without leaving a trace. And it was like knocking four quick times on the door of unhappiness. (59)

Blinded by tears and salt, reeling, Meursault's whole being tenses. The trigger gives. There it all started: in death, in murder. And that is also where the first part concludes. Two pages on, readers find Meursault in jail, enduring his trial.[8]

In this prison, Meursault loses sense of the relentless flow of time that brought him there, and he grapples with the inevitability of his death, "learn[ing] to remember" in the process. His trial and sentencing usher in his liberation, Meursault's only movement to a sense of being in the world that is more full bodied than the violent passivity he knew after Maman's death. While the sea and the sun arguably represent the "mythic religious symbols" of the Mediterranean world Camus studied at university, offering an immersion "[through which] everything is dissolved, all forms disintegrate, [and] all history is abolished," it is prison—not water—that offers Meursault this liberating dissolution/absolution (Viggiani 877). Time and history dissolve for Meursault in cycles of gray daylight as he, paradoxically, "learn[s] to remember." He nearly delights in the realization that he may live the rest of his life in the prison's timelessness because he can explore his memories. Life was already so full, revisiting memories could create the world anew.[9] Yet Meursault does not go so far as to refashion the world through memory; he does not go far at all. He relays his invigoration at the possibility of such an exercise, picking through memories here and there. Camus shares one memory, primarily, while referencing others. Although memories bring Meursault a sense of possibility, he is not free of distress about his impending death. And it is in one such time that he remembers: "I remembered a story Maman used to tell me about my father. I never knew him. Maybe the only thing I did know about the man was the story Maman would tell me back then: he'd gone to watch a murderer be executed" (Camus 110). Meursault's father attended the execution and came home in knots, distraught at what he had witnessed. Meursault remembers reviling his father. Now, however, he is struck: "How had I not seen that there was nothing more important than an execution, and that when you come right down to it, it was the only thing a man could truly be interested in? If I ever got out of this prison I would go and watch every execution there was" (110). The thought of escape, of watching other executions, is too much. It smothers what promise memory held for Meursault and leaves him with "poisoned joy ... curl[ed] up in a ball under the blanket" with his teeth chattering (110). Camus communicates none of this distress. Meursault may evoke identification from those who have felt numb or askance from societal norms, yet he does not invite fellow feeling.

Matter-of-factly, he proceeds to describe his vacillating emotional states until arriving at the climactic encounter with a priest. Just prior to the contest of theological and secular wills, though, Meursault shares a glimpse of the fruit of his newfound interest in memory. In stark contrast to David, Meursault's memory leads to effacement. Regarding Marie, his lover and fiancée, Meursault loses touch with his desire for her at the thought of her death. When Marie's letters stop, Meursault wonders whether she has found another man, how she is doing, and if—well, maybe—she has died, he thinks. The thought of her death snares his musing, and he is left in doubt: "How was I to know, since apart from our two bodies, now separated, there wasn't anything to keep us together or even to remind us of each other? Anyway, after that, remembering Marie meant nothing to me. I wasn't interested in her dead" (115). Meursault does not know whether his lover has died, yet the possibility snuffs out his thought. Meursault loses Marie's meaning, even without a telegram to confirm her death. Meanwhile, the prison chaplain has been calling, despite Meursault's repeated rebuffs, and the priest surprises the prisoner by coming at an unexpected time of day. Unsure as to why, Meursault plays host to the theological stranger in his cell.

The priest drives and drives at Christian deliverance, and Meursault pushes back until his eruption in anger carries him to accept the absurdity of his death. To get there, the men lock eyes; it's a "game" Meursault knows well (117), a game in which one man reaches out to the other to offer solace, albeit with a variety of religious trappings. The priest breaks the silence of their stares with a reflection on the men he has seen and helped over the years, sufferers all. Gazing around the prison cell, he implores Meursault to *see* his surroundings. See what? Meursault asks. Wearily, the priest replies: "Every stone here sweats with suffering, I know that. I have never looked at them without a feeling of anguish. But deep in my heart I know that the most wretched among you have seen a divine face emerge from their darkness. That is the face you are asked to see" (119). This is a prison in which the very stones "sweat with suffering," from which a face emerges in the dark. The face of God, the priest contends. Meursault has none of it. He has nothing of the afterlife, salvation. Maybe, Meursault scoffs, "maybe at one time, way back, I had searched for a face in [the stones]" (119). But the face he was "looking for was as bright as the sun and the flame of desire—and it belonged to Marie. [He] had searched for it in vain" (119). He had never seen anything emerge from the stones. Quietly after Meursault shouts, the priest wonders: why call me *monsieur* and not father. That, well, "that got me mad," Meursault recalls, "and I told him he wasn't my father; he wasn't even on my side. I grabbed him by the collar of his cassock. I was pouring out on him everything that was in my heart, cries of anger and cries of joy" (121). Meursault rails on, cry after cry about his certainty, the priest's certainty, the meaningless of it all moving like a "black wind rising" in both their futures. What did it matter? "Nothing, nothing mattered, and I knew why. So did he … what would it matter if he were accused of murder and then executed because he didn't cry at his mother's funeral?" (121). It would not matter to Meursault. It might matter to the priest, whom Meursault shakes with fists clenched around his collar. Where Camus employs "poetry" for the murder, in this fit of anger and joy he introduces ellipses:

> Couldn't he, couldn't this condemned man see … And that from somewhere deep in my future … All the shouting had me gasping for air. But they were already tearing the chaplain from my grip and the guards were threatening me. He calmed them, though, and looked at me for a moment without saying anything. His eyes were full of tears. (122; ellipses in original)

Meursault turns to sleep, and he wakes to stars.

In the peace of morning, Meursault finds gratitude and affection for Maman. He discovers a fount of gratitude in the prison cell and takes himself as walking to his death replete. As the sirens blast to announce departures "for a world that now and forever meant nothing to" him, Meursault returns to his memories and makes of them an imagination of his mother's final days:

> For the first time in a long time I thought about Maman. I felt as if I understood why at the end of her life she had taken a "fiancé," why she had played at beginning again ... So close to death, Maman must have felt free then and ready to live it all again. Nobody, nobody had the right to cry over her. And I felt ready to live it all again too. As if that blind rage had washed me clean, rid me of hope; for the first time, in that night alive with signs and stars, I opened myself to the gentle indifference of the world. (122)

Fictively and emotionally reunited with Maman, Meursault is ready to live again. Finding the gentle indifference "so much like myself—so like a brother, really—" Meursault feels that he "had been happy" in life and that he is now "happy again" (122). Grateful, grounded. Without much of the pain of mourning, this appreciation is the culmination of Maman's death for Meursault, his grieving process defined up to this point as indifference. From apathy to gratitude, Meursault skips sorrow and despair. Anger at the priest arguably sets him free. It is perhaps with an awareness of this anger that he wishes the crowd at his execution greet him "with cries of hate," like those leveled at Jesus on the day of his crucifixion (123). Without stating as much himself, Meursault's experience of learning to remember is like learning to value another person. He has, in short, learned to love his mother again, and his peace in memories and imaginings of her may guide him to the inescapable fate of his own death. Had he known such appreciation and love before, he may have never murdered a man. Regardless of the cause of death and the path to it, Meursault faces death as Camus liked to imagine Sisyphus: happy. No face emerges from the suffering stones. Time is relentless, or time dissolves; no matter. The great difficulty is to accept the dawn and the executioners who accompany it. The reward for such great difficulty, Camus would have us imagine, is happiness. To this, I imagine James Baldwin might raise an eyebrow.

III

Whether it is with the raise of an eyebrow or the wink of an eye, *Giovanni's Room* takes the arc of *L'Étranger* and bends it back on itself, inverting a role here and replacing a figure there. I have no evidence that Baldwin wrote David with Meursault in mind, but the resonances alone captivate me. Where Meursault ends, David begins and, after a night of tortured remembrances, ends yet again. The threat of the guillotine hangs over David's head, although it is his lover who must heed the executioner's instructions at dawn. Anticipating Giovanni's death—and feeling anything but happy—David already asserts one of his subtle, powerful differences from Meursault. Giovanni's death is both a murder and suicide to David— fatal harm done to his lover and to the most vital version of himself that he had known. David can neither ignore nor efface these forms of harm, in contrast to Meursault's casual disregard of his own murderous act. Rather, the pain demands of David a searing encounter with his own role in the violence.

In the process, David begins with an awareness akin to that which seemingly redeemed Meursault. He already knows that "the great difficulty is to say Yes to life" (*Giovanni's Room* 9). Though Meursault seemed to achieve the difficult task of saying "yes" to death, David's challenge may be more difficult. In imagining his lover's death as a death of his own, David hints at vaster conceptions of selfhood and love that Baldwin vigorously insisted his readers behold. Saying "Yes to life" has the ring of an existentialist sounding call to it, undeniably. Yet *Giovanni's Room*, like so many of Baldwin's writings, compels readers to confront how this affirmation, this commitment, requires interrelationship. Such a conviction is absent from Camus's absurdist heroism, not merely "dimmed" by a philosophical perseveration on "unavoidable individual choice" (Lapenson 199). By my reading, the way *Giovanni's Room* plays with David's awareness of the need to say "yes" takes readers into a writhing example of the sensuous interdependence that makes a person. "Life," as another of Baldwin's protagonists observes, "is many things, but it is, above all, the touch of another" (*Tell Me* 316). David simply and powerfully suffers the denial of life as such, and *Giovanni's Room* offers a winding path toward the possibility of difference.

Structurally, if Camus's text is a line or a march through time, Baldwin's is a taught spiral: a circle when viewed on end, a coiling spring when viewed along the axis from start to *fin*. With this spiral, Baldwin creates a more convoluted imprisonment for David, in both time and psyche. A moment opens to a lifetime of meaning when interrogating the past takes hold, and a simple Man-contra-the-Universe divide collapses in the terror and potential for heroism in self-appraisal. There are no weeping stones in David's prison, yet a face appears again and again. Giovanni's visage haunts him now and perhaps forever, appearing in the night with David's eyes closed or open.

A tale also presented in two parts, *Giovanni's Room* starts and ends in the present moment of David's vigil in the French countryside. Like *L'Étranger* and *Crime and Punishment* before it, Baldwin's first section concludes with a crime—or rather David's unshakeable conviction of criminality after meeting, falling for, and stumbling home with Giovanni. Prior to that, the opening pages quickly set the stage, defining David's isolation and the harm he caused Giovanni, his lover, and Hella, his erstwhile fiancée. Within a few pages, it is clear that, before dawn, whirlwinds and zephyrs of memories will carry readers to and fro in David's pain. San Francisco (where David's mother died), Long Island, New York (Brooklyn, Manhattan, *the* City), and Paris add to the scenery. Lovers and love-objects, deceased mother and emotionally absent father, and *le milieu* populate his memories. As Jacqueline Goldsby observes, the flashbacks in *Giovanni's Room* do "function as a medium of social history and ethical consciousness" in that they allow "social order [to be] distorted and restored at once" (35). They make the context and meaning that help readers "comprehend the damage that men ... like David unleash in the world; at the same time, we have reason to hope for predictable change at the close" of the text (35). Goldsby suggests that for *Giovanni's Room* hope rests with the readers in that "we suspect we will mourn Giovanni's unjust execution" (35).

This may be so, yet the text itself stops short of delivering change. Readers initially find David much as they leave him by the end: the guillotine hangs, dawn approaches, and inevitability sounds its steady beat, relentless like the train David imagines in the text's opening paragraphs. Life, the world, the train—it "will be the same, the people ... will be the same, and I [David] will be the same ... It will all be the same, only I will be stiller" (*Giovanni's Room* 8). When David ultimately tears up the note announcing Giovanni's execution in the book's last paragraph, we are left in this stillness with no clear vision of change. The same, only stiller, having arrived at the "most terrible morning" of his life, as the first sentence of the text instructs us (7). What lies in this stillness, and what does it offer?

After this mention of stillness on the second page, Baldwin wastes no ink laying out themes of mortality, time, and heroism predicated on both remembering and forgetting. He even sneaks in the loss of a mother. Crucially, though, Baldwin weaves these themes together with reflections on self-delusion and the impossibility of self-mastery. In the stillness, there may be no demonstrable change, yet there may be an opening. From the thought of stillness, the thought of Giovanni's death, Baldwin leads us to the first act of repentance that initiates the text's flow of memories: David confesses the lie he "told Giovanni but never succeeded in making him believe, that I had never slept with a boy before" (11). David had, and he states: "I had decided I never would again" (11). With this decision, readers encounter David's first attempt to choose—*to choose!* Giovanni later exclaims, *to choose!* Sartre and Camus demanded—to choose to live life as he saw fit. The choice, and the attempts to recreate it, prove devastating for David, for life is far more than his vision of propriety, from the events of the world to the unknown intimacies of his self.

David recalls his love and lust for Joey on the boardwalk, sensuous acts he "blamed on the heat," heat "banging from the walls of the houses with enough force to kill a man" (12). The heat of the Brooklyn streets flowed with that in his chest, becoming

> a great thirsty heat, and trembling, and tenderness so painful I thought my heart would burst. But out of this astounding, intolerable pain came joy; we gave each other joy that night. It seemed, then, that a lifetime would not be long enough for me to act with Joey the act of love. (14)

But, David shares, "that lifetime was short, was bounded by that night—it ended in the morning" (14). Within seven pages of the first Dell edition, David has performed the motif that recurs writ small and large throughout the text: a lifetime in a night, a life cut brutally short by dawn. The blade is not fear, the fear that turns David away from Joey and away from Giovanni. Life for David is cut short by his decision to act on that fear. He decided "to allow no room in the universe for something which shamed and frightened" him. And he "succeeded very well," for a time, "by not looking at the universe, by not looking at myself, by remaining, in effect, in constant motion" (30–31). David succeeded, that is until ushering in ruin, by combining the traits of Camus's absurdist heroes—Don Juan, the actor, the conqueror—stringing together affairs in acts of appearance to generate being, with the ultimate choice of action over contemplation. Deciding to abandon Joey, David set out on the course of creating a life and self through will alone.

Such an approach is not only untenable, *Giovanni's Room* argues, but also denies fundamental and mercurial aspects of relationships essential to identity. The deeper in his memories David goes in pursuit of himself and the origins of his pain, David does not find *a self* but many, many others: Hella, Giovanni, his father, his mother, and his aunt; Jacques, Guillaume, a sailor here, Joey there. David encounters himself through and with others, and what he finds retains an element of frightening mystery. As he remarks, "when one begins to search for the crucial, definitive moment, the moment which changed all others, one finds oneself pressing, in great pain, through a maze of false signals and abruptly locking doors" (16). Searching for an origin, even if one could be found, does not resolve the potential for violence and joy that lives in this mystery of causes. Yet now living with the pain, the stillness of anticipating Giovanni's death, David arrives at a new awareness of decision-making and willpower. In a voice that is hard to describe as anything other than that found in Baldwin's essays,[10] David observes a new humility in his pain and loss:

> I am—or I was one of those people who pride themselves on their willpower, on their ability to make a decision and carry it through. This virtue, like most virtues, is ambiguity itself. People who believe that they are strong-willed and the masters of their destiny can only continue to believe this by becoming specialists in self-deception. Their decisions are

not really decisions at all—a real decision makes one humble, one knows that it is at the mercy of more things than can be named—but elaborate systems of evasions, of illusion, designed to make themselves and the world appear to be what they and the world are not. (30)

Willpower becomes self-deception and decisions, in such a mode, become interpretive errors, misattributions of capacity. It is a challenge, here, to read Baldwin as "epitomiz[ing] Sartre's revolutionary understanding of sovereign will" (Clytus 73). One does not simply experience "the responsibility of self-creation to varying degrees" (Clytus 75). Rather, like David, like Baldwin, like me, "'one is a stranger to one self, and … one must deal with this stranger day in and day out'" (Baldwin, qtd. in Clytus 75). The necessary act of self-creation is not one of will and assertion so much as it is a dance with a mystery, letting what is known yield to the energy of the unknown.

Another way of considering this dance is via David's belief in a rare form of heroism, a heroism that parallels the task Baldwin gave himself a year earlier in 1955's "Notes of a Native Son." Where Camus identifies one holistic moment of embrace in a heroism predicated on affirmation, Baldwin demands a double move. Prompted by Jacques, a weary acquaintance in the realm of failed love, David reflects on the possibility of innocence in the form of personal Edens. "Nobody," Jacques observes, "can stay" (*Giovanni's Room* 35). David picks up with the thought and lays out two options, much as Meursault established in accosting the chaplain. David, like his author, ultimately refuses a dichotomy of choice and delivers a seemingly paradoxical ideal:

Perhaps everybody has a garden of Eden, I don't know; but they have scarcely seen their garden before they see the flaming sword. Then, perhaps, life only offers the choice of remembering the garden or forgetting it. Either, or: it takes strength to remember, it takes another kind of strength to forget, it takes a hero to do both. People who remember court madness through pain, the pain of the perpetually recurring death of their innocence; people who forget court another kind of madness, the madness of the denial of pain and the hatred of innocence; and the world is mostly divided between madmen who remember and madmen who forget. Heroes are rare. (36)

David, having courted the madness of forgetting for years, embarks on the quest to remember. In his stillness at the end, it is unclear if he is a hero. He may merely be a madman, yoked to one pole or the other. Nonetheless, he has traced a path toward the possibility of heroism in simultaneously remembering and forgetting. The implications appear self-defeating, for how may both remembrance and forgetfulness be maintained? One must remember, and one must forget—the same moments, the same pain, the same life—but how?

It is by a doubling akin to that which Baldwin outlined for himself and his readers after his father's death. It is by cultivating a capacity for more than apparent opposition. The day of the funeral was that of his youngest sister's birth and a day Harlem shook with riot and protest. Baldwin drew it all together to find meaning in the death, birth, and violent wrongs of society:

> It began to seem that one would have to hold in mind forever two ideas which seemed to be in opposition. The first idea was acceptance, the acceptance, totally without rancor, of life as it is, and men as they are: in the light of this idea, it goes without saying that injustice is a commonplace. But this did not mean that one could be complacent, for the second idea was of equal power: that one must never, in one's own life, accept these injustices as commonplace but must fight them with all one's strength. ("Notes" 84)

The characterization of life's charge is near Sisyphean, in Camus's sense. One must accept the boulder as it is and keep pushing against it, accept, and revolt. Yet Baldwin's elaboration spells out the difference in intimate, interpersonal terms. The fight for which one must bring "all one's strength … begins, however, in the heart":

> and it now had been laid to my charge to keep my own heart free of hatred and despair. This intimation made my heart heavy and, now that my father was irrecoverable, I wished that he had been beside me so that I could have searched his face for the answers which only the future would give me now. (84)

Like his protagonist, Baldwin's heart and history are central to the act of acceptance and refusing to accept. His heart and his stepfather, whom he so often loathed, are at stake. The indifference of the world be damned. As Ralph Ellison wrote of the blues, the heroism of both remembering and forgetting speaks of "an impulse to keep the painful details and episodes of a brutal experience alive in one's aching consciousness, to finger its jagged grain, and to transcend it, not by the consolation of philosophy but by squeezing from it a near-tragic, near-comic lyricism" (qtd. in Clytus 72).

Overwhelmed by remembrance at the end, David reaches for transcendence. Like Meursault's last night in the cell, David's last pages of reflection are full of Christian imagery and imagination. Dawn approaches, and thoughts of Giovanni consume David. Where Marie fell away from Meursault's mind and care, Giovanni becomes David's only care. David yearns for a lover to be there with Giovanni in his last hours, for someone to hold and comfort him. He yearns for such comfort himself. As the horizon lightens, as if in a trance, David's consciousness splits between his room and his imagination of Giovanni's cell; the walk to the guillotine that Meursault cannot provide readers is readily imagined by David. Gates swing open in David's mind before Giovanni. Or perhaps he still sits and watches the dawn: "Will he die alone? I do not know if death, in this country, is a solitary affair. And what will he say to the priest?" (*Giovanni's Room* 221). While David undresses, "Giovanni's face swings before [him] like an unexpected lantern on a dark, dark night." And

> His eyes—his eyes, they glow like a tiger's eyes ... I cannot read what is in his eyes: if it is terror, then I have never seen terror, if it is anguish, then anguish has never laid hands on me ... They pull him to the door of his cell, the corridor stretches before him like the graveyard of his past, the prison spins around him. Perhaps he begins to moan, perhaps he makes no sound. The journey begins. Or, perhaps, when he cries out, he does not stop crying; perhaps his voice is crying now, in all that stone and iron. I see his legs buckle, his thighs jelly, the buttocks quiver, the secret hammer there begins to knock. He is sweating, or he is dry. They drag him, or he walks ... down those metal stairs, into the heart of the prison and out of it, into the office of the priest. (221–22)

David glimpses his naked body in the mirror, and he sees a body "under sentence of death. It is lean, hard, and cold, the incarnation of a mystery ... trapped in my mirror as it is trapped in time" (223). With the silent shrieking of the dawn light, David imagines Giovanni thrown forward in darkness. David dresses and steps out into the morning "with the dreadful weight of hope" on his shoulders, finding the blue envelope announcing Giovanni's execution in his hand; he tears "it slowly into many pieces, watching them dance in the wind, watching the wind carry them away. Yet, [as he turns] ... the wind blows some of them back" (224). With that, we are left with neither the guillotine nor the comfort of starting again. If David's acts of remembrance amount to heroism when paired with his will to forget, it is a heroism certainly without triumph.

IV

And so what comes of reading Meursault and David alongside each other? What is important about the inversions of time and the convolutions of pain, manhood, and memory achieved by *Giovanni's Room*, when compared to the teleological metronome of *L'Étranger*? And how can we avoid conferring sainthood to men, or Baldwin in particular, when comparing the two works? I do not ask these questions rhetorically. I ask because I'm curious about the stakes involved. I believe Baldwin offers more truth and more possibility than Camus, yet I do not know how to gauge the impact of either author. Regardless, the importance I see pertains to the relationship between memory and, for lack of a better term, whiteness.

Baldwin went to great lengths to describe whiteness, and the White Man, as a myth prone to violent effacements of history, using turns of phrase that could run the risk of being dismissed as naïve attempts at post-racial thinking if uttered too casually these days. Yet when Baldwin wrote that "blackness and whiteness did not matter," it is clear in the context of his life and work that he was speaking of the ruse that such labels sprung from inherent, immutable truths of nature ("Notes" 84). Like prescriptions on sexuality, claiming nature was but a means of recreating power, obscuring the routine social work required to perpetuate social ills. From *The Fire Next Time* through to his last essays, 1985's "Freaks and the Ideal of American Manhood" chief among them, Baldwin contended with the grave error of refusing to confront one's history in the world. Of many past travesties, America's persistent sin was, and arguably remains, its inability to witness how the past lives on in the present. Though Baldwin leveled this criticism at those "who still insisted—in light of it all—that they were *white*" (Pavlić), Baldwin spoke generally of that American temptation to lose sight of the past in the mistaken supposition "that you or I have bled and suffered and died in this country in order to achieve Cadillacs" ("Uses" 62). By the time he wrote *No Name in the Street*, Baldwin saw these evasive temptations shaping global affairs, and he shared as much in his reflections on Camus.

From the vantage point of 1972, Baldwin writes in *No Name in the Street* of 1956 and the global implications of a white identity he had primarily written off as American. The year witnessed Fidel Castro land on the shores of Cuba, the nationalization of the Suez Canal, and, importantly for Baldwin and Camus, the Battle of Algiers. It was also the year Baldwin published *Giovanni's Room*. Though Baldwin neglected to mention the Algerians in his writing during the 1950s, by 1972 the bloody halt of the civil rights movement and the violence of the Vietnam War left Baldwin reaching back to his past for a vision of solidarity. His memory, as Robert Reid-Pharr notes in this volume, is faulty and partial; it elides truths, and it stumbles. It is utterly serviceable. Connecting his life and its history to the violence endured by Algerians in Algeria and France, Baldwin comes to one of his few mentions of Camus in print:

> I have said that I was almost entirely ignorant of the details of the Algerian-French complexity, but I was endeavoring to correct this ignorance; and one of the ways in which I was going about it compelled me to keep a

file of the editorial pronouncements made by M. Albert Camus in the pages of the French political newspaper, *Combat*. Camus had been born in Oran, which is the scene of his first novel, *The Stranger*. He could be described, perhaps, as a radical humanist; he was young, he was lucid, and it was not illogical to assume that he would bring—along with the authority of knowing the land of his birth—some of these qualities to bear on his apprehension of the nature of the French-Algerian conflict. (*No Name* 378–79)

Alas, like William Faulkner's commitment to a mythic Mississippi, Camus did not impress Baldwin. Despite a history of advocacy and journalism on behalf of Algerians from before the Second World War, a fact that Baldwin may have never known, Camus fails in Baldwin's appraisal due to the implicit boundaries of his humanism. Baldwin continues:

I have never esteemed this writer [Camus] as highly as do so many others. I was struck by the fact that, for Camus, the European humanism appeared to expire at the European gates: so that Camus, who was dedicated to liberty, in the case of Europeans, could only speak of "justice" in the case of Algeria. ("A legal means," said an African recipient, "of administering injustice.") Given the precepts upon which he based his eloquent discourses concerning the problems of individual liberty, he must have seen that what the Battle of Algiers was really about was the fact that the French refused to give the Algerians the right to be wrong; refused to allow them, so to speak, that "existentialist" situation, of which the French, for a season, were so enamored; or, more accurately, did not even dare imagine that the Algerian situation could be "existentialist"; precisely because the French situation was so extreme. (*No Name* 379)

Granted, at the time of the conflict in 1956, Baldwin was writing nowhere about the moral failings of French rule in Algeria. He did, however, witness firsthand the impact of material social change in postwar Europe. The Marshall Plan and colonial extortion demonstrated how quickly the world could change from a battle zone crossed with train tracks leading to concentration camps to a medley of civil societies with ever-broadening social welfare. The world could change quickly—and for the better. That is, when "the world" relied on colonial holdings overseas to remake itself. Worn and ever more worn by assassinations and halting change in the country of his birth, Baldwin maintains little generosity for a European sentiment he reads in Camus that disregards swaths of humanity with unintended ease.

Further enhancing his sense of a globalized white ignorance, Baldwin recollects attending a play in 1956 "that Camus translated and directed":

William Faulkner's *Requiem for a Nun* (*No Name* 79). For an evening, who knows, Baldwin was in the playhouse with Camus. There, too, he was unimpressed. Watching the play, Baldwin could see, and believed he understood, why "Faulkner may have needed to believe in black forgiveness" as the motive for the murderous event at the plot's center. Baldwin could imagine his way to an understanding of the Southern sensibility that sought and fabricated a kind of redemption in fiction. Baldwin "could see why Faulkner needed Nancy: but why did Camus need Faulkner? On what ground did they meet, the mind of the great, aging, Mississippi novelist, and the mind of the young writer from Oran?" (*No Name* 380). For one, they met on ground inherited from colonial settlers; they met on ground stably supporting the stance of a Meursault, the stance of Modern Man as conceived by a European colonialism and lauded by the Nobel Committee. Camus and Faulkner shared a conscience rightfully horrified by the atrocities of both world wars, yet it was a perspective that failed to incorporate, for example, the "widespread feeling among coloured people that there is a certain retributive justice in Belgium's present plight [in the Great War] on account of its treatment of the natives in the Congo Free State," as W. E. B. Du Bois described during the First World War (qtd. in Twomey 258). Camus, like Faulkner before him, suffers the error of "seeking to exorcise a history which is also a curse" (*No Name* 381).

If there is any hope for the absurd hero in the mix, it is in David's form, wrestling with the past. There are no exorcisms to be had; exorcism requires a denial of all the history that has made us who we are. In contrast, Meursault is too captivated by accepting the inevitability of his future, not only at ease with the harm he has caused but ignorant of it. The ability to turn from history, to consider its exorcism, or ignore its reality altogether reinforces the insidious attitude of whiteness Baldwin dissected time and again, not least of which with David. Facing history in Baldwin's way demands a reckoning with interconnection. David's agonizing night is one of confronting, over and again, his relationships, and it is the physical, sensual reality of constant relation that makes a self anything but a unified abstraction. To Baldwin, there is perhaps something more distressing, and more urgently real, in the awareness that a world of subjectivity versus objectivity itself evades a distressing, generative truth:

> It has always been much easier (because it has always seemed much safer) to give a name to the evil without than to locate the terror within. And yet, the terror within is far truer and far more powerful than any of our labels: the labels change, the terror is constant. And this terror has something to do with the irreducible gap between the self one invents— the self one takes oneself as being, which is, however, and by definition, a provisional self—and the undiscoverable self which always has the power to blow the provisional self to bits. ("Nothing Personal" 694)

In his prison cell, Meursault does not catch a glimpse of himself in this way. When not seized by his memories, David can look nowhere else but at the mirrors and reflective windowpanes of the villa to which he has fled. He endures the pain of having so long refused his undiscoverable self.

One may prefer Meursault's jubilation in life's richness to the paralysis of David's guilt. Nonetheless, of the two heroes, only David endeavors to fulfill the work Baldwin found necessary for change. Both figures are trapped, yet only Meursault suffers from the illusion of believing himself free. Both figures may be of European ancestry, born and raised on the colonized lands of America and Africa, yet Meursault remains, in Baldwin's phrasing, white. David exemplifies Baldwin's prized effort: to "examine and face your life," by which, if you can meet the task, "you can discover the terms in which you are connected to other lives, and they can discover, too, the terms in which they are connected to other people" (Baldwin, "Interview"). Meursault has no such notion of what he has done to others through his indifferent act of murder. He finds liberation in prison, because Camus mistook his trap as one of abstract morality and the challenge of living in the wake of God's death. Meursault could easily pull the trigger again. Like the America Baldwin addressed, Meursault "has no notion whatever—and this is disastrous—of what [he's] done to" himself; he has no notion of what he has done to others ("Interview"). He has not faced the terror within. His dungeon, surely, has not shaken.

David, blond though he may be, is shook and shakes to this day with each reading of *Giovanni's Room*. Written with an ability to regard his past and his wounding effect on others, David trembles. Perhaps his white mask is on the verge of slipping as he looks at his reflection in the window, though he remains trapped in the mirror. David suffers from a nearly debilitating stasis, to be sure, yet he accomplishes a confrontation with history and his past that Baldwin extolled time and again for a white America. Giovanni will die, Hella has deserted him, and he walks in a hungover stupor, but David has won for himself some semblance of honesty. Meursault achieves happiness in a prison cell; David demonstrates the kind of work necessary to the prison for himself and others. After David, Meursault is no longer "simply" a foreigner to a society that does not comprehend his grasp of the arbitrariness of life. He is no longer a mere individual standing trial by a populace more concerned with his lack of remorse at his mother's funeral than at the death of an Algerian man. Meursault, a mythic white man—perhaps an archetype of a colonizing psychology—is a man numb to his own grief, ignorant of the multitude of selves through which an individual comes to be.

David is not triumphant in his acts of memory; he hardly acts at all. His inability to love both himself and others leads to heartbreak and murder. Nonetheless, he is free of the delusion that safety may be achieved by demanding that life conform to an abstraction of manhood. That is, he is free of the belief that safety may be achieved at all, not least of all by refusing love. The consequences of such a belief have broken David open to the possibility of change. Grief lays him bare. We may not imagine him happy. Nor may we imagine him redeemed. But we may consider, for a moment, that David has achieved the possibility of change.

Notes

1 For an elaboration of Meursault's reenactment of Oedipus's legend, see Fletcher.

2 As Sartre or Sontag may have contended (Sontag).

3 See, for example, Abur-Rahman; Armengol; Brim; Kent; and Lapenson.

4 Prompted by Bruce Lapenson's footnoting, I brushed up on (neo)liberal individuality with Michael J. Sandel's *Liberalism and the Limits of Justice*.

5 Stephen D. Ross in *Literature and Philosophy* has an excellent consideration of how so many managed to read *L'Étranger* without a moral reaction to Meursault's murderous act.

6 Richard Webster, for one, argues as much about Sartre. Camus and Baldwin grew up awash in Christian cosmologies.

7 Us, our, we—the readers of *Time* magazine, *The New Yorker*, James Baldwin, Richard Wright, and Annie Proulx; the "our" and "we" of his essays that invariably included those who mistook themselves as white and those who, black, white, or otherwise, found Baldwin's sexuality an affront to their manhood. In Radiclani Clytus's words, it is a "we" that speaks "'objectively' (and thus inclusively) … [to expose] readers to the idea that black subjectivity [in the form of 'the Negro Problem' was] essentially a speculative trope in the minds of black and white Americans alike" (73).

8 With *L'Étranger*'s structure loosely evocative of *Crime and Punishment*, one half to build to the crime, the other for the punishment, there's likely an essay in comparing Camus's and Baldwin's interest in Dostoevsky as well.

9 It may be overly generous to state that revisiting memories could create the world anew, because neither Meursault nor Camus shares this act of remembering. We are simply told of its totality, the near fulfillment it might provide—as if Meursault were the cousin of Jorge Luis Borges's 1942 *Funes the Memorious*, the boy bedridden after a horse riding accident who could remember every moment of his life exactly as he lived it, a boy caught in a lifelong loop that would infinitely lead back through the moment he struck his head in the fall.

10 Perhaps one of the reasons Susan Sontag lumped Baldwin together with Camus as "husband-like" authors who combined the role of artist with civic conscience: "One sensed in Camus, as one senses in James Baldwin, the presence of an entirely genuine, and historically relevant, passion. But also, as with Baldwin, that passion seemed to transmute itself too readily into stately language, into an inexhaustible self-perpetuating oratory. The moral imperatives—love, moderation—offered to palliate intolerable historical or metaphysical dilemmas were too general, too abstract, too rhetorical."

Works Cited

Abur-Rahman, Aliyyah I. "'Simply a Menaced Boy': Analogizing Color, Undoing Dominance in James Baldwin's *Giovanni's Room*." *African American Review*, vol. 41, no. 3, 2007, pp. 477–86. *JSTOR*, jstor.org/stable/40027408. Accessed 3 Sept. 2018.

Armengol, Josep M. "In the Dark Room: Homosexuality and/as Blackness in James Baldwin's *Giovanni's Room*." *Signs*, vol. 37, no. 3, Spring 2012, pp. 671–93. doi: 10.1086/662699.

Baldwin, James. *Collected Essays*. Library of America, 1998.

Baldwin, James. *The Cross of Redemption: Uncollected Writings*. Pantheon Books, 2010.

Baldwin, James. "Freaks and the American Ideal of Manhood." Baldwin, *Collected Essays*, pp. 814–29.

Baldwin, James. *Giovanni's Room*. Alfred A. Knopf, 1956.

Baldwin, James. Interview with Studs Terkel. 1961. *YouTube*, uploaded by thepostarchive, 21 Oct. 2015, youtube.com/watch?v=Ke6G3sEdj-s. Accessed 4 Sept. 2018.

Baldwin, James. *No Name in the Street*. Baldwin, *Collected Essays*, pp. 349–475.

Baldwin, James. *Nobody Knows My Name*. Baldwin, *Collected Essays*, pp. 137–289.

Baldwin, James. "Notes of a Native Son." Baldwin, *Collected Essays*, pp. 63–84.

Baldwin, James. "Nothing Personal." Baldwin, *Collected Essays*, pp. 692–706.

Baldwin, James. *Tell Me How Long the Train's Been Gone*. Alfred A. Knopf, 1968.

Baldwin, James. "The Uses of the Blues." Baldwin, *The Cross of Redemption*, pp. 57–66.

Brim, Matt. *James Baldwin and the Queer Imagination*. U of Michigan P, 2014.

Camus, Albert. *The Stranger*. 1942. Translated by Matthew Ward, Knopf Publishing, 1989.

Clytus, Radiclani. "Paying Dues and Playing the Blues: Baldwin's Existential Jazz." Elam, pp. 70–84.

Elam, Michele, editor. *The Cambridge Companion to James Baldwin*. Cambridge UP, 2015.

Fletcher, John. "Interpreting *L'Etranger*." Special issue of *The French Review*, vol. 43, no. 1, Winter 1970, pp. 158–67. doi: 10.2307/487573.

Goldsby, Jacqueline. "'Closer to Something Unnameable': Baldwin's Novel Form." Elam, pp. 25–40.

Horowitz, Louise K. "Of Women and Arabs: Sexual and Racial Polarization in Camus." *Modern Language Studies*, vol. 17, no. 3, Summer 1987, pp. 54–61. doi: 10.2307/3194734.

Kent, Jessica. "Baldwin's Hemingway: *The Sun Also Rises* in *Giovanni's Room*, with a Twist." *Twentieth-Century Literature*, vol. 63, no. 1, Mar. 2017, pp. 75–93. doi: 10.1215/0041462X-3833474.

Lapenson, Bruce. "Race and Existential Commitment in James Baldwin." *Philosophy and Literature*, vol. 37, no. 1, Aug. 2013, pp. 199–209. doi: 10.1353/phl.2013.0002.

Maher, Eamon. "Camus' Meursault: The Only Christ That Modern Civilisation Deserves?" *Studies: An Irish Quarterly Review*, vol. 87, no. 347,

Autumn 1998, pp. 276–81. *JSTOR*, jstor.org/stable/30091922. Accessed 3 Sept. 2018.

McMurray, George R. "Albert Camus' Concept of the Absurd and Juan José Arreola's 'The Switchman.'" *Latin American Literary Review*, vol. 6, no. 11, 1977, pp. 30–35. *JSTOR*, jstor.org/stable/20119099. Accessed 24 Aug. 2018.

"The Nobel Prize in Literature 1957." *Nobel Prize*, Nobel Media AB, nobelprize.org/prizes/literature/1957/summary. Accessed 28 Aug. 2018.

Pavlić, Ed. "Baldwin's Lonely Country." *Boston Review*, 29 Mar. 2018, bostonreview.net/race/ed-pavlic/baldwins-lonely-country. Accessed 24 Aug. 2018.

Reid-Pharr, Robert F. "Effective/Defective James Baldwin." *Of Latitudes Unknown: James Baldwin's Radical Imagination*, edited by Alice Mikal Craven, William E. Dow, and Yoko Nakamura, Bloomsbury, 2019.

Ross, Stephen David. *Literature and Philosophy: An Analysis of the Philosophical Novel*. Appleton-Century-Crofts, 1969.

Sandel, Michael J. *Liberalism and the Limits of Justice*. Cambridge UP, 1998.

Sontag, Susan. "The Ideal Husband." Review of *Notebooks, 1935–42*, by Albert Camus. *The New York Review of Books*, 26 Sept. 1963, nybooks.com/articles/1963/09/26/the-ideal-husband/. Accessed 24 Aug. 2018.

Twomey, Christina. "Framing Atrocity: Photography and Humanitarianism." *History of Photography*, vol. 36, no. 3, Aug. 2012, pp. 255–64. doi: 10.1080/03087298.2012.669933.

Viggiani, Carl A. "Camus' *L'Etranger*." *PMLA*, vol. 71, no. 5, Dec. 1956, pp. 865–87. doi: 10.2307/460515.

Ward, Matthew. "Note on Translation." *The Stranger*, by Albert Camus, translated by Ward, Knopf Publishing, 1989, pp. v–vii.

Webster, Richard. *Why Freud Was Wrong: Sin, Science, and Psychoanalysis*. Basic Books, 1995.

9

James Baldwin's Black Power: *No Name in the Street*, Fanon, Camus, and the Black Panthers

James Miller

Introduction

At the First International Congress of Black Writers and Artists, held at the Sorbonne in 1956, Richard Wright, Frantz Fanon, and James Baldwin gathered under one roof for the first and only time. Wright and Fanon presented papers, while Baldwin wrote about the conference for *Encounter* in his essay "Princes and Powers." The essay gave a detailed account of some of the papers he heard at the conference, including those by the then luminaries of *négritude*, Léopold Senghor, Alioune Diop, and Fanon's fellow Martinican, Aimé Césaire.[1] It is not known if Baldwin heard Fanon's paper on "Racism and Culture," which asserted that the "biological" racism that had prevailed in the nineteenth and early twentieth centuries was giving way to a cultural racism exemplified by calls to defend "western values" (Macey 287–90). Fanon had yet to become the voice of third world revolution. His paper was not mentioned in the transcripts made by *Présence africaine* of conference debates, and at the time there was no special reason for Baldwin—who was almost certainly unaware of *Peau noire, masques blancs* (1952; *Black Skin, White Masks*)—to have referred specifically to Fanon.

In 1972, Baldwin published his long essay *No Name in the Street* in which he articulates his own version of Black Power, an ideology that, by this point, had largely replaced the integrationist ethic of the first stage of civil rights.[2]

This chapter hopes to situate Baldwin's essay within the intellectual climate of the period in order to show that the ideas outlined in *No Name in the Street* owe much to Fanon's *The Wretched of the Earth* (1961) and represent a departure from Baldwin's earlier position and an expansion of his radical imagination, part of a wider call for "resistance, intervention, compassion and struggle" (Nancy 148). After looking at how Baldwin revises, adapts, and to some extent distorts Fanon's ideas through debates about Camus, Faulkner, and the Algerian situation, we move on to his discussion of the Black Panthers, arguing that Baldwin uses the Panthers to articulate a very personal and American ideal of blackness as a critical-utopian construct.

Fanon was a major influence for many Black Power activists. Eldridge Cleaver famously said that "every brother on a roof top" could quote Fanon, whilst Stokely Carmichael and Charles Hamilton quote extensively from *The Wretched of the Earth* in their introduction to *Black Power* (1967). However, the reciprocal influence between Fanon and radical African American thought goes back to include Richard Wright. Wright and Fanon corresponded, and according to Fanon's biographer David Macey, Wright's novels were a profound influence on Fanon (Macey 127, 192–93).[3] Michel Fabre supports this view, stating

> It is significant that [Wright's] deepest influence on a non-American black writer should have been Frantz Fanon whose West Indian heritage made him, more than any African, aware of the complexities of the black Western intellectual caught between white masks and black skin. (211)

This chapter will discuss the following: the influence of *The Wretched of the Earth* on *No Name in the Street* and the extent to which *No Name in the Street* departs from Baldwin's earlier and more nuanced interpretation of postcolonial identities, particularly "Stranger in the Village," through a close reading of Baldwin's discussion of Camus and Camus's interpretation of Faulkner's play *Requiem for a Nun* (1950). Finally, we look at Baldwin's discussion of the Black Panthers in order to show how he recuperates a complex understanding of African American identity as a potential immanent within a dialectic of struggle and recognition that is both particular to the United States and germane to wider problems of postcolonial nationhood and identity.

No Name in the Street and *The Wretched of the Earth*: Reciprocities of influence

No Name in the Street is split into two sections—"Take Me to the Water" and "To Be Baptized"—and Baldwin uses the first part to provide background, through a politically nuanced retelling of his experiences in

France during the Algerian War and in the Deep South during the civil rights movement, for his support of the Black Panthers in the second. As these titles show, Christianity remains a primary reference for Baldwin. The essay itself takes its title from the book of Job ("His remembrance shall perish from the earth and he shall have no name in the street" [18:16–18]), whilst the section titles draw a comparison between baptism into the Christian fold and Baldwin's assertion of a much more radical political perspective. The essay was intended as a sequel to *The Fire Next Time* and is also heavily autobiographical in tone. Much of it laments the murders of Martin Luther King Jr., Medgar Evers, and Malcolm X—a sort of farewell to the first wave of civil rights activists—whilst heralding the next generation of African American militants, especially the Black Panthers. Baldwin was friends with Huey Newton and Bobby Seale by this time.[4] The essay touches on a wide range of issues around the experience of justice for both the African American and "Third World" subject, focusing on the arrest for murder of a friend of Baldwin's called Tony. Indeed, much of the essay chronicles Baldwin's failure to get his friend off the hook, and this narrative—which suggests Tony's experience is emblematic of the experience of African American men in the United States in general—is interwoven with a wider engagement with civil rights and the fight for independence in the third world.

By 1972, Baldwin had read Fanon. In *No Name in the Street*, he states that "Fanon," "Mao," and "Che" "have something to say to the century" and can be "read with profit," although he does distance himself from their "doctrinaire position" ("No Name" 541). Certain key elements of *The Wretched of the Earth* have a special relevance to *No Name in the Street*. The first is violence. For Fanon, violence was the means by which the colonized subject achieved recognition within the racist, colonial system (see Gordon 62; Gibson 115–17). Fanon called violence a "cleansing force" that "frees the native from his inferiority complex and from his despair and inaction" (*Wretched* 74). According to Fanon, "violence ... ruled over the ordering of the colonial world." Therefore, violence would mobilize the masses and introduce "into each man's consciousness the ideas of a common cause, of a national destiny and of a collective history" (31, 73). The violence of the "native" is the moment when "the native" decides "to embody history in his own person," which allows a "new man" to emerge (31).[5] Violence enables the colonized to enter into the history of the colonizer.

No Name in the Street picks up on this idea. Baldwin appears to concur with what Sartre referred to in his introduction to *The Wretched of the Earth* as "the moment of the boomerang" (17) by arguing that such violence was a "prospect white people ... have brought on themselves" through their acceptance and complicity with the racist structure of American society ("No Name" 551). As a result, "it is not necessary for the black man to hate a white man, or to have any particular feelings about him at all, in order to realize he must kill him" (550). This rather icy acceptance of racial violence was unprecedented for Baldwin, a way of registering his outrage at the cruelty of America's racial history and his dismay toward the ongoing violence of the time. Few critics have considered the implications of this statement, and those who do tend, like Horace Porter, to look askance, inaccurately dismissing it as an "extraordinarily despairing statement" that "could easily have been written by a Black Muslim" (167).

Exasperated by the failure of peaceful tactics to quench the violence perpetuated by American racists, Baldwin vents his frustration (Leeming 220, 228). He shows he understands those who, like the Panthers, felt they had no choice but to take up arms:

> I know what I would do if I had a gun and someone had a gun pointed at my brother, and I would not count to ten to do it and there would be no hatred in it, nor any remorse. People who treat other people as less than human must not be surprised when the bread they have cast on the waters comes floating back to them, poisoned. ("No Name" 551)

Baldwin ironically reworks the Old Testament reference "Cast thy bread upon the waters: for thou shalt find it after many days" (Ecclesiastes 11:1) in order to suggest that white violence produces black violence in return. He does, however, shy from advocating such action in more explicit terms, couching even this advocacy with a biblical, rather than political, language of vengeance. The discussion of the Black Panthers that concludes this essay shows how Baldwin's support for the Panthers avoids consideration of Huey Newton's Maoist assertion that "power" comes from the barrel of the "gun" (Newton 12). Although Baldwin makes emotive and rhetorical statements that suggest why African Americans might resort to such action, he shies away from a concrete discussion of such tactics.

The second key idea behind *The Wretched of the Earth* is the necessity of repudiating Western civilization: "All the Mediterranean values," claims Fanon (selecting those least useful to his vision of collective struggle), "the triumph of the human individual, of clarity and of beauty—becomes lifeless, colourless knick-knacks" during the fight for independence (*Wretched* 36). Fanon argues that an appeal to "Western values" is another form of oppression: these values are "affirmed" with a "violence" and an "aggressiveness" that suppresses indigenous culture and negates the humanity of "the native" (33). This sense of European culture as experienced within the colonial context as a monolithic, repressive force bears upon Baldwin's rejectionist posture, although he is dealing with the more involved situation of the African American. As a result, it is the more ambiguous concept of racial identity, rather than land, that must be liberated.

Fanon goes on to stress the necessity of third world autonomy: "The Third World ought not to be content to define itself in the terms of values which have preceded it ... the under-developed countries ought to do their utmost to find their own particular values and methods and a style which shall be peculiar to them" (78). Impressive as this may sound, Fanon struggles to define where these new values would come from or emerge from within the colonized nation. Although nationalism was an idea produced by the fact of occupation, it was also an imported European ideal, a contradiction Fanon struggled to conceive in dialectical terms (Gibson 203; see also Appiah 82–88). As Albert Memmi understood, all that is "real and verifiable is that the colonized's culture, society and technology are seriously damaged" (158). Fanon's vision of how revolutionary struggle transforms national culture was inaccurate. Although his method was criticized by strict Marxists, he anticipated revolution as leading to a socialist-type, secular society based on reason rather than religion (Macey 478–82).[6]

The problem of where these "particular values," "methods," and "style" would come from is important, not least because Fanon claimed the struggle would rid "the native" of tribal loyalties and superstitions. His view reflected a Marxist reason of history. Such opinion argued that just as an agricultural economy would be replaced by industrialization, so an age of superstition would be replaced by one of reason. *The Wretched of the Earth* draws on the abstract framework of group action derived from Sartre's *Critique de la raison dialectique*. Macey notes, "The fundamental ambiguity of *Les Damnés de la Terre* is that, while Fanon constantly prophesies the victory of the people, the theoretical model he adopts necessarily implies that the group unity on which that victory is based cannot be sustained" (478, 487). Despite his attempt to disavow Western influences, Fanon's model depends on a Marxist theory of the dictatorship of the proletariat transferred to the colonial peasant. Fanon failed to understand the importance of Islam in shaping the revolutionary consciousness of the Algerian. After 1962, the "Manichean world" of colonialist and native would be replaced not by a new, third world style socialism but by a bitter struggle between secular military power and Islamic fundamentalism (see Clancy-Smith). The prophesied new communist man of Algeria never materialized. Whilst Baldwin's approach was also bound up with these contradictions, his emphasis on witness and recognition over ideology and on identity rather than territory allowed for a more recuperative approach, arguably one better attuned to the specific complexities of the struggle in the United States.

This essay will now closely read one such moment where Baldwin's radical imagination engages with Fanon's ideas—via debates about Camus, Faulkner, and the Algerian War of Independence—to better demonstrate how his language offers a rhetorical solidarity with the third world.

Baldwin, Camus, and Faulkner

Baldwin initiates his rejection of Euro-American history and culture with a partisan interpretation of the work of Camus, Faulkner, and what he considers to be their flawed attitude toward Algeria, civil rights, and the concept of justice itself. He argues that they typify a refusal—characterized by his essay as intrinsic to white, Euro-American society—to recognize the legitimate demands of the African American or third world subject. The essay will be closely read in order to analyze this rejection and to consider the extent to which Baldwin is able to support his assertion: "The Algerian and I were both, alike, victims of this history ... their destiny was *somehow* tied to mine, their battle was not theirs alone but was my battle also" ("No Name" 470; emphasis added). The question is whether a connection between the African American and third world subject, fudged in this case by Baldwin's evasive use of "somehow," is credible. The reality of Baldwin's American identity complicates his simplistic division of the world into a battle between "those placed within history and those dispersed outside" (474). A Puritan American suspicion of Europe and a Christian faith in the ultimate righteousness of the poor coupled with a violent rhetoric drawn from Fanon's *The Wretched of the Earth* give this part of Baldwin's essay its particular power.

No Name in the Street revisits Baldwin's expatriate days in Paris in order to politicize the experience. He reinterprets his time in Paris to argue that his experiences in Europe helped him to understand that American racism was part of a wider structure of colonial exploitation. When he first arrived, Baldwin states he was "almost entirely ignorant of the details of the Algerian-French complexity" and sought to amend his ignorance by keeping a file of Camus's "editorial pronouncements" in *Combat* ("No Name" 471). However, he quickly discovers that for Camus, "European humanism appeared to expire at the European gates: so that Camus, who was dedicated to liberty in the case of Europeans, could only speak of 'justice' in the case of Algeria" ("No Name" 471).

There are several factual inaccuracies behind this argument. First, Baldwin gets his dates mixed up: he did not arrive in Paris until November 11, 1948 (Campbell 50). Camus, however, resigned from *Combat* in 1947. The editorials to which Baldwin refers were all written between 1944 and 1947 (Camus 8–9). Baldwin knew little French at the time, certainly not sufficient to read *Combat* had he chanced upon any back issues. Apart from "Neither Victims nor Executioners" translated and published by Dwight Macdonald in the August 1947 edition of *politics*, the first comprehensive selection of *Combat* editorials to be translated into English did not appear until 1991. Baldwin knew Macdonald and so it is conceivable that he read this edition or was familiar with some of Camus's arguments. Camus does write about justice in these editorials under titles such as "*Combat* Wants to Make Justice Compatible with Freedom," but he is concerned mostly with France, the Nazi occupation, and the new society he hoped would emerge after liberation (Camus 57–58).

Furthermore, the only reference in these editorials to "our colonies" and "justice" contradicts Baldwin's suggestion that "justice"—as applied by the French—was incompatible with Algerian demands for liberty. Camus states: "We will find support from our colonies only when we have convinced them that their interests are our interests and that we do not have contrary policies, one giving justice to the French people, the other consecrating injustice in our empire" (65). In this article, Camus's "justice" does not make a distinction between France and its "colonies" (although Camus does not mention Algeria by name). Quite the opposite: Camus argues France and its colonies have mutual interests, a position that contests the absolute division between the West and the third world that Baldwin presents in his essay. That said, the fundamental issue of whether France had any rights to "colonies" or an "empire" at all is left unquestioned in Camus's editorials.

Although he distorts Camus, there is some basis for Baldwin's critique. Despite mistakenly mentioning *Combat*, it seems more likely that Baldwin, writing fifteen years later, is actually thinking of some of the articles about Algeria that Camus wrote for *L'Express* throughout 1955 and 1956. During this period, Camus's position embroiled him in controversy with the French Left. Baldwin must have been aware of these arguments while living in Paris. In this instance, his assertion that Camus was unaware of the role of "French power" in making Algeria "French" is more accurate ("No Name" 472). According to Ronald Aronson, Camus refused in his *L'Express* articles to recognize the importance of the FLN (Front de Libération Nationale) or the legitimacy of their demands for independence. Camus "seemed blind to the intentions of the Algerian insurrection" and called for fresh elections under the supervision of the French government despite acknowledging that the colonial administration was responsible for subverting elections held in 1948 (Aronson 187).

Furthermore, as Aronson demonstrates, Camus revised his prewar views on Algeria. In 1955, he changed the wording of a 1939 statement, replacing references to "colonial conquest" and "the conquered people" with "colonisation" and the "colonised" (Aronson 186–88). As Camus's early *Combat* editorials made clear, a conquered people (the French) reserved the right to use violence to resist their conquerors (the Nazis). But with regard to Algeria, Camus muted this position, softening the experience of colonialism for the Algerians in order to undermine the legitimacy of their use of counterviolence against the *colons*. Of course, as one born and bred in Algeria, Camus was in a very difficult position. The division between colonizer and colonized was not one he could easily rationalize.

Baldwin might have also been thinking of a statement Camus made shortly after he received the Nobel Prize. Challenged by an Algerian student at a question-and-answer session at Stockholm University to break his self-imposed silence and give a view on the crisis, Camus replied by asserting: "I must also condemn a terrorism that is carried out blindly, in the streets of Algiers, for example, and may one day strike my mother or my family. I believe in justice, but I will defend my mother before justice" (qtd. in Aronson 211–14; Todd 378–82). By situating himself within his tribe, and by affirming his family over abstractions, Camus rejected a justice for the Arabs that would be unjust to the French Algerians. Camus's proposed settlement to the crisis always left French Algerian rights intact. He even went so far as to assert that "There has never yet been an Algerian nation," a denial of the fundamental demands of the Arabs that differed little from the resistance of the pied-noir (qtd. in Aronson 214). Similarly, when Baldwin writes, "the Algerians were not fighting the French for justice ... but for the power to determine their own destinies," he suggests Camus's concern with "justice" is a means of evading the real issue: the Algerians' desire for independence ("No Name" 472).

Baldwin was uninterested in the finer feelings of those he felt sided with oppressive forces and ignores the very real difficulty of Camus's position as a French Algerian.[7] Making his attack, Baldwin avoids engaging with the fact that Camus's aversion to violence was a considered position reached as a result of his disillusionment with the postliberation purges in France. Nor does he appreciate that Camus was trying to reconcile his divided loyalties as a French Algerian, or even that the violence in Algeria meant Camus's anxiety for his mother's safety was only human. Arguably, Camus's divided loyalties— as both Frenchman and Algerian—meant he was closer to Baldwin's position as an African American than Baldwin was prepared to recognize.

Baldwin turns to Faulkner via Camus's adaptation of *Requiem for a Nun* (1950) (Izard and Hieronymus 43). In *Requiem for a Nun*, Temple's maid, Nancy, is accused of murdering Temple's baby (Faulkner, *Requiem* [Random House] 63). Nancy knows Temple has been having an affair with a gangster called Pete and that the couple is planning to elope. Nancy accuses Temple of planning to "drop" her baby "into a garbage can" or else of abandoning it while her husband is away, before she then apparently murders the infant herself (Faulkner, *Requiem* [Chatto] 164). Baldwin calls Faulkner's "fable" a "preposterous bore" and is unconvinced by Nancy's sacrifice "to arrest her mistress's headlong flight to self-destruction" ("No Name" 472). He asks, "why did Camus need Faulkner," implying Camus was attracted to the vision of justice or "black forgiveness," which he thinks Faulkner is trying, unsuccessfully, to present in the work.[8] Unlike Camus, who was apparently "not interested in the racial questions in the story, but rather the problems of suffering and redemption," Baldwin interprets the play in strictly racial terms (Todd 357). He writes that "black Nancy may have murdered white

Temple's white baby out of pure, exasperated hatred" and suggests Faulkner "suspects" that "revenge" not redemption is the true meaning of the play ("No Name" 472). By stressing the color of the protagonists above all else, Baldwin interprets Nancy's crime as a slave uprising that unmasks the hypocrisy and false benevolence of the South.

Baldwin builds on what he considers to be the play's concern with redeeming the South. He writes that Faulkner wants to save the "old order," a broad term used to encompass Faulkner's South, Camus's French Algeria, and European culture in general:

> He [Faulkner] is seeking to exorcise a history which is also a curse. He wants the old order, which came into existence through unchecked greed and wanton murder, to redeem itself without further bloodshed— without, that is, any further menacing itself—and without coercion. This, old orders never do, less because they would not than because they cannot. They cannot because they have always existed in relation to a force which they have had to subdue. This subjugation is the key to their identity and the triumph and justification of their history, and it is also on this continued subjugation that their material well-being depends. (473)

Baldwin makes an implicit analogy between colonial Algeria and segregated Mississippi. But exactly how in specific historical and political terms the "Algerian and the black American problem" are similar is never specified by Baldwin (475). He tries to affirm a connection between the African American and third world revolutionary, but his inability to account for the fundamental differences between these situations forces him to offer solidarity more rhetorical than substantive. By the same measure, his language in this piece presents a homogenous view of Euro-American "history" set in absolute opposition to what Baldwin calls "a force." Carmichael and Hamilton also used this expression to describe what they saw as the parity between the African American and third world radical (xiii). Baldwin picks up on their use of this term, but unlike in *Black Power*, he is much more explicit about the connection between "black people" and "the Third World."

Baldwin sets Euro-American "history" against the "millions of people" on the other side. Such language would suggest that Baldwin had absorbed Fanon's polarized apprehension of the colonial situation. He represents history, as experienced by the third world poor, as a triad of oppression that encapsulates the enclosed world—servitude, incarceration, execution— endured by Nancy in Faulkner's play:

> One may see that the history, which is now indivisible from oneself, has been full of errors and excesses; but this is not the same thing as seeing that, for millions of people, this history—oneself—has been nothing but an intolerable yoke, a stinking prison, a shrieking grave. ("No Name" 473)

The problem with this structure is that it has the effect of substituting a complex dialectical system of oppositions with a more binary one. As Baldwin understands and represents elsewhere in his fiction, the history of white Europeans and Americans is more than just "error" and "excess." Furthermore, he chooses to ignore the fact that Euro-American history has never been a homogenous structure of material wealth accumulated entirely as the result of racial and colonial subjugation. His refusal to recognize class or other divisions within European history suggests he shared Fanon's disenchantment with the potential of the working class to oppose their society.[9] But it also shows Baldwin's reluctance to articulate a more sophisticated analysis of how economic exploitation really works. He relies on a blanket judgment derived from Fanon, but his polemic lacks Marxist insights into capitalist relations of production. Race, not economics, remains Baldwin's primary means of understanding the situation. While this was a potent model with which to interrogate the contradictions within the United States, Baldwin struggles to apply it to a global context.[10] By casting the third world subject as either an oppressed victim or as a revolutionary fighting for the right to enter history, Baldwin reiterates a limited, and in some senses very Western, understanding of what it means to be African or Asian.

By framing issues of historical representation in terms of an absolute opposition between exploiter and exploited, Baldwin's account is subject to further simplifications:

> It is not so easy to see that, for millions of people, life itself depends on the speediest possible demolition of this history, even if this means the leveling or the destruction of its heirs. And whatever this history may have given to the subjugated is of absolutely no value, since they have never been free to reject it; they will never even be able to assess it until they are free to take from it what they need, and to add to history the monumental fact of their presence. The South African coal miner, or the African digging for roots in the bush, or the Algerian mason working in Paris, not only have no reason to bow down before Shakespeare, or Descartes or Westminster Abbey, or the cathedral at Chartres: they have, once these monuments intrude on their attention, no honorable access to them. Their apprehension of this history cannot fail to reveal to them that they have been robbed, maligned and rejected: to bow down before that history is to accept that history's arrogant and unjust judgment. ("No Name" 473–74)

Baldwin tries to speak for the poor of the third world, suggesting the South African "coal miner," the African peasant, and the Algerian laborer are alike because of their shared exclusion from the monuments of European civilization. His argument retains a Western sense of history defined as monuments, artifacts, and great men, a list of cultural achievements that says rather more about his ambivalent relationship with European culture than it does about African attitudes toward such monuments. While it is indeed true that the poor of Africa have, at least in part, been "robbed, maligned, and rejected" as a result of slavery, colonialism, and the International Monetary Fund, Baldwin avoids the technicalities of how colonialism and economic exploitation actually operate. His notion that an African peasant is forced, somehow, to "bow down" before Chartres Cathedral is a rather crude personification that trivializes the complicated role of Christianity in legitimating colonialism (and also ignores the role of the Christian church in helping to end slavery in the United States) and overestimates the value of these monuments to the third world poor. It presents a narrow conception of the relationship between European and African cultures that was actually contradicted by Baldwin's own experiences.

Baldwin last referred to a similar list of European icons, including "the cathedral at Chartres," in the essay "Stranger in the Village" (1953). In that essay, Baldwin used the culture shock of expatriation to reflect on his sense of alienation as an African American from Europe, but even more so from Africa. He emphasized his alienation by exaggerating the extent to which Europeans shared a common heritage, asserting the "most illiterate" Swiss peasant was "related, in a way that I am not, to Dante, Shakespeare, Michelangelo, Aeschylus, Da Vinci, Rembrandt and Racine" ("Stranger" 83). This Pantheon of very different Italian, English, Ancient Greek, Dutch, and French poets, playwrights, artists, philosophers, and architects expressed his ambivalent feelings toward European high culture (83). But by 1972, disillusioned by the assassinations of King and others, Baldwin's vexed relationship to these icons of European civilization had hardened. Despite the fact that he knows far more about Shakespeare than the life of a South African miner, his rhetoric in this passage creates an anti-European stance that sees the whole of that history in terms of malign oppression.

Despite his polemical tone, Baldwin offers some close analysis in the manner of Fanon. He draws a parallel between the colonized bourgeoisie, "someone educated by, and for, France," and "some of 'our' niggers" ("No Name" 474) to argue that just as the "*évolué* from Dakar" is "much more likely to be a spiritual citizen of France" unable to "convey the actual needs of his part of Africa," so the African American bourgeoisie "become spokesmen for 'black' capitalism" (474). Baldwin dismisses this class in much the same way as Fanon asserts that the "national bourgeoisie" of the colonial nation "identifies itself with the Western bourgeoisie from whom it has learnt its lessons" (*Wretched* 123). Despite trying to follow Fanon's investment in the revolutionary potential of the peasantry, Baldwin's anxiety towards "Shakespeare," "Descartes," and "Westminster Abbey" shows a concern with cultural capital quite alien to the third world worker on whom so many of his expectations now rest.

Baldwin understands that "dialogue" between the colonized and the colonizer "cannot avoid the root possession of the land and the exploitation of the land's resources" ("No Name" 474), just as Fanon wrote: "For a colonised people the most essential value, because the most concrete, is first and foremost the land" (*Wretched* 34). However, while the Algerian "knew exactly where home was," for the African American, "there was no place for us to go: we *were* home" ("No Name" 461). The Algerian could use nationalism as the basis of a revolutionary consciousness and as a means of breaking with the influence of Europe. But as Baldwin was all too aware, the African American cannot break with his nation so easily. He needs something as "concrete" as "the land" on which to base his appeal. *The Fire Next Time* spurned the separatist solution of the Nation of Islam as unrealistic, and elsewhere in *No Name in the Street* he expresses unhappiness with the idea of the return to Africa.

Solidarity with the third world is performed through generalizations that conflate very different issues and by the changing mode of address adopted in the passage as Baldwin shifts from the white, Western "oneself" of "this history" moving through to the "they" of the South African miner and Algerian mason before finally ending with a third world "one" that demands "one's own land" on "one's own terms" (474). The passage concludes in the first person, with Baldwin appearing as a spokesman of the third world, claiming: "for I *know* my gods are real: they have enabled me to withstand you" (475). Again, as Baldwin was steeped in the same religion that had fashioned Chartres Cathedral, these "gods" are left undefined. The binary structure of Baldwin's argument is reiterated by the declaration of faith in this concluding sentence. He confuses the colonial struggle for land with the need for the African American to achieve greater power as an interest group, much as he blurs the need of newly independent nations to assert a positive cultural identity by aligning this with the African American's desire to reappropriate their color as a signifier of positive cultural difference. His anxiety toward European culture expresses a much more individual concern with issues of identity that has little in common with Fanon's view of colonial struggle. Ironically enough, despite his rhetorical rejection of Europe, in the same year that *No Name in the Street* was published, Baldwin made his permanent home in the south of France (Leeming 312–15). Clearly, the hostile racial climate of the United States was far more of an actual problem for Baldwin than "Balzac," "Descartes," and "Chartres." Baldwin's attempt to unify himself with the third world revolutionary remains a rhetorical exercise, written for the benefit of a Euro-American audience and using the Euro-American genre of the autobiographical essay.

Although *No Name in the Street* is weakened by the violence of Baldwin's argument, this is not the end of the essay. In the second half, he retreats from the international perspective adopted in the first and returns to the American context. The rest of this essay will concentrate on Baldwin's remarks about the Black Panthers to show how he uses them as a more concrete means of articulating his sense of Black Power.

Baldwin and the Black Panthers

Baldwin's discussion of the Panthers concentrates on their community-orientated actions. He describes these programs as "antidotes to the demoralisation" of the ghetto and as "techniques of realization." The Panthers are also called a "force," which, as we noted earlier, was the same term Carmichael and Hamilton used in *Black Power* to designate the third world. The Panthers are "a new force," "a great force for peace and stability in the ghetto," "a force working toward the health and liberation of the community" and "a force which sets itself in opposition to that force which uses people as things" ("No Name" 536–37). Baldwin's use of the word "force" keeps his rhetoric relatively free from many of the clichés of the debate, while remaining in tone with the more generalized and emotive approach adopted in his essay.

Baldwin follows Newton's efforts to align the Black Panther Party (BPP) with third world revolutionaries, calling the Panthers "the native Vietcong" and the ghetto the "village in which the Vietcong were hidden" (537). Comparisons between the struggle to maintain order at home and the overseas situation were made by all sides of the political spectrum during the late 1960s. Michael W. Flamm notes that "an important theme, particularly for many on the right, was that the country could not contain the communist menace in South Vietnam unless it could contain crime in the streets, protests on the campuses, and riots in the cities—and vice versa" (111).

Again, Baldwin sidesteps the overtly ideological content of such debates and ignores Newton's attempt to draw an ideological parallel between the BPP and third world Marxist revolutionary fighters (Newton 31–33). Instead, he also shows his enduring sense of an exceptionalist American nationality by affirming his belief in an "indigenous socialism, formed by, and responding to, the real needs of the American people," going on to claim that this "'Yankee Doodle type'" socialism is "not a doctrinaire position." He bases his assertion on "the necessity for a form of socialism" on moral rather than ideological grounds, declaring that "the world's present economic arrangements" are "sterile and immoral" and "doom the rest of the world to misery" ("No Name" 541). Once more, Baldwin's Christian ethics emerge at a moment when he is most pressed to grapple with tangible, political issues.

However, this is not necessarily a weakness, particularly if we consider the fact that the Panthers' reputation better rests on their community-based activism rather than their conflation of Marxist ideology with intrinsically American notions around the right to bear arms.[11] Baldwin's discussion of the Panthers reiterates his moral and ethical concept of blackness as a "tremendous spiritual condition." He claims: "when the black man's mind is no longer controlled by the white man's fantasies, a new balance or what may be described as an unprecedented inequality begins to make itself felt." By reclaiming their identity, Baldwin suggests the African American complicates the structures of (mis)recognition that define American society and so throw the white American into confusion: "for the white American no longer knows who he is, whereas the black man knows them both" (550). Baldwin conceives of Black Power as a skeptical consciousness able to question and challenge white ideologies of identity and history: the moment when "the black glories in his newfound color ... and asserts ... the unanswerable power and validity of his being" induces what Baldwin calls a "fear" in "the white" (550). We can understand this as a moment of troubling but truthful recognition for the white American, which will prepare the way for a genuine integration, one that will transform the preexisting power relations (social and sexual as well as political) that currently define the spectrum of black and white recognition.

At the very end of his essay, Baldwin suggests another parallel between America and the third world. Both Africa and America are called "confusions" and "mysteries." Both continents are still "chained to Europe," and it is through this connection that his rejection of European and Euro-American culture should be understood. Baldwin recasts the suspicion and perplexed fascination toward Europe that marked early essays like "Stranger in the Village," but this time his exceptionalist sense of American identity becomes an exclusively black province. He argues that the "conditioned ... fantasy" and "brainwashing" of white America's "adolescent ... self-love" prevent white America from engaging in a more substantial integration, one that would "have the effect of reordering all our priorities, and altering all our communities" to change not only the segregated nature of American society but also the orientation of American foreign policy to one of sympathy and support for the third world (543).

Conclusion

Articulating his sense of Black Power, Baldwin returns to the problems of whiteness that inform his early work. Although the polemical nature of the essay forces him into an increasingly polarized understanding of the relationship between Euro-American culture and the poor of the third world, his sense of America's racial problem remains dialectical. His emphasis on Black Power and blackness as a source of value invariably returns to issues of white power and white identity, with race ultimately circumscribed within a wider narrative of an ideal American sociopolitical-sexual selfhood conceived as a potential still waiting to be achieved. As a result, *No Name in the Street* represents a powerful articulation of Baldwin's transnational, radical imagination, a valuable attempt to resolve the contradictions between integration or separation, racial solidarity or national identity that plague the work of other, more explicitly ideological Black Power thinkers.

Notes

1 For a discussion of Senghor's and Césaire's contributions to the conference, see King 246–50.

2 There has been very little sustained discussion or close reading of *No Name in the Street*. Stanley Macebuh, in *James Baldwin: A Critical Study* (1973), and Yoshinobu Hakutani, in his essay "*No Name in the Street*: James Baldwin's Image of the American Sixties" (1988), have provided two of the longest discussions, although these pieces avoid close reading or a sustained consideration of the intellectual context behind his essay. More recent criticism, such as the anthologies *James Baldwin Now* (1999) and *Re-viewing James Baldwin* (2000) or critical works including *James Baldwin's Later Fiction* (2002) by Lynn Orilla Scott and *James Baldwin's God* (2003) by Clarence E. Hardy III either omit the essay altogether or relegate it to a few pages of anecdotal summary.

3 Macey shows how in *Black Skin, White Masks*, Fanon based much of his understanding of American racism on a rather narrow interpretation of the fiction of Wright and Chester Himes, especially *If He Hollers Let Him Go* (1945).

4 Bobby Seale confirmed to me in an email that Baldwin visited him whilst he was incarcerated and that the Panthers read Baldwin's work: "James Baldwin was a very good friend. He visited me in jail three times when I was a political prisoner for two years. So was Ossie Davis and Gordon Parks, et al. After the BPP in 1976 and 1977 my crew and I visited James often in New York. James wrote the introduction to my autobiography: *A Lonely Rage*. He actually suggested the 'Lonely Rage' title after he read that manuscript which my wife Leslie and I wrote. In the early sixties days: 62, 63, 64, yes, James Baldwin was part of my [our] protest movement reading but his writings were never 'out-front' primary to cause us to organize. It was WEB DuBois *Souls Of Black Folk* and *Black Reconstruction* that were more important. Even LeRoi Jones' *Blues People* and especially Herbert Apthacker's dissertations; all of Frantz Fanon's works (*The Wretched Of The Earth*). These were the primary reading for myself as the founding Chairman of the Black Panther Party in October 1966" (Seale, Email to author).

5 Hannah Arendt notes: "Violence is justified on the ground of creativity" (172).

6 Sartre affirmed this goal, heralding the promise that colonialism would be "replaced by socialism" (*Wretched* 20).

7 Other commentators were more sympathetic. Memmi wrote of Camus: "It must be understood that his situation is by no means easy; it is not intellectually or emotionally easy to have all of one's family on a side that is morally condemned" (qtd. in Todd 382).

8 Faulkner's treatment of race is too broad a theme to consider at length, but he made many other statements regarding his situation as a white southerner that reveal his position to be far more complex and considered than Baldwin allows in this instance.

9 Fanon wrote: "the workers of Europe have not replied to these calls; for the workers believe, too, that they are part of the prodigious adventure of the European spirit" (*Wretched* 253).

10 Manning Marable notes that, in the context of the United States, "the oppressed perceive domination through the language and appearance of racial forms, although such policies and practices always served a larger class objective" (217).

11 See Seale, *Seize the Time*, especially p. 413 on the Free Breakfast for Children program; p. 414 on free community medical care; p. 415 on community caucuses; pp. 416–17 on liberation schools; and pp. 419–21 for community control of the police.

Works Cited

Appiah, Kwame Anthony. *In My Father's House: Africa in the Philosophy of Culture*. Methuen, 1992.

Arendt, Hannah. *Crises of the Republic*. Harcourt Brace, 1969.

Aronson, Ronald. *Camus and Sartre: The Story of a Friendship and the Quarrel That Ended It*. U of Chicago P, 2004.

Baldwin, James. *The Fire Next Time*. Penguin, 1964.

Baldwin, James. "No Name in the Street." Baldwin, *The Price of the Ticket*, pp. 449–552.

Baldwin, James. *The Price of the Ticket: Collected Non-Fiction 1948–1985*. Michael Joseph, 1985, pp. 79–91.

Baldwin, James. "Stranger in the Village." Baldwin, *The Price of the Ticket*, pp. 79–90. Originally published in Harper's Magazine, Oct. 1953.

Campbell, James. *Talking at the Gates: A Life of James Baldwin*. Faber and Faber, 1991.

Camus, Albert. *Between Hell and Reason: Essays from the Resistance Newspaper Combat 1944–1947*. Translated by Alexandre De Gramont, Wesleyan UP, 1991.

Carmichael, Stokely, and Charles V. Hamilton. *Black Power: The Politics of Liberation in America*. Jonathan Cape, 1968.

Clancy-Smith, Julia, editor. *North Africa, Islam and the Mediterranean World: From the Almoravids to the Algerian War*. Frank Cass, 2001.

Fabre, Michel. *The World of Richard Wright*. UP of Mississippi, 1985.

Fanon, Frantz. *Black Skin, White Masks*. 1952. Pluto Press, 1986.

Fanon, Frantz. *The Wretched of the Earth*. 1961. Penguin, 2001.

Faulkner, William. *Requiem for a Nun*. Adapted for the stage by Ruth Ford, Random House, 1951.

Faulkner, William. *Requiem for a Nun*. Chatto and Windus, 1953.

Flamm, Michael W. *Law and Order: Street Crime, Civil Unrest, and the Crisis of Liberalism in the 1960s*. Columbia UP, 2005.

Gibson, Nigel C. *Fanon: The Postcolonial Imagination*. Polity, 2003.

Gordon, Lewis R. *Fanon and the Crisis of European Man: An Essay on Philosophy and the Human Sciences*. Routledge, 1995.

Izard, Barbara, and Clara Hieronymus. *Requiem for a Nun: Onstage and Off*. Aurora Publishers, 1970.

King, Richard H. *Race, Culture and the Intellectuals 1940–1970*. Johns Hopkins UP, 2004.

Leeming, David. *James Baldwin: A Biography*. Alfred A. Knopf, 1994.

Macey, David. *Frantz Fanon: A Biography*. Picador, 2000.

Marable, Manning. *Beyond Black and White: Transforming African-American Politics*. Verso, 1995.

Memmi, Albert. *The Colonizer and the Colonized*. 1957. Earthscan Publications, 2003.

Nancy, Jean-Luc. *The Sense of the World*. U of Minnesota P, 1997.

Newton, Huey. *To Die for the People*. Edited by Toni Morrison, Writers and Readers Publishing, 1999.

Porter, Horace A. *Stealing the Fire: The Art and Protest of James Baldwin*. Wesleyan UP, 1989.

Seale, Bobby. Email to author. 8 July 2003.

Seale, Bobby. *Seize the Time: The Story of the Black Panther Party and Huey P. Newton*. Hutchinson, 1970.

Todd, Olivier. *Albert Camus: A Life*. Translated by Benjamin Ivry, Alfred Knopf, 1998.

PART FOUR

James Baldwin and Changing Communities: Recontextualizing Baldwin's Legacy

10

Continuing a Legacy: James Baldwin, Ta-Nehisi Coates, and the African American Witness

Marcus Bruce

The central question that lies at the heart of Ta-Nehisi Coates's 2015 *New York Times* bestselling book, *Between the World and Me*, concerns the intellectual, psychological, and practical challenge of living in a black body in the United States. "How should one live within a black body," Coates writes, "within a country lost in the Dream, is the question of my life, and the pursuit of this question, I have found, ultimately answers itself" (*Between the World* 12). Ostensibly a letter to his fifteen-year-old son, Coates's book, comprised of three separate essays, is in part an attempt to explain to his son, and his readers, how he has gone about answering this question, especially in the wake of a number of high-profile police assaults and murders of African Americans, the failure of the justice system to indict violent police actions, and the rise of the Black Lives Matter movement. The book is less a polemic or an apology for his life than it is a form of "bearing witness," an account and an extended testimonial (to his son and to his readers) of his search for answers to his question and the manner in which he has lived his life. Coates's particular form of bearing witness has led some observers to draw a comparison between Coates and James Baldwin, a writer noted for his fierce, unwavering, and bold accounts of his life and his struggle to define himself.

Coates is partly responsible for this comparison. In a number of interviews, Coates confessed that he had drawn inspiration from James Baldwin's now-classic 1963 book of essays, *The Fire Next Time* (Adams). A cursory glance at the two texts reveals a number of noticeable similarities. Both texts adopt the format of epistles that use the biographical details of each author's life as a lens through which to see the experience of African Americans. Both texts address the next generation of African Americans and serve as practical guides on how one can and should go about living in a country where the experience and the humanity of African Americans are often unrecognized or misunderstood. Both texts offer accounts of the challenges of being black, or living in a black body, in the United States of America. Yet one further similarity invites a closer inspection of the connections between the two texts and their authors.

Both Baldwin and Coates distinguish themselves as writers with the unique ability to bear witness to specific historic moments, situations, and problems in American life viewed from the perspectives of their individual lives as black men. In doing so, they not only reveal the unacknowledged and unrecognized lives of African Americans but also show the deadly disparities between American ideals, promises, and dreams and the realities of daily life in America for African Americans. For Baldwin, the historic occasion observed by *The Fire Next Time* was the one hundredth anniversary celebration of the Emancipation Proclamation in 1963, an event which he viewed through the lens of growing up as a young African American male in Harlem, anxious for his life, fearful for his prospects, and painfully conscious that the freedoms promised to all Americans were routinely withheld from African Americans (Baldwin, *Fire* 10). For Coates, the historic moment chronicled in *Between the World and Me* comes in the form of a question, often implied but never directly asked, occasioned by the troubling yet endlessly repeated social media images of African Americans being violently arrested, assaulted, and murdered: how does one live in a black body in America? Coates answers by bearing witness and giving an account of his life as a young black male surviving on the streets of Baltimore, a tenacious and voracious student in pursuit of answers at Howard University, and an aspiring writer struggling to confront, interrogate, and form a response to these proliferating forms of violence. He views this response as a vital one upon which his very life depends.

None of these similarities between the two texts and writers, nor their differences for that matter, went unnoticed by the media, readers, writers, and scholars (Alexander). In a now-famous, frequently repeated, and much-discussed blurb that accompanied the publication of *Between the World and Me*, Toni Morrison, Nobel Prize-winning African American author, pronounced the book "required" reading and further confessed that while she had been "wondering who might fill the intellectual void that plagued me after James Baldwin died," she was no longer in doubt. "Clearly," Morrison declared, "it is Ta-Nehisi Coates." The "language" of Coates's journey, Morrison declared, and the "visceral, eloquent, and beautifully redemptive" and examination of "the hazards and hopes of black male life" were both profound and revelatory (Cover). Toni Morrison's remarks, brief though they may have been, also seemed to suggest something more substantive between Baldwin and Coates than just a similar format and target audience, or a shared set of problems, questions, and concerns. For Morrison, Baldwin's life and writings represented a thoughtful response to the challenges of living as a black person in American society and constituted a specific set of survival techniques, cultural practices, and established traditions that had become a part of African American culture and could be passed on from one generation to the next. Coates's writings marked a revival of the cultural practices and traditions of which Baldwin had been an exemplar.

Morrison's declaration was echoed in the praise and widespread media attention received by the book. Yet her comments also provoked a number of more critical and dismissive remarks from prominent African American intellectuals, most notably the African American scholar, activist, and public intellectual Cornel West. West questioned what he considered to be the uncritical reception of the book and the comparison—albeit from a figure as prominent and well-respected as Toni Morrison—of the new writer Coates with the venerated Baldwin. "Baldwin was a great writer," wrote West, "with profound courage who spoke truth to power." "Baldwin's painful self-examination," West continued, "led to collective action and a focus on social movements." By contrast, West insisted, "Coates's fear-driven self-absorption leads to individual escape and flight to safety." For West, the comparison between Baldwin and Coates was premature and prompted more by the skill with which each writer crafted his text and distinguished his voice. The comparison offered little insight on either the social and political commitments of each writer or their individual conceptions of the role writers should play as activists. For West, Baldwin was a bold civil rights activist who had marched with Dr. King and others, spoken at public events advocating civil rights, and encouraged others to take similar risks and organize for collective action. Coates, in West's estimation, was no activist and certainly not one in the tradition of Baldwin. Here the comparison failed. According to West, Coates was at best "a clever wordsmith with journalistic talent" (West).

In this chapter, I examine the ways in which Coates's 2015 book, *Between the World and Me*, is the continuation of an African American cultural practice of which James Baldwin was an exemplar. Specifically, I discuss how Coates's work uses Baldwin's *The Fire Next Time* to bear witness to his own experience, which is at once a painful and individual account. He shows how he has attempted to answer the question that forms the central concern of *Between the World and Me*: how should one live within a black body within a country lost in the American Dream? "Black people need witnesses in this hostile world," Baldwin declared in the documentary film *I Am Not Your Negro*. "I am a witness. In the church in which I was raised, you were supposed to bear witness to the truth" (*I Am Not Your Negro*). In what sense, I ask, does Coates participate in the cultural practice of bearing witness?

Bearing witness

Bearing witness is a complex set of practices, born within the African American church yet dispersed and practiced throughout African American culture and especially in its literature. Baldwin manifested this practice of bearing witness in his written work, his public addresses, and his political activism. Long after Baldwin had left the church, there remained something of the fiery Pentecostal preacher and the prophet in his writings and public speeches. Baldwin at times merely appeared to have left the institution of the church only to pursue a larger literary mission and embrace a wider audience as a prophetic figure within the United States, France, and Turkey. While Coates makes no pretense to being a preacher or a prophet—he actually rejects religious belief and practice—he does tenaciously, candidly, and courageously bear witness, to his son, a new generation of African Americans, and his readers alike, to the continuing challenge of living in, and caring for, a black body in the twenty-first century. In a day and age when aspects of the lives and experiences of African Americans in the United States remain a mystery to their fellow citizens, and their accounts of frequent harassment and assault by the police evoke both surprise and denial, despite the prevalence and frequently repeated disturbing images on social media, Coates's individual account of a life in a black body can be a form of activism, a challenge to narratives that neither recognize nor represent black lives. According to Michael Eric Dyson, "Coates need not ever speak at a rally to be heard ... especially by those who are fed by his ravenous intellect and who drink in his considerable insight. His writings compose a powerful moral force for good; his words aid a thinking populace to find its ethical orientation and its justification for action."

More specifically, bearing witness is a form of testimonial that draws its power, poignancy, and usefulness from the degree to which it represents and gives voice to a range of discriminatory experiences that are not commonly acknowledged or represented and that run counter to more recognized social beliefs and practices. Hence the contemporary African American cultural expression and practice called "the talk"—a conversation in which black parents inform their children on how to handle "encounters" with the police—identifies a specific "practice" designed to address a common occurrence among African Americans that is rarely understood by white Americans: the intimidation of, assaults against, and murders of African Americans by police officers. The talk points to realities and events that are denied or rarely acknowledged but that have grave consequences for black folks and black bodies. The talk bears witness to the realities of police violence against black bodies and develops a strategy and techniques for surviving, coping, and thriving. The talk has entered popular culture through *The New York Times* in articles like Dana Canedy's "The Talk: After Ferguson, a Shaded Conversation about Race" that offers an African American mother's reflections on and concerns for her eight-year-old son, and an episode of the popular television show *Black-ish* entitled "Hope" where three generations within one African American family argue and struggle over how to understand, explain, and respond to the reoccurring images and unsettling reports of violence against African Americans. Coates and his book *Between the World and Me* are featured as another way to have the talk with black children about the politics of race in America. The episode, itself a form of bearing witness, was both evidence and confirmation of a cultural practice, in this instance conversations among African Americans about how to understand and handle encounters with the police, rarely seen or discussed in public.

The question is not whether Coates fills the intellectual void left by Baldwin but in what identifiable and observable ways does he continue the African American cultural practice of bearing witness so brilliantly illustrated in the life, career, and writings of James Baldwin. Again, I turn to Toni Morrison for insight. Using Morrison's comments in a December 20, 1987, *New York Times* tribute to Baldwin, entitled "James Baldwin: His Voice Remembered; Life in His Language," I identify three ways in which Coates follows in the tradition of Baldwin as a "witness," a tradition that not only requires one to bear witness to themselves and to the truth but also to bring attention to the example, courage, and knowledge of previous exemplars who have pointed the way (Morrison, "James Baldwin" 27). First, the epistolary autobiographical manner in which acknowledging the example and the practices of other African American exemplars allows individuals to find and develop their own voice. Standing between Baldwin and Coates, Morrison bears witness to the manner in which Baldwin's "restructuring" of American English to "accommodate our complicated passion" not only enabled her to find her voice but gave her "a language to dwell in" (27). Baldwin's style, as I demonstrate, functions in a similar fashion for Coates. Second, Morrison emphasizes "the journey" and the courage that each writer displays: Baldwin, who became "a stranger in the village" and wrote about "the courage to live life in and from its belly as well as beyond its edges" (27) and Coates, whose "visceral, eloquent and beautifully redemptive" journey offers an account of the "hazards and hopes of black male life" (Morrison, Cover). Each writer bears witness to an individual journey that is less about defining or representing the experience and culture of an entire group of people than it is an offered account, examination, and rigorous interrogation of oneself and the world in which one lives. This interrogation, Morrison notes, yields the "lived reality" of

African Americans and becomes a process in which each new generation engages (Morrison, "James Baldwin" 27). Finally, Morrison considers each writer and their work "revelatory." The journey and reflections drawn from posing questions and engaging with the problems associated with "living in a black body" ultimately reveal the content, character, and wisdom of one's witness that can, and does in the case of Baldwin and Coates, invite and encourage emulation and appropriation. "Yours was a tenderness of vulnerability," writes Morrison of Baldwin, "that asked everything, expected everything and provided us with the ways and means to deliver. That is why I was always a bit better around you, smarter, more capable, wanting to be worth the love you lavished and wanting to be steady enough to witness the pain you had witnessed" (27). Bearing witness encourages each individual to express his or her humanity and provides reasons for continuing the struggle.

A language to dwell in

Bearing witness reveals its own distinctive use of language, one that conveys the unacknowledged, unrecognized, and despised experience of African Americans in contrast to the known world and the larger narratives of American society and culture that have been constructed. Morrison writes that Baldwin gave her "a language to dwell in" by "decolonizing it" so that she and others "could enter it, occupy it, [and] restructure it in order to accommodate our complicated passions ... our lived reality" (Morrison, "James Baldwin" 27). Both Baldwin and Coates use the form of a letter to the next generation to bear witness to the necessity of reclaiming and trusting their own experience as African Americans. Baldwin's detailed, descriptive, and unsettling account of the limited, dire, and frightening prospects of a young African American growing up in Harlem serves as an example of how bearing witness gives voice, language, and form to realities often denied. Coates's similar accounts of the neighborhoods and streets of Baltimore provide vivid portraits of a world in which knowing the language—the right head nods, walk, and physical gestures—enabled young black men like himself to save their lives, protect their bodies, and survive another day (*Between the World*).

In *The Fire Next Time*, Baldwin offers advice and counsel to his nephew James on the one hundredth anniversary of the Emancipation Proclamation of 1863, a celebration, he notes with irony, that has come "one hundred years too early" (10). While the historic occasion is given but brief mention at the end of the letter, the entire book is an extended reflection on how to be free, the necessity of defining freedom for oneself, and the redefinition of what freedom means to African Americans. Baldwin informs his nephew James that the "details and symbols of your life have been deliberately constructed to make you believe what white people say about you" (8), yet, Baldwin insists, James must trust his own experience and learn "how to handle" white Americans (6). To believe and trust in something besides one's own experience is to invite spiritual and even physical death.

In the essay that follows his letter, Baldwin gives an autobiographical account of his painful struggle, both as an African American among white Americans *and* among African Americans, to learn how to trust his own experience. He had initially sought refuge in the practices and institutions of religion from the world and the people he saw around him in Harlem. Then he tried to escape from the intimation of his own desires and sexuality. Finally, he gained peace from the despair occasioned by his discovery of the limited prospects of a young black man in America. At each phase, Baldwin turned to his own instincts for solutions. In *The Fire Next Time*, Baldwin is just as wary of the peculiar authority, security, and promises offered in the words and the vision of Elijah Muhammad and the Nation of Islam as he is of the white world's limited expectations and conceptions of African Americans. Yet Baldwin insists that in challenging the white world's assumptions (27), definitions (9), and standards (22), African Americans are compelled to acknowledge that "the universe has evolved no terms" for their particular and unique existence in the United States of America and that they must do so themselves, naming the nature of the fears and prejudices they encounter, the painful and "deadly struggle" (37) that ensues within and without and the strategies that must be adopted to address them.

Morrison finds that Coates takes a similar approach in *Between the World and Me*, in the "visceral, eloquent, and beautifully redemptive" language of Coates's journey that takes the form of a quest to answer the singular yet complex question of living in a black body (Cover). Coates's book also takes the form of a letter to the next generation, in this instance his fifteen-year-old son, informing him of what Morrison calls the "hazards and hopes of black male life" (Cover) but revealing to him the special burden, responsibility, and struggles of African Americans (Coates, *Between the World*). Though Coates assures his son that the journey itself will provide answers to the central question of how to live in a black body in America, it is a journey that he must take himself. He too must discover and create his own language for the experiences and struggles that will be distinctively his own yet representative of the struggles of other African Americans. "You are a black boy," Coates informs his son, "and you must be responsible for your body in a way that others boys cannot know. Indeed," Coates continues, "you must be responsible for the worst actions of other black bodies, which, somehow, will always be assigned to you" (71). By way of example, Coates gives an account of how his mother taught him his "earliest acts of interrogation, of drawing myself into consciousness" (29). The objective was not only to teach him how to be responsible for himself but to discover his own humanity in a way denied and misrepresented by the world around him.

This responsibility requires not only learning but creating another language for the range of violent and discriminatory experiences unique to African Americans. Coates relates how learning "to survive," to navigate the streets of Baltimore, and to shield his body (23) meant he had to learn a language of head nods and handshakes that granted him passage through a neighborhood. "You must find some way to live within the all of it," Coates insists as he describes what it meant for him "to be black in the Baltimore of his youth," where he was confronted daily with "the elements of the world—the guns, fists, knives, crack, rape and disease" (17). Yet the process that began with his mother's lessons in self-interrogation, in reading his father's books on African and African American heritage, were combined with his three-year education at Howard University. His disciplined study of "the craft of writing as the art of thinking" (48) were steps toward not only what Morrison calls "a language to dwell in" ("James Baldwin" 27) but also the reclamation and "total possession of my body but by some other route which I could not before then have imagined" (Coates, *Between the World* 48).

Morrison's astute observance that both Baldwin and Coates create "a language to dwell in" ("James Baldwin" 27) is confirmed by the manner in which each writer bears witness to the need for and capacity of African Americans to create and fashion a language that conveys the unrecognized and distinctive features of their own experience, their understanding of freedom, and their contributions to the formation of American society. Just as white Americans have "invented" themselves, so too must African Americans imagine, invent, write, and fashion a language for themselves that recognizes them and conveys their lived realities.

Courage

Bearing witness speaks of and exhibits a form of courage necessary for the individual and the writer who must pursue answers to questions that only their own experience can provide. "Trust your own experience," Baldwin advises his nephew (Baldwin, *Fire* 8). Baldwin and Coates not only boldly venture out beyond the assumptions, definitions, and symbols of a white world that has set the boundaries and parameters of their lives, their prospects, and their destinies, but also courageously shoulder the burden and responsibility for their own lives. Both Baldwin and Coates also speak of seeking refuge for a time in some institution such as the Pentecostal church for the young Baldwin or Howard University, the Mecca and epicenter of African American culture for the young Coates. Yet ultimately, they display and bear witness to the courage necessary to venture beyond such institutions to face and confront their pain, fears, need for answers, and responsibility for their individual lives, a courage that is at once both a requirement and a product of struggle.

In order to create the language tailored to the needs of black folk, Baldwin and Coates ask questions, hard questions, that go beyond the initial answers regarding how to live in a black body. Each boldly considers anew the meaning of freedom, American identity, and humanity in the context of a nation that fails to recognize the basic rights or humanity of African Americans. "Yours was the courage," writes Morrison of Baldwin, "to live life in and from its belly as well as beyond its edges, to see and say what it was, to recognize and identify evil but never fear or stand in awe of it" ("James Baldwin" 27). For Morrison, Baldwin's journey into a village in the Swiss Alps, not unlike Coates, who takes his readers on a journey into "the hazards and hopes of the black male life" (Morrison, Cover) requires courage and willingness to explore, discover, and ultimately reveal the distinctive problems, challenges, shared humanity, and features of African American experience that necessitates and serves as the occasion for a new language. According to Morrison, African Americans must be willing to ask difficult questions regarding the attitudes of white Americans, the persistent violence meted out against African Americans, the meaning of freedom for African Americans, and the usefulness of dominant tropes about African Americans and American society.

We see this kind of "interrogation" in *The Fire Next Time* and *Between the World and Me*: both are probing and relentless investigations of American fears and stereotypes regarding black bodies and their impact and enduring effects on the psychology, lives, and prospects of African Americans. Baldwin is merciless in his identification of and challenge to American assumptions about African Americans and candid about how the inculcation of such beliefs can, and often does, destroy and undermine the confidence and humanity of African Americans. He uses his own life as an example for his nephew and candidly recalls the "prolonged religious crisis" of his fourteenth year (Baldwin, *Fire* 15).

In the second and longer essay of *The Fire Next Time*, entitled "Down at the Cross: Letter from a Region in My Mind," Baldwin offers an account of how, at the same age as his nephew, he had begun considering his life, its prospects, and its challenges. As an African American teenager growing up in the predominantly black community of Harlem during the late 1930s, Baldwin considered his options so bleak—as a prostitute, a pimp, a drug dealer, or an impoverished laborer—that he sought refuge in the African American church. He soon discovered that this retreat could not protect him from the terrors represented by the streets of Harlem and the white world or the fear within him of his own anger, sexuality, and unfilled aspirations. The religious language did give Baldwin a way to articulate, frame, and talk about his own unique and distinctive experiences as he would so ably demonstrate in his first novel, *Go Tell It on the Mountain*, a fictional account of his life that demonstrated his imaginative, skilled, and adept use of religious language to integrate and express his own complex understanding of the integration of a gendered, sexual, cultural, and national identity. Yet Baldwin would leave the relative safety of the church once he discovered within himself the courage to acknowledge that the institution of the church could not protect him from himself nor from the things he feared in the world around him. The message conveyed both to his nephew and his readers is one of his courage to take the journey, to ask the difficult questions, to enter the church seeking answers, and to leave the church once he had arrived at a new understanding of himself. Baldwin gained courage precisely when he became responsible for and the custodian of his own life, committed to both understanding and trusting his own experience. This witness becomes his legacy.

In his account of the question of how to live in a black body, Coates invites his son to take up the conscious pursuit of the question that has already begun to trouble and shape his young life and to be courageous in his navigation of life and in the manner in which he chooses to live in a black body in the United States of America. Coates offers his own mother and grandmother as examples of a continuing legacy of courageous individuals who have sought their own answers to troubling questions and who taught Coates how to examine his own life, seek his own answers, and develop his own response and sense of responsibility.

At a critical moment when his son despairs and seeks refuge from the unsettling news that police have again been found innocent in the assault and death of another unarmed young black man, Coates admonishes him, "You must never look away from this" (*Between the World* 10). This moment and others like it are the crucial juncture where the central question is made personal—how do *I* live in a black body?—in the form of a "visceral" experience of racism that "dislodges brains, blocks airways, rips muscles, extracts organs, cracks bones, breaks teeth" (10), in the serial and unrelenting acts and representations of violence that portend a tragic and destructive end to all black bodies. It is at once a terrible and unsettling insight regarding life in America for an African American yet one that serves as the moment to introduce the example, the witness, and the legacy that Coates has to offer his son. Inviting his son to struggle with the images, realities, and questions before him, Coates embodies what Morrison called Baldwin's gift of courage, the gift that requires that we see life for what it is, "to see and say what it was, to recognize and identify evil but never fear or stand in awe of it" ("James Baldwin" 27). The invitation, encouragement, and witness of the father to the son to engage in "the struggle" also imparts a special wisdom: the discovery of that portion of life—his own struggle to understanding the realities before him—that is within his control *and* the new sense of freedom and self-consciousness that come with each effort to understand. This, "the struggle to understand," Coates declares, "is our only advantage over this madness" (*Between the World* 106).

The courage to take the journey, to make the effort to explore and answer the question of how one should live in a black body, is potentially available to all and strongly advocated by both Baldwin and Coates. In a sense, bearing witness as a cultural practice has no set forms, regulations, or laws, only exemplars and examples of how others have gone about answering the questions. Baldwin and Coates tell the stories of their individual lives and, in doing so, bear witness to the next generation. They point out and identify the terrain that is covered, the questions that are asked, and the problems and challenges that arise. Their accounts also bear witness to the courage and self-knowledge that comes with the struggle to understand and is finally its own reward.

Vulnerability

Finally, bearing witness, as Morrison shows in what she considers a third gift from Baldwin, reveals the vulnerability and humanity of African Americans who, like other Americans, set out on a journey into a world in which no one is safe, innocent, promised an untroubled life, guaranteed answers to their questions, or even confident of a peaceful end. Both Baldwin and Coates give accounts of journeys where they discover that the struggle to understand how to live as a black person in American society yields not only personal insight but a more acute sense of the humanity they share with others. The struggle to understand what has isolated African Americans from other Americans reveals what they have in common. For Baldwin, it is, among other things, discovering how inextricably linked are the lives, the freedoms, and the destinies of black and white Americans, who must learn to live with and love each other or perish in the fire next time, the enduring rage, hatred, and violence that leads them in ongoing conflict. For Coates, the journey deepens the overwhelming sense of the precariousness and uncertainty that surrounds his own life and that of his son's yet provides confirmation of their fundamental human right to be alive. It is precisely here that Morrison illustrates how this particular form of bearing witness can be a source of inspiration, love, and encouragement to others who are pursuing their own questions, seeking their own language, and summoning the courage to continue their journey.

This is the most complex gift yet of the practice of bearing witness. Baldwin's example and willingness to reveal his vulnerability, express tenderness, offer his love, and allow others to witness his pain served as an invitation for Morrison and others to respond in kind and more fully express their own humanity. Baldwin and Coates insist that their progeny must embrace their own humanity, fragility, and vulnerability in all their complexity. "You can only be destroyed," Baldwin informs his nephew James, "by believing that you really are what the white world calls a nigger." "Take no one's word for anything, including mine," he continues, "but trust your experience" (*Fire* 4). The entire purpose of creating a language to dwell in and asking and pursuing difficult questions is to live more fully as a human being beyond the boundaries and stereotypes of American symbols specifically designed to "make you believe what white people say about you." *The Fire Next Time* thus bears witness to Baldwin's profound humanity, his fears, his anxieties, and his stumbling yet tenacious pursuit of a way to more fully embrace his own humanity in all its complexity.

For Coates, there are truths that await all of those who ask the question of how to live in a black body and who find the courage to take the journey to discover answers. While Coates confesses that he can neither save his son from the dangers that await him nor answer for him how he should live in a black body, he can bear witness to a discovery made in asking the question pursuing an answer. Quoting the words of a black mother whose son has died as a result of police violence, Coates admonishes his son, telling him that despite the struggle and violence that await him, "You exist. You matter. You have value. You have every right to wear your hoodie, to play your music as loud as you want. You have every right to be you. And no one should deter you from being you. You have to be you. And you can never be afraid to be you" (*Between the World* 113).

In their vulnerability, candor, and profound and heartrending confessions, Baldwin and Coates offer the next generations and their readers something previously denied to them: evidence of their fragile yet enduring humanity. For Morrison, Baldwin's willingness to reveal his vulnerability becomes an invitation to be more fully herself and to explore and write her own complex humanity. She discovers new forms of self-acceptance and the confidence to express herself. Coates's confessions of his deepest fears and anxieties to his son and his readers regarding the limits of his power as a man and a father serve also as an invitation and encouragement to explore the limitations and range of possibilities for being human. Ultimately, for Baldwin and Coates, bearing witness to their humanity is both an act of liberation from the assumptions, stereotypes, and beliefs about African American white Americans and a revelation of what is humanly possible.

A new birth of freedom

On a warm Tuesday afternoon in June 2016, at the University of Paris 8 located on the edge of Paris near the *banlieue* of Saint-Denis, Ta-Nehisi Coates gathered with a sizeable crowd of faculty, students, and visitors for a nearly four-hour conversation on the occasion of the French translation and publication of his book *Between the World and Me*, entitled *Une colère noire* (A Black Anger). At the beginning of the gathering, Coates, seated on a stage with a panel of faculty and students, briefly addressed the audience as their featured speaker and honored guest, speaking fluent French. On one or two occasions when English words, phrases, and idioms seemed more suited to his purpose, he spoke in English and a translator did her best to convey his meaning in French. Yet, whether in French or in English, Coates spoke with a thoughtfulness, understanding, and intensity that moved faculty, students, and listeners even when they may not have fully understood the words. He was bearing witness to his own experience and his deepening understanding of the challenges, problems, and similarities between the question that had driven him (how to live in a black body) and the French panelists seated beside him and the audience gathered before him.

Though the occasion was ostensibly the publication of his book, Coates was seated on a stage with a panel of faculty and students, each of whom represented French citizens whose ethnic, religious, and cultural identities are seldom discussed or acknowledged under French law. French Arabs, Africans, and Muslims, the panelists were women and men who clearly viewed *Une colère noire* as an occasion to voice their anger and frustration with life in France and as an invitation to share their own accounts of what it was like to experience discrimination, police violence, social and economic isolation, and invisibility in French society. In a lecture hall that seated an overflowing crowd of nearly three hundred people, the audience sat listening to each panelist engage with Coates in an extended discourse on what it was like to live in a black or brown body in a culture that acknowledged neither their heritage nor their experience.

After his presentation and the remarks by the other speakers, Coates did something that went beyond merely summarizing his book or giving an account of his own experience. He listened and responded to the audience. This was something that evoked the spirit and the legacy of James Baldwin who, during his sojourn in France, in essays such as "Black Meets Brown" and novels such as *Giovanni's Room*, had used his voice and pen to make visible, represent, and empower Algerians in the years following the Algerian War. Like Coates, Baldwin listened, and in doing so, he used his writing to fulfill his sense of responsibility, drawn and cultivated from a lifetime of exploration and commitment, to write it all down and to be a witness.

Coates listened and, in doing so, gave each of the panelists a stage and a rare opportunity to give voice to a range of experiences that are not often heard, discussed, or acknowledged in a public context in France. Just as Morrison had found her voice and language in Baldwin's words and writing, the French faculty, students, and members of the audience who gathered with Coates for over three hours now "found life in his language" and a book that encouraged and even gave them license "to restructure it in order to accommodate their complicated passion." More than a clever wordsmith, more than a journalist, Coates's bearing witness to his own experience was a new demonstration of a complex and enduring practice of African American culture and the occasion for a new birth of freedom that he and those gathered before him had been seeking.

And, as Baldwin would insist:

his responsibility, which is also his joy and his strength and his life, is to
defeat all labels and complicate all battles by insisting on the human riddle,
to bear witness, as long as breath is in him, to that mighty unnameable,
transfiguring force which lives in the soul of man and to aspire to do his
work so well that when the breath has left him, the people—all people!—
who search in the rubble for a sign or a witness will be able to find him
there. ("Why I Stopped")

Works Cited

Adams, Tim. "Interview: How Ta-Nehisi Coates's Letter to His Son about
    Being Black in America Became a Bestseller." *The Guardian*, 20 Sept. 2015,
    theguardian.com/books/2015/sep/20/ta-nehisi-coates-interview-between-the-
    world-and-me-black-america. Accessed 25 Aug. 2018.
Alexander, Michelle. "Ta-Nehisi Coates's 'Between the World and Me.'" *The New
    York Times*, 17 Aug. 2015, nytimes.com/2015/08/17/books/review/ta-nehisi-
    coates-between-the-world-and-me.html. Accessed 25 Aug. 2018.
Baldwin, James. *The Fire Next Time*. Vintage International, 1993.
Baldwin, James. "Why I Stopped Hating Shakespeare." *James Baldwin: The Cross
    of Redemption: Uncollected Writings*, edited by Randall Kenan, Pantheon
    Books, 2010.
Candey, Dana. "The Talk: After Ferguson, a Shaded Conversation about Race."
    The New York Times, 13 Dec. 2014, nytimes.com/2014/12/14/sunday-review/
    dana-candey-the-talk-after-ferguson-a-shaded-conversation-about-race.html.
    Accessed 25 Aug. 2018.
Coates, Ta-Nehisi. *Between the World and Me*. Random House, 2015.
Dyson, Michael Eric. "*Between the World and Me*: Baldwin's Heir?" *The Atlantic*,
    23 July 2015, theatlantic.com/politics/archive/2015/07/james-baldwin-tanehisi-
    coates/399413/. Accessed 25 Aug. 2018.
"Hope." *Black-ish*, season 2, episode 16, American Broadcasting Company, 24 Feb.
    2016. Television program.
I Am Not Your Negro. Directed by Raoul Peck. Magnolia Pictures, 2017.
Morrison, Toni. Cover endorsement. *Between the World and Me*, by Ta-Nehisi
    Coates, Random House, 2015.
Morrison, Toni. "James Baldwin: His Voice Remembered; Life in His Language."
    The New York Times, late city final ed., 20 Dec. 1987, sec. 7, p. 27.
Standley, Fred L., and Louis H. Pratt, editors. *Conversations with James Baldwin*.
    UP of Mississippi, 1989.
West, Cornel. "In Defense of James Baldwin." *Facebook*, 15 July 2016, 6:53 p.m.,
    facebook.com/drcornelwest/posts/10155807310625111. Accessed 25 Aug. 2018.

11

Baldwin, the "Arab", and the End of the West

Bill V. Mullen

In his 1994 book *Representations of the Intellectual*, Edward Said offers a provocative connection between African American political history and his own commitments to Palestinian self-determination: "there can be little doubt," writes Said, "that figures like Baldwin and Malcolm X define the kind of work that has most influenced my own representations of the intellectual's consciousness. It is a spirit in opposition, rather than in accommodation, that grips me because ... the challenge of intellectual life is to be found in dissent against the status quo at a time when the struggle on behalf of underrepresented and disadvantaged groups seems so unfairly weighted against them. My background in Palestinian politics has further intensified this sense" (xvii).

In the case of James Baldwin, Said could have looked in any number of places for inspiration. For example, in his 1972 book *No Name in the Street*, in part a memoir of his years in Paris, Baldwin draws his own comparative perspective between himself in exile and North African migrants to the city. "The Arabs were together in Paris," writes Baldwin, "but the American blacks were alone ... I will not say that I envied them, for I didn't, and the directness of their hunger, or hungers, intimidated me; but I respected them, and as I began to discern what their history had made of them, I began to suspect, somewhat painfully, what my history had made of me" (*No Name* 25).

This essay argues for the centrality of the Arab, and the Arab world, in James Baldwin's evolving comprehension of race, colonialism, and the real and discursive weight of Western empire under capitalist modernity.

It demonstrates how Baldwin's exile from the United States to Paris in 1948 began his comprehensive reconsideration of the contours of Western imperialism through voluntary affiliation with Arab anti-colonial movements in North Africa; Arab and Muslim dispossession in France, the United States, and Turkey; and direct, sympathetic relationships to the Palestinians in their historical displacement from Palestine after 1948. Much as it was for his fellow New York intellectual Edward Said, the "Arab" was pivotal to Baldwin's apprehension of what he called in 1968 "the very last form of imperialism— Western imperialism" and of his complex disidentification with Europe and the West as, in Baldwin's words, "a frame of reference, a standard-bearer, the classic model for literature and civilization" (Elgrably and Plimpton 246). Baldwin's writings on Palestine, especially from 1966 to 1979, concretize a nascent understanding of the region's colonial history as a critical apex of Western conjuring. In the case of the Israel–Palestine conflict in particular, Baldwin's understanding is best articulated as what Said called "Zionism from the standpoint of its victims" (Said, "Zionism"), with Zionism here standing in for the historical project of European and Western colonial rule. Indeed, Baldwin's late writings, I will argue, including his play *The Welcome Table*, should be understood as fables of affiliation to this perspective: in the character of Mohammed in that play, Baldwin found historical analogue, and apotheosis, of Afro-Arab subordination and deterritorialization, and a vehicle for expressing what might be called the terminal geopolitical drama in his journey out of the West, namely, "statelessness" as a historically produced condition of empire. Through the figure of the Arab in *The Welcome Table*, in other words, and through what Said might call a joint or "contrapuntal" making of Afro-Arab history, Baldwin came to express one of his most salient, and prophetic, articulations of our modern moment.

*

Baldwin's understanding of crossroads in Afro-Arab history is prefigured by the originary moment of his exile. In *No Name in the Street*, Baldwin famously recalls his "escape" from America as boundaried by two versions of the Occident: the first, Europe, to which he flees, the second, Israel, his road not taken. "Four hundred years in the West had certainly turned me into a Westerner—there was no way around that," he writes. "But four hundred years in the West had also failed to bleach me—And if I had fled, to Israel, a state created for the purpose of protecting Western interests, I would have been in yet a tighter bind: on which side of Jerusalem would I have decided to live?" (*No Name* 42). We should note firstly Baldwin's appreciation of his "strange birth" into exile in 1948 as concurrent with the imperial world's laying down of a new colonial mark—partition—across Palestine. Here, Baldwin's perspicacious reading of the creation of the state of Israel *as* colonial project likely reflects his political training of the 1940s.

This was his self-avowed period as a "Trotskyite" with the Young People's Socialist League, which stood independent of both the Communist Party and even the popular Black Left—like Du Bois—in uncritical support for the creation of Israel. Rather, Baldwin comprehends a future theme of his work in 1948, namely, that both Jews and Palestinian Arabs may be metonymic of his own displacement from America and that in living as an outsider within the West, he is his own signifier of *apartheid*.

Hence it would not be long before arriving in Paris that Baldwin would consider the newly minted South African state—created the same year as Israel—as one point on a figurative Maginot Line of postwar colonial power extending from Palestine in the west of Asia to Vietnam in the southeast. Making this axis visible from his Paris bunker, significantly, was the Algerian. The French, he notes, were "still hopelessly slugging it out in Indo-China" when he arrived. "The Arabs," Baldwin writes, "were not a part of Indo-China, but they were part of an empire visibly and swiftly crumbling, and part of a history which was achieving, in the most literal and frightening sense, its *denouement*" (*No Name* 25). Meanwhile, the beginnings of the Algerian independence war in 1954 are marked by Baldwin as anti-colonial symmetry, an effort to "bring the French to another Dien Bien Phu" (26). Significant to my larger essay, Baldwin concentrates his analysis of French repression in Paris on the police. Baldwin's witnessing of gendarmes beating an "Arab peanut vendor" and hurling North Africans into local prisons is meant to recall, in context, the Setif massacre of May 8, 1945, in which French colonial police killed 103 Algerian demonstrators, and the 1952 house arrest of Messali Hadj for organizing mass protests in Paris. Indeed, by the time of his 1955 essay "Equal in Paris," an account of his own arrest, the police and the French criminal system had come to stand in for the colonial apparatus binding into one the joint "histories" of the Afro-Arab with which I began this essay. We know this because Baldwin recognizes in Paris prison demographics the nature of what we have come to call today disproportionate (i.e., *not* equal) incarceration, a phenomenon that begins to break down his perception of the differential treatment between the "American blacks" and the Arabs he had initially noted on his return to Paris at the end of the summer of 1952. In jail, the self-imposed "gap," as Baldwin calls it, between the "realistic" North African inmates acculturated to repression and his neophyte carceral self dissolves in the mockery Baldwin understands the discursive "West" makes of both parties. The laughter Baldwin hears in the courtroom at the description of his alleged theft of a *drap de lit* (bed sheet) is, he concludes, "the laughter of those who consider themselves to be at a safe remove from all the wretched," a laughter that is "universal and can never be stilled" ("Equal" 116).

Baldwin carried memories of seeing Algerians and other non–northern Europeans, including Jews, "corralled into prisons" in Paris when he ventured to Israel in 1961. Interesting for our purposes, he also carried in his luggage the unfinished manuscripts for both *Another Country* and extensive notes for "Down at the Cross," the essay published in *The New Yorker* in 1962 as "Letter from a Region in My Mind" and then in 1963 as *The Fire Next Time*. He arrived in Tel Aviv as a guest of the Israeli government, touring the Negev desert, Haifa, and a kibbutz near the Gaza Strip. As Keith Feldman notes, Baldwin's primary response to his visit was a deepened and self-reflective ambivalence elicited by partition. Baldwin is tormented by the apartheid geography of the region—hostile Muslim citizens surrounding an Israeli state "forced to control the movement of Arabs." Thus though Israel does function as a "homeland, however beleaguered," Baldwin wrote, "you can't walk five minutes without finding yourself at a border … and of course the entire Arab situation, outside the country, and above all, within … the fact that Israel is a homeland for so many Jews … causes me to feel my own homelessness more keenly than ever" (qtd. in Feldman ix). For Feldman, the 1961 Israel visit is precursive and predictive of Baldwin's declaration to Margaret Mead some ten years later—"You have got to remember … that I have been, in America, the Arab at the hands of the Jews" (Mead and Baldwin 193)—a quotation to which we shall return. Yet what can be said definitively here is that Baldwin apprehended the Israel visit as a real and symbolic turning point in understanding the physical and ideological contours of what Alex Lubin has called the "Afro-Arab Political Imaginary." As Baldwin wrote later, "When I was in Israel, it was as though I was in the middle of *The Fire Next Time*. I didn't dare go from Israel to Africa, so I went to Turkey, just across the road" (qtd. in Feldman viii).

Baldwin's insistence that to be in Israel was to be in the midst of American racial chaos begins to map more clearly his evolving ideas of race, the Arab, and occidental modernity. The conceptual link is provided by Baldwin's deliberate meditation in *The Fire Next Time* on ties between Arab and African American dispossession. Indeed the bridge between Baldwin's Palestine travel and the Harlem "region" of his 1962 essay is provided by what we are meant to see as temporal and geographical borders of his argument: the first, early in the essay, refers to Tunisians who, Baldwin argues, "were quite right in 1956—and it was a very significant moment in Western (and African) history—when they countered the French justification for remaining in North Africa with the question 'Are the *French* ready for self-government?'" (*Fire* 316), and the second, near the end of the essay, when Baldwin reflects affirmatively on Elijah Muhammad's contention that

> no people in history had ever been respected who had not owned their land … For everyone else has, *is*, a nation, with a specific location and a flag—even, these days, the Jew. It is only "the so-called American Negro" who remains trapped, disinherited, and despised, in a nation that has kept him in bondage for nearly four hundred years and is still unable to recognize him as a human being. (328–29)

What binds these moments of dispossession for Baldwin are imperialism and ethnonationalist conquest—Kipling's "white man's burden," which serves as an epigraph to the essay. Thus Baldwin marks the development of racism as a historical process linked to claims for statehood and nationalist ideologies. This is the significance of Baldwin's observation that "White Christians have … forgotten several elementary historical details. They have forgotten that the religion that is now identified with their virtue and their power—'God is on our side,' says Dr. Verwoerd—came out of a rocky piece of ground in what is now known as the Middle East before color was invented" (*Fire* 312). Thus in the case of North Africa, it is the "Christian" claim to land and territory masquerading as and masking French ethnonationalist supremacy over the Arab other; in Nazi Germany, it is Aryan genocide against the Jew; in South Africa, it is the Afrikaaner conquest of indigenous South African blacks; and in Harlem, it is the Jewish merchant and landlord who has himself become "white" by contributing to the long deterritorialization of the Negro. Yet because he has come to terms with the rise of the Nation of Islam (NOI) in his essay, it is to the historical relationship between the Christian "West" and its Oriental nemesis that Baldwin fixes as a turning point in history. Baldwin puts this most succinctly in this brief allegory of the Enlightenment:

> The Christian church itself—again, as distinguished from some of its ministers—sanctified and rejoiced in the conquests of the flag, and encouraged, if it did not formulate, the belief that conquest, with the resulting relative well-being of the Western populations, was proof of the favor of God. God had come a long way from the desert—but then so had Allah, though in a very different direction. God, going north, and rising on the wings of power, had become white, and Allah, out of power, and on the dark side of Heaven, had become—for all practical purposes, anyway—black. (*Fire* 313)

Baldwin's reflections here help us understand more fully how his encounter with Arab separation in Israel cited earlier made him feel his own "homelessness" more powerfully, and how "Letter from a Region of My Mind" may be read as Baldwin's early epistle to the world from America's own "Palestine," Black America. Indeed, to be "in the middle of *The Fire Next Time*" in Israel was for Baldwin to be in a clash of colonial history in the broader West, now taking the form at home of the NOI's own challenge to the American Occident's, and Christendom's, histories of conquest and *reconquista*. Here, it is also important to note for my larger argument how Baldwin's characterization of the NOI returns repeatedly to the question of land and territory. In keeping with his assertion elsewhere in the essay that "whoever questions the authority of the true faith also contests the right of the nations that hold this faith to rule over him—contests, in short, their title to his land" (*Fire* 319), Baldwin singles out moments from his encounter with the NOI where the struggle for a homeland prevails.

For example, Baldwin cites Malcolm X's words on the formation of Israel as an entrée into the NOI's own discourse on black dispossession:

> When Malcolm X, who is considered the movement's second-in-command, and heir apparent, points out that the cry of "violence" was not raised, for example, when the Israelis fought to regain Israel, and, indeed, is raised only when black men indicate that they will fight for *their* rights, he is speaking the truth. The conquests of England, every single one of them bloody, are part of what Americans have in mind when they speak of England's glory. In the United States, violence and heroism have been made synonymous except when it comes to blacks, and the only way to defeat Malcolm's point is to concede it and then ask oneself why this is so. (*Fire* 320)

Baldwin's intriguingly paradoxical turn of phrase "when the Israelis fought to regain Israel" reveals, even unconsciously, fissures opened up in his thinking on Israel's historical formation, as it relates to its Arab Palestinian inhabitants as well as to the valence of violence in state formation. If Israeli statehood depended upon the use of violence, why not, then, the justifiable use of violence by the Jew's colonial Other, the Muslim? Yet rather than advocating for violence as a strategy, Baldwin parses the NOI's arguments about the return of Southern states in the historic "Black Belt" as "back payment" for slavery. While Baldwin doubts the efficacy of such a strategy, or the willingness of the United States to concede territory, he endorses the rational center of the argument as a counterweight to US settler colonial history:

> All this is not, to my mind, the most imminent of possibilities, but if I were a Muslim, this is the possibility that I would find myself holding in the center of my mind, and driving toward. And if I were a Muslim, I would not hesitate to utilize—or, indeed, to exacerbate—the social and spiritual discontent that reigns here, for, at the very worst, I would merely have contributed to the destruction of a house I hated, and it would not matter if I perished, too. One has been perishing here so long! (329–30)

As it turns out, Baldwin concludes his long spatial meditation by driving towards Lake Michigan. In a poignant *denouement* to his journey from a Harlem dotted by "dark, noisome ghetto streets, into the hovels where so many have perished," Baldwin offers a summary of his discussion with the young NOI chauffeur of his car: "The driver and I started on our way through dark, murmuring—and, at this hour, strangely beautiful—Chicago, along the lake. We returned to the discussion of the land. How were we—

Negroes—to get this land?" (332–33). It is impossible to know if Baldwin includes in his thinking Chicago's own history of black settlement dating to its founding by the fur trader Jean Baptiste Point Du Sable, but there is little doubt that the question of dispossession, deterritorialization, and occupation hangs over the totality of *The Fire Next Time*. Finally, vis-à-vis his American book as a parable of his Israel journey, Baldwin puts this most starkly, and presciently, in his advisement that even in America, a single nation working in harmony is preferable to two populations in perennial conflict.

Yet Baldwin himself was in a fighting, and typically prophetic, mood as he concluded *The Fire Next Time*. Just four months after his Israel trip, in December 1961, he reflected in an interview with Studs Terkel on the meaning of the "relationship between American Negroes and Africans and Algerians in Paris" by arguing that he had begun to see that "the West—the entire West—is changing, is breaking up, and that its power over me, and over Africans, was gone" (Terkel 20). In between Baldwin's trip and the interview had occurred the Algerian massacre in Paris on October 17, an event Baldwin references, somewhat out of chronology, in *No Name in the Street*. Four months after the Terkel interview, Algeria would declare its independence. Meanwhile, in Cairo in May 1964, the Palestinian Liberation Organization (PLO) was formed at the Arab League's Cairo summit convened by Gamal Abdel Nasser. As Alex Lubin and Keith Feldman have noted in recent books, the PLO's initial statement of the "right of the Palestinian Arab people to its sacred homeland Palestine" and its initial charter "cast in the vernacular of third world anticolonialism" had a decisive impact on the decisions by the Student Nonviolent Coordinating Committee (SNCC) and the Black Panther Party (BPP) to include Palestinian liberation in their own platforms of demands for black freedom. The original 1964 PLO charter had also articulated a new criticism of Zionism as a "colonialist movement in its inception," later revised after the 1967 Six-Day War as "organically associated with international imperialism" (Feldman 36). The latter coinage was especially meant to link the Palestinian liberation struggle to ongoing anti-racist, anti-imperialist movements in Latin America, South Africa, and Southeast Asia.

Much of Baldwin's writings on race and the Arab world carry the inflection of these geopolitical turns. In both his writings on the United States, and more explicitly in his post-1967 writings on the Middle East, Baldwin amplifies and centers Arab, especially Palestinian, dispossession as a metonymy for Western imperial hegemony. For example, Baldwin's July 1966 essay, "A Report from Occupied Territory," builds its trope of "occupation" out of the sustained violence and hyper-policing of black communities across the United States, and by comparison between this localized militarism and the US war against the Viet Cong in Vietnam. As Baldwin memorably puts the matter, "They are dying there like flies; they are dying in the streets of all our

Harlems far more hideously than flies" ("Report" 738)—the same symbol
he would use to describe Algerian bodies dumped into the Seine during
the Algerian massacre. The essay's use of the trope of "occupation," in the
contemporary context, would also have resonated with anyone familiar
with the PLO's charter description of Palestine as stolen indigenous land,
the word codifying Baldwin's geographical expressions of black and Muslim
dispossession limned earlier in "Letter from a Region in My Mind."

One year after Baldwin's essay, in 1967, SNCC's newsletter published
"'Third World Round-Up' The Palestine Problem: Test Your Knowledge."
Among its thirty-two talking points was criticism of a US government that
had "constantly supported Israel and Zionism by sending military and
financial aid"—a tacit embrace of the PLO charter on Zionism—along with
an allegation with blatantly anti-Semitic overtones that Jewish wealth—
the Rothschild's—"control much of Africa's mineral wealth" (Lubin 118).
Baldwin's April *New York Times Magazine* essay, "Negroes Are Anti-Semitic
Because They're Anti-White," attempted to walk back from anti-Semitism
in some quarters of black radical affiliation with Palestinian liberation,
while fashioning an alternative conception of Zionism, what Said might
call "Zionism from the standpoint of its victims." Baldwin returns to
an analysis of the formation of the state of Israel by way of juxtaposing
Jewish inclusion, and African American exclusion, from the making of the
imperial West: "It is doubtful" writes Baldwin, "that the Jews could have
won their battle had the Western powers been opposed to them. But such
allies as the Negro may have are themselves struggling for their freedom
against tenacious and tremendous Western opposition" ("Negroes" 745).
Baldwin does not here name these allies, but the framework of separation
he describes manifests in the theme of "landlessness" and displacement we
noted in "Letter from a Region of My Mind." Of the US African Americans
of the diaspora, Baldwin writes, "He is a pariah in his own country and
a stranger in the world. This is what it means to have one's history and
one's ties to one's ancestral homeland totally destroyed" ("Negroes" 745).
Baldwin's positing of Harlem's Jews as contributing to the making of a
"burning house" for the African American climaxes thusly: "He is singled
out by Negroes not because he acts differently from other white men, but
because he doesn't. His major distinction is given him by that Christendom,
which has successfully victimized both Negroes and Jews. And he is playing
in Harlem the role assigned him by Christians long ago: he is doing their
dirty work" (746).

Two things are especially noteworthy vis-à-vis my theme: first, Baldwin's
essay is pivotal for understanding and illuminating Baldwin's 1970
declaration to Margaret Mead cited earlier: "You have got to remember ...
that I have been, in America, the Arab at the hands of the Jews," an assertion
whose meaning can only obtain in a contrapuntal context of African America
as America's Palestine. As Baldwin elaborated to Mead, "the creation of the

State of Israel was one of the most cynical achievements—really murderous, merciless, ugliest and cynical achievements on the part of the Western nations" (Mead and Baldwin 78). And second, Baldwin's essay is meant to draw a distinction between Judaism as a *religion* and Zionism as a strategy of Western colonial history.

Indeed, these two themes adumbrate and animate much of Baldwin's writing on "The Arab" and the Arab world between 1967 and 1979 especially. It is an era, we should note, bookended by the Six-Day War, in which Israel seized the West Bank, the Gaza Strip, and the Golan Heights, and thus became a turning point for many African Americans in their apprehension of the "problem" of Palestine, and Jimmy Carter's 1979 decision to fire Andrew Young from his position as UN ambassador because of his decision to meet with a delegation of the Palestinian Liberation Organization. In between these events, African American support for Palestinian claims for self-determination swelled well past the SNCC and the BPP to include "mainstream" figures like Jesse Jackson and a wide range of black intellectuals. For example, on November 1, 1970, fifty-six people signed a *New York Times* advertisement by the Committee of Black Americans for Truth in the Middle East called "An Appeal by Black Americans against United States Support of the Zionist Government of Israel." The ad located its critique of Zionism as a colonial and racial relationship and as what Alex Lubin calls a "proxy for U.S. empire in Southeast Asia and in Africa" (119).

This context helps to illuminate a string of Baldwin's observations throughout the 1970s on events in the wider Arab world. Central to these observations is a continuous honing of Baldwin's earlier themes of dispossession and displacement with an issue particular to the Palestinian struggle, namely, citizenship and "statelessness." We have noted earlier, for example, Baldwin's 1972 affirmation in *No Name in the Street* of his decision not to flee to Israel in the late 1940s for fear of divided, or what might be called binational, affiliation. There is also this declaration from *No Name in the Street* that

> any real commitment to black freedom in this country would have the effect of reordering all of our priorities, and altering all our commitments, so that, for horrendous example, we would be supporting black freedom fighters in South Africa and Angola, and would not be allied with Portugal, would be closer to Cuba than we are to Spain, would be supporting the Arab nations instead of Israel, and would never have felt compelled to follow the French into Southeast Asia. (178)

In Baldwin's 1979 novel *Just Above My Head*, Hall Montana meditates on the politics of hijacking and terrorists. The passage is generic in content, making no references to specific hijackings or persons, but several clues indicate that Baldwin is talking about Palestinians, most likely the hijackings in 1970, 1972, and 1976 by the Popular Front for the Liberation of Palestine (PFLP), one of which seized a plane headed for London. The PFLP, a Marxist-Leninist anti-imperialist group, emerged out of a break with the PLO. About the arrival of "hijackers and terrorists" on the contemporary scene, Baldwin writes,

> the people in the seats of power have only themselves to blame. Who indeed, hijacked more than England has, for example, or who is more skilled in the uses of terror than my own unhappy country? Yes, I know: nevertheless, children, what goes around comes around, what you send out comes back to you. A terrorist is called that only because he does not have the power of the State behind him—indeed, he has no State, which is why he is a terrorist. (*Just Above My Head* 342)

Both the initial English "hijacking" of Palestine and the stateless PFLP's demand for a single, binational country likely hover around the edges of Baldwin's fictional account of imperial chickens coming home to roost.

But it is Baldwin's 1979 *Nation* essay, "Open Letter to the Born Again," that is the apotheosis of his thinking on the question of the Arab, and the Palestinian, in the contemporary world. I would argue that it is a critical document on the history of Zionism in the West. In it, Baldwin is both furious in his denunciation of Western anti-Semitism and unbound in his open solidarity with Palestinian self-determination as a disruption or break in Western history's manifest destiny. The occasion for the essay was Baldwin's outrage at Jimmy Carter's aforementioned firing of UN ambassador and former Martin Luther King Jr. adviser Andrew Young for his decision to meet with Yasser Arafat and members of the PLO. In it, Baldwin links his own rupture with Christian fundamentalism to Christianity's own role in the persecution and betrayal of Jews. More pointedly, he aligns Carter's dismissal of Young with imperial gerrymandering in the Middle East dating to the Balfour Declaration and the history of "broken promises" known by both Jews and Palestinians. Notes Baldwin, "The Zionists— as distinguished from the people known as Jews—using, as someone put it, the 'available political machinery,' i.e. colonialism, e.g. the British Empire—promised the British that, if the territory were given to them, the British Empire would be safe forever" ("Open Letter" 785). Here, Baldwin closes in on his essay's theme, "betrayal," noting the priority of Western colonial, not Jewish, interests in the Zionist project, and importantly for this essay, the fact that "The Palestinians have been paying for the British colonial policy of 'divide and rule' and for Europe's guilty Christian conscience for more than thirty years." There is, Baldwin writes, "no hope" of peace in the Middle East without "dealing with the Palestinians." The essay then closes, full circle, to what might be called Baldwin's "apartheid" theme with which I began this essay, noting that the collapse of the shah of Iran's regime "not only revealed the depth of the pious Carter's concern for 'human rights,' it also revealed who supplied oil to Israel, and to whom Israel supplied arms. It happened to be, to spell it out, white South Africa" (786–87).

With "Open Letter to the Born Again," Baldwin renounces both Christian Zionism and settler colonial Zionism as secret sharers in the domination of the Afro-Arab world. For Baldwin, Andrew Young is a Palestinian Christ on the international cross of Anglo-American Middle East imperialism, one who has become a "hero, betrayed by cowards" (787). Baldwin's stringent stance against both anti-Semitism and what we would now call anti-Islamophobia in the essay effectively calls out the West's own peculiar history of Orientalist disdain for the Jew in days past, and the Arab in days present. Likewise, the essay's rhizomatic history of Western "broken promises"—of forty acres and a mule to the slave, of abandoned state treaties to the Indian, of Balfour to the Jews, of Palestinian dispossession—draws together into a singular totality a composite portrait of what Baldwin once called, self-referentially, "bastards of the West." It is towards Baldwin's final reckoning and place of the Arab in this schema to which I turn briefly in my closing.

*

Magdalena Zaborowska, in her superb book on Baldwin's Turkish decade, refers to Baldwin's last finished work, his play *The Welcome Table*, as a "last testament" to major life themes, including exile, erotics, and the multiple identities of the diasporic black subject. I wish to supplement Zaborowska's astute reading by arguing that it is the figure of the Algerian gardener Mohammed in the play who is a catalyst for Baldwin's primary theme: dispossession. While the play offers a sequence of characters permanently displaced by politics, war, sexual crisis, or gender traumas, it is the figure of Mohammed, the play's servant, whose "unwelcomeness" at the *Welcome Table* is Baldwin's deepest figuration of dispossession. Indeed, Mohammed's location in the "rambling stone house" that contains the play's actions is marked frequently as a literal outsider: he spends significant time in the garden, enters the dramatic action almost always as an instrumental attendant, and provides a literal denouement to the action by leaving the house (and the stage) when he drives the erstwhile matriarch and original owner of the house, Madame LaFarge, away into the night. The symbolic double departure of the fallen expatriate from Algiers—driven out of the country first by the national liberation struggle and second by Mohammed's escort—is shorthand for the play's theme of decline and fall: from colonial grandeur, from theatrical careers, from revolutionary movements, from houses and homes. At a broader level, the text is a playful, sardonic signifier for a terminus, and crossroads, in the West's history of revolutions, from 1789 Paris to 1954 Algiers. This is captured in the symbolism of the ninety-five-year-old Madame LaFarge's birthday, possibly her last, which all have come to commemorate, and in this exchange between Mohammed and Peter David, a black American journalist, about Mohammed and Edith's working relationship in Algiers:

> MOHAMMED. "In my country—when she was home, there—she never serves us cake."
> PETER. "You ever hear of a French Queen, called Marie Antoinette?"
> MOHAMMED. "She was—beheaded?"
> PETER. "She ran out of cake."

The exchange between Peter and Mohammed and their presence in the play points to several sources for *The Welcome Table* germane to my theme. Some time after 1958, Baldwin began work on "Les évadés," a planned story about American, Algerian, and French characters in Paris during the spring/early summer of that year. The story—never completed, but notes for which exist in the Baldwin papers at the Schomburg Center—focuses on two characters: Boona, an Algerian in Paris, whose brother had been tortured to death in Algeria during the resistance, and Ralph, a black journalist for CBS who has come to Paris to cover the effects of the Algerian uprising on the French. The action takes place in the spring of 1958, during what Baldwin calls "the time of the revolt of the generals in Algeria" ("Évadés"), a reference to a hastily arranged election that spring meant to ramp up the French state's military commitments against the Algerian uprising and which resulted in the election of Charles de Gaulle.

In *The Welcome Table*, the presence of journalist Peter David—along with Daniel, an ex–Black Panther now in exile—provides Baldwin an opportunity to explore the symbiotic relationship between African Americans confronting American racism and empire at home (Baldwin began the play in 1967 during the time of the Vietnam War and the year the BPP chapter was founded in Oakland) and the corresponding conditions in France for exiles like himself. Indeed, in both "Les évadés" and *The Welcome Table*, French colonial power in North Africa forces to the surface parallels between racist regimes—French and American—and their exercise of power on the bodies of blacks and Algerians. This is the knowledge garnered by Ralph in "Les évadés." In his "man in the street" interviews in Paris, he learns "there have been so many incidents that every Algerian in Paris is suspected of being a terrorist." When he goes to the small village of Roubaix to conduct interviews about the Algerian War, he is told, "You make the mistake ... of thinking that they [the Algerians] are like you. But they are not like you. They are savages still" ("Évadés"). Shortly thereafter, Ralph is sitting in a café among Algerians when he is roughly stopped by a French policeman with a gun and forced to show his papers. Moments later, as Algerians are being herded into paddy wagons and arrested, the police knock at Ralph's door and try to grab him. By implication, Ralph's skin color has made him a potential "terrorist" and honorary Algerian. Baldwin's notes for "Les évadés" conclude with Ralph and the Algerian Boona, now friends, driving together through Paris discussing whether they have the correct "papers" to get past the police.

"Les évadés" is itself a companion in topic and theme to a second unpublished Baldwin text, the essay "Paris, '58," also available in draft form in the Baldwin archives at the Schomburg. The essay is drawn from handwritten notes taken that year on the same events represented in the manuscript—the Algerian resistance in North Africa and in the streets of Paris, the rounding up of Algerians by the police, and the hardening of French racist attitudes towards the anti-colonial natives. Like the character of Ralph, the essay shows Baldwin awakening to the corresponding treatment of blacks and Algerians as the latter make known their demands for equality: "I remembered," writes Baldwin, "that American Negroes had not been hated as long as they were slaves; they began to be hated when they were slaves no longer. And the French did not hate Algerians ten years ago. They scarcely knew that Algerians existed. But they are beginning to hate them now" ("Paris, '58"). The essay also brings Baldwin full circle to explore connections between race revolts in 1958 in France and the United States. While predicting of the Algerian struggle that "Time is working on his side and against the French," Baldwin writes, "it is the history of Europe which makes white a proud color. And it is because Americans were Europeans once, have never gotten over it, nor learned how to deal with it, that Little Rock, as much as Formosa or Algeria, menaces the future of everyone now living" ("Paris, '58").

Both "Les évadés" and "Paris, '58" resound in meaningful ways in the textual action of *The Welcome Table*. Baldwin's decision to end the play with Mohammed driving Madame LaFarge out of the house, and the play, bespeaks the text's anxious, cyclical postcolonial thematic about the declension of Western empires. Their overturning is echoed by signs and symptoms of the erosion of the "other" Western hegemon in the play's French setting—the United States—whose dominance as described totters under challenge by militants like the Panthers, imperial overreach suggested via allusion to US political crimes in Guatemala (the 1954 coup), Chile (the 1973 coup against President Allende), and both South Africa and Palestine, briefly referenced in the text. Thus the play examines what might be called imperial fatigue, the ennui of "rootless cosmopolitanism" and exile as conditions generated by historical processes of national conquest, imperial domination, anti-colonial resistance, and displacement. As Regina, Edith's oldest friend, puts it, "I hope to God I never see another flag, as long as I live. I would like to burn them all—burn every pass-port." In so saying, the play's other aging grand dame expresses an ambivalence about the inevitability of *statelessness*.

Which returns us to Mohammed: he is *The Welcome Table*'s subaltern nomad, waiting in the wings of modernity's rituals of self-aggrandizement for, well, cake. As such, Mohammed embodies statelessness as a condition of lack, of national unbelonging, the condition of being, as Baldwin put it in the title of his final, unpublished, and incomplete novel about Mohammed himself, without papers. Indeed, according to James Campbell and David Leeming, the novel *No Papers for Mohammed* was to be Baldwin's book based on his own frightening encounter with French immigration authorities—one perhaps fictionalized in Ralph's near apprehension by the police in "Les évadés"—and on the case of an Arab friend deported to Algeria. Campbell also notes that the novel was to capture Baldwin's "personal conundrum" that his residency in Turkey coincided with the "first waves of Turkish immigrants flooding into Germany and Switzerland," a conundrum exacerbated by Baldwin's recognition of himself as "master of the plantation," as he put it in an interview, in his relationship to his own Algerian gardener upon whom his book was to be based (271). This scattered paper trail around *No Papers* then—including the unpublished "Les évadés" and "Paris, '58"—serves as ineffable but proper coda to Baldwin's riddle of the Arab with which I began this essay, namely, "as I began to discern what their history had made of them, I began to suspect, somewhat painfully, what my history had made of me." Clearly Baldwin saw in his X-ray examination of the Afro-Arab condition the skeleton not just of Western history but the master-slave dialectic played out on the backs of he who the former Black Panther Daniel calls, in *The Welcome Table*, "My Algerian brother." Baldwin's quest to represent the Arab then, as always, is a quest for freedom from the real and discursive political structures by which the West was won. Today, we might recognize fortress Europe, Donald Trump's Muslim ban, the Israeli apartheid wall—even the Arab Spring—as residual forms of those structures, and Baldwin and Said as brothers under the skin. We might also recognize in Baldwin a most radical impulse to explain our own present to ourselves, and to give us the tools, once again, to dismantle and rebuild the master's burning house.

Works Cited

Baldwin, James. "Equal in Paris." *Collected Essays*, Vintage, 1998, pp. 101–16.
Baldwin, James. "Les évadés." James Baldwin Papers, box 56, folder 11. Unpublished manuscript.
Baldwin, James. *The Fire Next Time. Collected Essays*, Vintage, 1998, pp. 291–348.
Baldwin, James. *Just Above My Head*. Delta, 1979.
Baldwin, James. "Negroes Are Anti-Semitic Because They're Anti-White." *Collected Essays*, Vintage, 1998, pp. 739–48.
Baldwin, James. *No Name in the Street*. 1972. Vintage, 2007.

Baldwin, James. "Open Letter to the Born Again." *Collected Essays*, Vintage, 1998, pp. 783–87.

Baldwin, James. "Paris, '58." James Baldwin Papers, box 44, folder 1. Unpublished manuscript.

Baldwin, James. "A Report from Occupied Territory." *Collected Essays*, Vintage, 1998, pp. 728–38. Originally published in *The Nation*, 11 July 1966.

Baldwin, James. *The Welcome Table*. James Baldwin Papers, box 138. Unpublished manuscript.

Campbell, James. *Talking at the Gates: A Life of James Baldwin*. Viking, 1991.

Elgrably, Jordan, and George Plimpton. "The Art of Fiction LXXVIII: James Baldwin." *Conversations with James Baldwin*, edited by Fred L. Standley and Louis H. Pratt, UP of Mississippi, 1989, pp. 232–54.

Feldman, Keith P. *A Shadow over Palestine: The Imperial Life of Race in America*. U of Minnesota P, 2015.

James Baldwin Papers. Schomburg Center for Research in Black Culture, New York Public Library.

Lubin, Alex. *Geographies of Liberation: The Making of an Afro-Arab Political Imaginary*. U of North Carolina P, 2014.

Mead, Margaret, and James Baldwin. *A Rap on Race*. Lippincott, 1971.

Said, Edward W. *Representations of the Intellectual: The 1993 Reith Lectures*. Vintage, 1996.

Said, Edward W. "Zionism from the Standpoint of Its Victims." *Social Text*, no. 1, Winter 1979, pp. 7–58. doi: 10.2307/466405.

Terkel, Studs. "An Interview with James Baldwin." *James Baldwin: The Last Interview and Other Conversations*, by James Baldwin, edited by Quincy Troupe, Melville House, 2014, pp. 1–34.

Zaborowska, Magdalena J. *James Baldwin's Turkish Decade: The Erotics of Exile*. Duke UP, 2009.

12

Effective/Defective
James Baldwin

Robert F. Reid-Pharr

I am a bit embarrassed by what I am about to say. I hesitate and stutter as I prepare myself for the simple, straightforward, and none too surprising revelation that I intend to write a biography—or something approximating a biography—of the famed novelist, playwright, and essayist James Baldwin. What discomfits me is not that there are already a fair number of biographical treatments of the maestro: Fern Eckman's 1966 *The Furious Passage of James Baldwin*; W. J. Weatherby's 1989 *James Baldwin: Artist on Fire*; Karen Thorsen's 1989 film, *The Price of the Ticket*; James Campbell's 1991 *Talking at the Gates*; Herb Boyd's 2008 *Baldwin's Harlem*; and more important still, the key 1994 text *James Baldwin: A Biography*, written by David Leeming, Baldwin's onetime assistant and the only individual to have received full access to the Baldwin papers. Nor am I particularly troubled by either the voluminous amount of Baldwin criticism or the very many interviews, speeches, and debates of the artist recorded on film, video, and audio and in print. What does bother me, however, what provokes that nagging embarrassment and guilt of which I have just spoken, is that I am frankly suspicious of the practice of biographical writing. The idea that there is something extra, a certain *je ne sais quoi* that might be ascertained by the careful student rifling through the detritus left behind in the wake of a great artist's passing, has always seemed to me somehow vulgar, an affront to the truth, the heft, one is wont to say, of the public archive that intellectuals, particularly progressive and politically committed intellectuals, struggle to produce and bequeath. Read a thick biography of a hero and you are likely to find yourself trapped within a sort of textual schizophrenia stretched between hagiography and distrust, in which the protocols of what the late Eve Sedgwick termed "paranoid reading" are very much on display (123–52). We seek an essential veracity underwriting the famed individual's life, a truth understood to be obscured, hidden, and denied by the very art that our beloved forebear struggled to produce. We hysterically ask, "Was he or wasn't he? Did she or did she not?"—the stated intentions of the always already suspect subject be damned.

Still, I am a man of my times. I listen daily to the irritated drums of dissent sounding just outside my office door. I am as aware as anyone that the nature of life, or rather the question of how to weigh and value human subjectivity and ontology—subjectivity and ontology defined by discourses of race, gender, sexuality, and class—dominate this nation's political and cultural discourse. Walk in the fullness of the day through the smugly pleasant streets of a liberal New England town, and one finds hanging from all the proudest of the proud steeples ever more grand and insistent reminders that "life matters." What gives me pause, however, is not how often it seems that I am, in fact, the only visible representative of the particular variety of life being named, but instead that the dialogue that the banners are meant to provoke seems to be one in which I can never fully participate, in which I am an object to be discussed but never a subject to be directly hailed or interpolated. I suspect then that there is something profoundly complex about the announcement of life, black life, gay life, queer life, female life, working life, intellectual life, within *popular* culture, the culture of biography, that it is wildly important to examine and understand as we try to stumble though difficult and interesting times toward something approximating the beloved community.

I will amend my earlier claims then to say that my desire is not so much to reveal the truth of James Baldwin as it is to understand the nature, the history if you will, of his celebrity. I want to know what it is that motivates our interest in understanding the hidden scripts that reveal the logic of the connections between his public persona and what we name, with only a bit of winking, his personal life. Even as I turn to the wealth of archival materials that Baldwin left in his wake, I still recognize that what drives the will to unveil and truly know Baldwin is not so much the belief that there are some remarkable secrets waiting to be told, but instead that we are all somehow clumsily and only half-consciously aware that the means by which one might announce and analyze life, including black, female, and queer life, are at once awkward and imprecise, politicized and vulgar. Indeed, we can only begin the process of coming to understand the nature of human life by attempting to access those deeply complex historical and ideological structures that demarcate the presumed limits of what is possible for us to know and imagine.

I should state here that my thinking on these matters is largely dependent upon the work of those many individuals who have attempted to theorize

the complexity of the political/ethical/discursive/ideological/cultural/social/
biological morass lumped inelegantly under the label "human." Speaking
of the generative tension that lies between "Man" and the (human) animal
body that supports this concept, Giorgio Agamben writes that

> Man exists historically only in this tension: he can be human only to the
> degree that he transcends and transforms the anthropophorous animal
> which supports him, and only because, through the action of negation,
> he is capable of mastering and, eventually, destroying his own animality
> (it is in this sense that Kojève can write that "man is a fatal disease of the
> animal"). (12)

The strange neologism "anthropophorous" holds my attention in this
passage. Agamben names the Man-bearing animal, a creature that though
proximate to and intimate with Man should never be seen or hailed. To do
so would risk revealing the obvious lie of a fundamental distinction between
Man and Man bearer. It would disrupt the "action of negation," the pursuit
of mastery and destruction that Agamben suggests as a primary engine of
modern society. Man exists. He transcends and transforms, masters and
destroys. It seems in fact that Man's never-ending attempts to confront and
destroy animality sponsor the flexibility, creativity, and vigor necessary for
his ever-proliferating creative projects. In contrast, the anthropophorous
animal does only one thing. It supports. Irritatingly, it consistently fails to
perform the only other task that has ever been asked of it. It will not die.

Or to state the matter as plainly as I can, the continued dominance of man
over woman, white over black, master over slave, colonizer over colonized
has never been simply a matter of avarice, but also an artifact of a set of
complex ideological structures in which the most vulgar forms of abuse and
exploitation are made to appear natural, inevitable, as things never to be
noted or remarked. What is needed from people of color, females, and queers
is not only that we unceasingly support the projects of so-called Western
humanism, not only that we *not* resist, but also that we never announce
in our speech, our bearing, the complexity of our culture that anything is
amiss. One must learn to take a punch and yet not say "ouch." Here I mean
to do nothing more complicated than to name the structure of the shocking
fear and hostility between black and white, female and male, immigrant
and native that one might readily see simply by turning the knobs on one's
television set to the "on" position. Again, the battles that we witness taking
place are at once structural *and* ideological. Or to rush toward one of
my major claims, the hostility directed toward the black, the brown, the
female, and the queer, the very hostility that is so easily—and innocently—
announced from the grandest of this nation's many grand stages, is in large
part driven by an only partially recognized or understood anxiety created
by the fact that subordinate communities, anthropophorous animals all,

seem to be willfully abandoning their traditional roles, retreating from their supporting postures. The virulence one hears in a presidential candidate's railing against *the* blacks in *the* ghettos is a product not so much of a hatred of black individuals and communities (though hatred aplenty there surely is), but instead an inchoate fear that once those individuals and communities have escaped their bounds and quit their traditional responsibilities, there cannot be any stable ground on which to announce the peculiarity and preciousness of the ever so reverently worshipped totems of American culture: wealth, whiteness, masculinity. One should always remember then that the winds of change do not move us all at the same speeds or in the same directions.

The genius of James Baldwin was that he got remarkably close to understanding the mechanics of all this. He understood, particularly during the period between 1954 and 1970 when the US civil rights movement was at full throttle, that progressive intellectuals needed to hail and defend the structural changes then taking place in the country while also modeling new forms of subjectivity and *inter*subjectivity for individuals and communities with no clear understanding of how they might continue to operate in a world in which basic social protocols were being called into question. He had, that is, to address the matter of what black and white identity actually were—or could be—once the fetters binding the two together began to fray and rot. The difficulty, however, was that he was hardly alone on this particular playing field. No matter the eloquence of his speech or the clarity of his vision, he was never fully in control of the protocols of celebrity that helped to establish and maintain his career.

What I propose, therefore, is not only that we treat Baldwin's celebrity as a script that might be adequately unpacked using the standard tools and protocols of literary and cultural criticism, but also that we recognize that much of the fascination with Baldwin's person—a fascination that peaked with the November 17, 1962, publication of "Letter from a Region in My Mind" in *The New Yorker* and began to wane as early as 1968 with the lukewarm reception of his fourth novel, *Tell Me How Long the Train's Been Gone*—was itself yet another example of the fretful nature in which American culture continuously announces, consumes, discards, and recycles presumably new versions of black subjectivity, "New Negrohood," if you will, as part of an effort to celebrate specifically American forms of modernity and forward thinking while also disallowing radical disruptions of hegemonic and commonsensical notions of the proper limits to individuality and communality.

In a remarkable series of eight articles published in *The Boston Globe* between April 14 and April 21, 1963, journalist Bryant Rollins lays out for his readers what would quickly become the standard narrative of Baldwin's life. Rollins informs us that Baldwin was a boy preacher whose incredible abilities to inspire, exhort, and testify were very much on display in both his prose and his public speaking. He then explained Baldwin's desperate need to escape the vulgar racism of New York and New Jersey for the considerably less hostile environment of Paris. And perhaps even more importantly, it was while Baldwin lived in France from 1948 to 1956 that he became aware of the fact that he was as American as any white Texan. We are reminded as well that Baldwin was a relentlessly truthful writer, one who often did his best work in the wee hours of the morning. Still, as even the most casual student of Baldwin and his work will surely recognize, Rollins tells us very little that Baldwin himself did not continually announce and rehearse throughout the course of his long and distinguished career. What I find truly fascinating about the articles, however, is the information placed at the margins. Indeed, even as the process of lionization starts to wear thin, to sound tinny and grating on the ear, Rollins, a Pulitzer-nominated reporter and columnist for *The Boston Globe* and later an editor with *The New York Times* and the executive editor of *The Amsterdam News*, clearly understood that Baldwin's celebrity was not simply a factor of the author's many talents but also a multifaceted and communal effort to find an articulate representative of mid-twentieth-century African American political and social insurgency.

In the last article of the series, published on April 21, 1963, Rollins quotes William Shawn, the famously reticent editor of *The New Yorker* from 1952 to 1987, on Baldwin and his essay "Letter from a Region in My Mind." "We at the New Yorker do not print articles of opinion, and if we had looked upon Baldwin's piece as being that, we would have not published it," Shawn begins.

> However, we considered it to be, in a highly unorthodox way, news. We regularly run letters from Paris, letters from London and Berlin, and so on, and we decided to call this article, "Letter From a Region in My Mind," to convey our feeling that the article was, indeed a report on what was going on in one area of James Baldwin's mind, and, thus, possibly on what was going on in the minds of many Negro Americans … Baldwin, because of his special literary powers, was able to express something that has been vaguely sensed by many people for a long time, though never before put into words … It required his particular combination of poetry, social situation, eloquence, and passion to describe what it is to be a Negro in America today … We were all aware that the piece would probably stand as some kind of event historically. The essential experience of being Negro in present-day America has now been recorded once and for all, and it had to be done by a Negro … It had to come from someone who had gone through it. (Rollins A64)

I fear that the only way that one can read these lines at all is to read them badly. The theatrical certainty that Shawn marshals in defense of his decision to publish "Letter from a Region in My Mind" provokes one to fits of sophomoric giggling. Baldwin's piece is not opinion but news. His mind is a district much like Paris, London, and Brazil. More remarkable still, Shawn claims, presumably with neither fingers nor toes crossed, that Baldwin's trenchant and beautifully rendered critique had been "never before put into words." Yet by the early 1960s Richard Wright had published *Native Son*, *Black Boy*, *The Outsider*, *Savage Holiday*, *The Long Dream*, and *Eight Men*; Ralph Ellison had won the 1953 National Book Award for *Invisible Man* and published many of the essays that would be collected in his 1964 *Shadow and Act*. Lorraine Hansberry's wildly successful play *A Raisin in the Sun* made her in 1959 the first black female playwright to have a work mounted on Broadway while Gwendolyn Brooks's *Annie Allen* had won the 1950 Pulitzer Prize for Poetry. Even the ever-prolific Langston Hughes had in 1958 published his *Selected Poems*, a collection that Baldwin himself reviewed.

The point of all this, those eight articles penned by Rollins and the rare interview with William Shawn, was, in fact, to remark Baldwin as at once representative and peculiar, archetypal and odd, the very conceptual monstrosity we conjure when we use the word synecdoche. "The essential experience of being Negro in present-day America has now been recorded once and for all," we are informed. The profound shift in black subjectivity and ontology that followed quick on the heels of the 1954 Supreme Court Brown v. Topeka Board of Education decision had been accounted for with but a single voice. In the process, both *The New Yorker* and the smug self-satisfaction that it continues to represent were reaffirmed and restabilized.

If you have followed my arguments thus far, you will understand that part of what I attempt here is to name Baldwin himself as a sort of rarified anthropophorous animal. Even and especially as he is celebrated as an exceptional, even superior, (black) individual, his celebrity is built—at least in part—on the ways in which he is imagined to announce and support protocols of racialism that have been at once modernized and invigorated. Thus the many profiles, interviews, and photographs of the artist can be said to be soothing for his audiences, evidence that the potential radicalism within the latest articulation of New Negro identity might be channeled through a lucid spokesman capable of translating so-called black rage into registers that might be understandable to the middlebrow elites associated with *The New Yorker*. Thus the appearance of the author's smiling face on the May 17, 1963, cover of *Time* magazine announces a sort of liberal relief and hopefulness, a belief that by acknowledging the logic and depth of feeling imbedded in both "Letter from a Region in My Mind" and the classic 1963 work *The Fire Next Time*, there might be a chance to usher in an era of desegregation without terribly disrupting basic political, social, and economic structures. Or to state the matter gracelessly, by celebrating the eloquence and elegance of James Baldwin, the country might be able to ignore the contradiction made apparent by the fact that Baldwin's fire-breathing essay was printed alongside an advertisement for a $150,000 set of pearls.

As a theoretical matter, however, I'd like to push beyond Agamben's extremely clever concept of anthropophorous animality by suggesting that the fixity, indeed the brittleness, of the idea begins to give way when we place it within the specific historical, social, and cultural contexts that produced James Baldwin. I will say from the outset that when I first read Agamben on this matter, I was reminded of nothing more exotic than New World slavery. There is a wealth of material both modern and ancient that speaks to the idea of the black (non)subject as a sort of only half-articulate being, one that supports the clear expression of dominant culture and society without somehow ever really participating in it. There is also an equally broad body of work that demonstrates the ways in which the messy living humanity of enslaved persons constantly disrupted the proper manifestation of these same protocols. Each time the black is imaged, the rules of engagement ever so slightly slip and falter. In the case of Baldwin, his status as a representative Negro had to be filtered through both his race radicalism and the matter of his difficult prose and his queer, never quite properly tamed body. Take too many photographs or conduct too many interviews of and with the author of the 1956 classic homosexual novel *Giovanni's Room* or the even more disruptive 1962 work *Another Country*, and one is very likely to be forced to rethink what type and quality of support this representative Negro is, in fact, able to offer.

The many celebratory profiles of Baldwin written after 1962 are marked by a remarkable amount of clumsiness, uncertainty, derision, and indeed fear in the descriptions that they offer. Baldwin is inevitably described as slight, ugly, fey, and nervous even as he is ceremoniously hailed as an extraordinary intellectual and a vibrant leader of his race. In an astonishing dispatch written by Roger Stone of *Time* magazine entitled "The Shadow Was a Nigger, Take One" and posted from the magazine's San Francisco bureau on May 9, 1963, we find a bewilderingly clear expression of the surprise and anxiety that Stone experienced when witnessing the Baldwin legend in the flesh.

> James Baldwin, an eloquent pixy with a sharp tongue, is fond of telling a beautiful story with a quick twist. One of his current stable is about how he was walking along a quiet street in a pretty town on a sunshiny day. As he strolled along, he suddenly saw, on a quiet patch of green lawn, a father swinging his tiny, pretty daughter in the air. "It didn't last for more than a second," says Baldwin. "But it was an unforgettable touch of beauty, a glimpse of another world. Then I looked down and saw a shadow. The shadow was a nigger—me."

You will forgive me if I am not fully able to collect myself at this juncture. It is not so much that I am offended, but instead that there is no proper or predictable way for me to read and unpack the codes that structure the logic of these seven surprisingly simple sentences. Is an "elegant pixy" a faggot? Are beautiful stories with sharp twists black queer nonsense? Do quiet streets and green lawns on which fathers swing tiny, pretty daughters in the air bespeak some unspoiled white Nirvana? The only certainty here is that shadows and niggers are one and the same. But even this bit of stability is undermined by Stone's report that it is James Baldwin himself who has provided this staggeringly unruly prose.

It is important to remember that this dispatch was designed to praise Baldwin. "Baldwin has been somewhat of a shadow, a fugitive and ill-formed writer," Stone announces. He then assures us that Baldwin's "shadow is fast lengthening in the twilight of diehard segregation," that "little Jimmy Baldwin is achieving full stride. ... [And] in the flash of lightning that has followed 'The Fire Next Time,' he has suddenly become the American Negro's number one spokesman." I think it best here that we focus not so much on intention as need. The fugitive and the ill-formed must be captured and normalized, pressed to the service of forms of racial liberalism that might reiterate the most basic social and ideological structures of the dominant society. There is something telling about the fact that Stone continually references a diminutive James Baldwin. Little Jimmy is a pixie growing into a not yet properly established manhood. Thus there is still time for guidance, still room for proper definition. Indeed, Stone comes just short of suggesting that without some form of policing and control, Baldwin's celebrity might cause a fundamental threat. "There is, in fact, a rapidly ascendant cult being constructed around James Baldwin," he notes, "a movement that sees his intellectual vigor as a step forward from the conditioned reflex action that has characterized much of the past civil rights movement among Negroes." Quoting a San Jose doctor, Stone goes on to inform us that "Civil Rights has moved into an existential phase."

That is to say, Baldwin's articulation, both the clarity of his speech and writing as well as the limpness of his body, the prominence of his eyes, his sparing consumption of food and stout intake of alcohol, all matters that Stone meticulously indexes in his profile, suggest new forms of black subjectivity about which there can be no certainty and for which there are no standard means of appraisal. Baldwin's persona is treated, therefore, as not so much queer as monstrous, a thing trembling between past and present, the beautiful and the dreadful. Stone announces with equal measures of bravado and enmity that "As a couple of Negro men watched Baldwin in action this week, one leaned across to the other and whispered, 'You know, he's the ugliest man I ever saw.'" With the thin cover of his never named black interlocutors in place, Stone proceeds to describe Baldwin as "short and slight" with "buggy eyes and a craggy, plastic-man face that, as he talks, contorts into unimaginable crevasses."

[Baldwin] bounces, jitters, thrusts his hands abruptly into his pockets and then waves them in the air. He is nervous and agile and light. But what he lacks in appearance he surely makes up for in the nimbleness of his mind and the power of his speech: if he tends to overstate his case, it is perhaps his overwhelming zeal to get his message across. Warm and possessive of an uncommon degree of humanity, Baldwin has a face that could soon be forgotten. Not so his lengthening shadow, as it steals across the nation. (Stone)

I would like to pause for a moment to note the resonance of Stone's description of Baldwin's speech, intellect, and body with similar descriptions of black subjectivity taken from popular culture, particularly the minstrel stage. To be sure, blackface minstrelsy was built upon the display of caricatures of black subjectivity and physicality in which the black was not only figured as a type that was physically awkward and ugly, with impossibly dark skin, unkempt wooly hair, and thick, often bright red lips, but also as a figure with a penchant for extreme and erratic forms of dress, movement, and dialect. I want to be careful, however, not to suggest that Roger Stone and the many other commentators whom I take him to represent were simply old-fashioned racists. Instead, I would aver that the minstrel character was—and is—so fascinating precisely because of its modernity. Nineteenth- and twentieth-century blackface minstrelsy was directly concerned with what to make of the legions of black individuals whose dress, speech, and public bearing demonstrated both movement away from the presumed simplicity and docility of their slave forebears and a desire to participate fully in the fast-paced changes in style and technology that are seemingly the greatest hallmarks of American culture. As Eric Lott has capably demonstrated, the blackface minstrel confirmed equal measures of white antipathy and adoration, love, and apprehension for African American subjectivity and culture.

Fern Eckman, one of Baldwin's earliest biographers, offers a dramatic description of young James Baldwin's obsessive reading and rereading of Harriet Beecher Stowe's 1852 masterpiece, *Uncle Tom's Cabin*, a work that the young author famously critiqued and rejected in his groundbreaking 1949 essay, "Everybody's Protest Novel." Eckman suggests that what so attracted Baldwin to *Uncle Tom's Cabin* was

that stock comedy figure, Topsy, who must have struck the boy as his feminine counterpart. She was exactly his age and, like him, a misfit, isolated, ridiculed, repugnant to those around her. She had his own round eyes, his own solemnity, his own quickness and keenness (she even learned to read, as he had with magical speed), his own generosity, and his own misery. (41)

I would add here that, like Baldwin, Topsy was a figure whose affect and intellect suggest a creature who exists outside of time, one who "never was born" and "just grew." That the character was a staple of the minstrel stage should itself demonstrate the American fascination and discomfort regarding the idea of a black subjectivity that cannot be easily assimilated to the prevailing logics of racial distinction. Moreover, as I have argued throughout this essay, I am not attempting to name some ancient reality, but instead a process that continues to dictate the ways in which we narrate black and queer subjectivity, both the celebrated and the obscene.

It is important, however, that we recognize that James Baldwin himself was very much aware of all this. In the last interview of his life, he confessed to Quincy Troupe that "It's difficult to be a legend. It's hard for me to recognize *me*. You spend a lot of time trying to avoid it ... it's unbearable the way the world treats you ... especially if you're black ... and you are not your legend, but you're trapped in it" (Troupe 189). The sobriety that we see on display in this quotation, the flat-footed acceptance of the fact that one enters into the public sphere via highly scripted—and policed—forms of interlocution demonstrates habits of thought to which Baldwin had become accustomed, and in which he actively participated, from very early in his career. In an autobiographical statement submitted to his publishers at Alfred A. Knopf in May 1953 on the verge of the release of his first novel, *Go Tell It on the Mountain*, one sees the author struggling toward not only a theory of literature and the practice of writing but also the matter of how one might function as an engaged (black) intellectual when so much in the common sense of American and European life viciously resisted either accepting— or even imagining—such an aberration. From the very first sentence of the document, we find Baldwin seeming at once to resist and acquiesce to the deeply calcified narratives of black life that framed his own efforts as a novelist. "The story of my childhood is the usual black fantasy," he begins, "And we can dismiss it with the restrained observation that I certainly would not consider living it again." Reiterating the critique that he had offered four years prior in "Everybody's Protest Novel," Baldwin complains that

> One of the difficulties about being a Negro writer ... is that the Negro problem is written about so widely. The bookshelves groan under the weight of information, and everyone therefore considers himself informed. And this information, furthermore, operates usually (generally, popularly) to reinforce traditional attitudes. ("Autobiographical Note")

That is to say, no matter the room into which the Negro writer walks, he is always imagined to be a known entity. Thus his vocalizations can never be said to be discourse per se, but instead repetitions of deep and constant realities already adequately demonstrated by the very darkness of his body. Playing this particular discursive game for all its worth, Baldwin closes the statement by turning himself into a sort of cipher, one whose family story is "the usual black fantasy." We find that the author has no particular interests other than food and drink, laughter and conversation, and "a morbid desire to own a sixteen-millimeter camera" ("Autobiographical Note"). He likes neither Bohemia nor those who are too earnest, but he does "love America more than any other country in the world," no matter that in May 1953 he was at the tail end of a more than eight-year absence from his beloved homeland.

Again I find myself embarrassed by what I am about to say. I would like to be able to demonstrate to you that the legacy of James Baldwin is one of unremitting resistance to the discursive and ideological structures that I have attempted to demonstrate. In the end, however, I cannot imagine such an easy escape. If you believe as I do that white supremacy and woman hating are not aberrations but instead deeply imbedded aspects of American and indeed Western culture, then it becomes impossible to imagine any subject, any subjectivity, that is not already implicated and sullied by and within these same ugly structures. I will beg you for a bit more of your graciousness then as I make but one more stop in the archive of celebrity, of popular biography, if you will, that I have been at pains to demonstrate.

I turn to Baldwin's much underappreciated 1972 work, *No Name in the Street*, both because it is perhaps the closest thing to a fully realized autobiographical statement that he ever published and because it is deeply flawed. I have in mind the arresting image that Baldwin provides of Dorothy Counts, one of four children who helped to integrate the Charlotte-Mecklenburg public school system in 1957.

In the fall of 1956, I was covering for *Encounter* (or for the CIA) the first International Conference of Black Writers and Artists, at the Sorbonne, in Paris. One bright afternoon, several of us, including the late Richard Wright, were meandering up the Boulevard St. Germain, on the way to lunch. Much, if not most of the group was African, and all of us (though some only legally) were black. Facing us, on every newspaper on that wide tree-shaded boulevard, were photographs of fifteen-year-old Dorothy Counts being reviled and spat upon by the mob as she was making her way to school in Charlotte, North Carolina. There was unutterable pride, tension, and anguish in that girl's face, as she approached the halls of learning, with history, jeering, at her back.

It made me furious, it filled me with both hatred and pity, and it made me ashamed. Some one of us should have been there with her! I dawdled in Europe for nearly yet another year, held by my private life and my attempt to finish a novel, but it was on that bright afternoon that I knew I was leaving France. I could, simply, no longer sit around in Paris discussing the Algerian and the black American problem. Everybody else was paying their dues, and it was time I went home and paid mine. (*No Name* 383)

Like James Baldwin, I am profoundly moved by the images that were taken of Dorothy Counts on the morning of September 4, 1957, as she made her historic approach to the campus of Harding High School in Charlotte, North Carolina. Taking place on the same day that Daisy Bates led nine black students to the doors of Central High in Little Rock, Arkansas, Counts's presence on the near west side of Charlotte was designed to challenge resistance to the 1954 Brown v. Topeka Board of Education decision by using exceptional young black people as the vehicles by which to break the schoolhouse color line. One must make sense, however, of the fact that Baldwin so seriously fumbled the details of his encounter with Counts's photograph. The Congress of Black Writers and Artists (an event that Baldwin styles as a conference) was held in 1956, a year before Counts entered Harding High School. That is to say, though Baldwin undoubtedly meandered up the Boulevard St. Germain in the company of Richard Wright and other black notables and though he was surely confronted by the remarkable photographs of Dorothy Counts's noble march, these two events did not, in fact, take place on the same day. Instead, Baldwin produced a factually inaccurate, if perfectly serviceable, memory in which he demonstrated with piercing clarity the complexities of history and ideology that I am now at pains to demonstrate. It is in this sense that I would ask us to examine the contours of our most precious aesthetic structures. It is nearly impossible to stop looking at the at once unsettling and beautiful photograph of Dorothy taken by Don Sturkey of *The Charlotte Observer*. One is enthralled by the young woman's style, her remarkable composure; that great length of arms trailing delicately by her sides; her immaculately pressed hair; those reading glasses hanging nonchalantly about her neck; a tasteful red and yellow checked dress made especially for the day bunches tightly at a slender waist only to burst into the exuberance of an overfull skirt. And even more remarkably, the young woman wears an immaculate cream colored ribbon hanging half the length of her body, reminding even the dullest among us that the child had been prepared for either triumph or sacrifice. Or to state the matter slightly differently, Baldwin and the others who proclaimed Counts's heroism, understanding all too well the mechanics of publicity and publication, celebrity and celebration did what it is seemingly inevitable for engaged intellectuals to do. They turned their precious subject into a shadow, bent her striking image once again toward the status of Man bearer in order to announce the very break with the vulgar protocols of racism and misogyny that the elegant young woman's singular march was designed to disrupt.

My desire to write a biography of James Baldwin, including my willingness to announce his failures, the instances in which his work and his actions reiterated structures of feeling and thought that functioned to maintain hierarchies of race, gender, class, and sexuality, is motivated in no way by pessimism. Instead, nearly a quarter century after the publication of Orlando

Patterson's masterful study *Slavery and Social Death*, I find myself fascinated by the question of what counts as social rebirth. Immersing myself in both the recently opened Baldwin archives as well as the competing ideological, social, and discursive structures that underwrite Baldwin's legacy, I find that the name "Baldwin" so attracts—and perplexes—because it marks a spot at which a remarkable intellect and a singular life have slipped the yoke, become unruly, if not fully uncontrollable. Restricted but not tamed, buried but not dead, Baldwin's biography is best approached not as a thing but instead as an unsettled process in which the grand authority exhibited in Baldwin's prose and oratory is continually challenged by both admirers and detractors alike. Thus the theoretical question that must stand at the center of Baldwin studies is how we might make sense of the fact of a black intellectual who, though interred decades before, still resists easy consumption. Nigger, shadow, genius intellectual; Baldwin never quite properly inhabits any of these identities. Instead he bequeaths us the gift of radical uncertainty, the promise of revolutionary discomfort.

Works Cited

Agamben, Giorgio. *The Open: Man and Animal*. Translated by Kevin Attell, Stanford UP, 2004.

Baldwin, James. Autobiographical Note to Alfred A. Knopf, Inc. May 1953. Dick Fontaine Papers, Paper and Film Outtakes Collection, Houghton Library, Harvard U, box 17, folder 6.

Baldwin, James. *No Name in the Street. Collected Essays*, edited by Toni Morrison, Library of America, 1998, pp. 349–476.

Eckman, Fern Marja. *The Furious Passage of James Baldwin*. M. Evans, 1966.

Lott, Eric. *Love and Theft: Blackface Minstrelsy and the American Working Class*. Oxford UP, 1993.

Patterson, Orlando. *Slavery and Social Death: A Comparative Study*. Harvard UP, 1982.

Rollins, Bryant. "James Baldwin, Author Extraordinary VIII: Can America Escape 'The Fire Next Time'?" *Boston Globe*, 21 Apr. 1963, p. A64.

Sedgwick, Eve. *Touching Feeling: Affect, Pedagogy, Performativity*. Duke UP, 2003.

Stone, Roger. Roger Stone Dispatch to Time Magazine, San Francisco Bureau. 9 May 1963. Time: The Weekly Newsmagazine Dispatches, 1 May–1 July 1963, Houghton Library, Harvard U, item 608.

Troupe, Quincy. "Last Interview (1987)." *James Baldwin: The Legacy*, edited by Troupe, Simon and Schuster, 1989, pp. 186–212.

CONTRIBUTORS

Marcus Bruce is Professor of Religious Studies at Bates College in Lewiston, Maine. A 1977 graduate of Bates, he earned a Masters and a PhD in American Studies from Yale University in 1990. He is also an Alumni Fellow at the W. E. B. Du Bois Institute at Harvard University. He is the author of *Henry Ossawa Tanner: A Spiritual Biography* and is currently writing a book on African Americans at the Paris Exposition of 1900 entitled *The Ambassadors: W. E. B. Du Bois, the Paris Exposition and the Problem of the 20th Century*.

Alice Mikal Craven is Professor of English and Comparative Literature at the American University of Paris and Chair of the Department of Film Studies. She is coeditor of *Richard Wright: New Readings in the 21st Century* (2011) and *Richard Wright in a Post-Racial Imaginary* (2014). She has published on authors and filmmakers including James Baldwin, Bertolt Brecht, Jean-Luc Godard, Chester Himes, Raul Ruiz, and Richard Wright. She is author of *Visible and Invisible Whiteness: American White Supremacy through the Cinematic Lens* (2018).

William E. Dow is Professor of American Literature at the Université Paris-Est (UPEM) and Professor of English at The American University of Paris. Professor Dow is Associate Editor of *Literary Journalism Studies*. He is also author of the book *Narrating Class in American Fiction* (2009), and coeditor of *Richard Wright: New Readings in the 21st Century* (2011) and *Richard Wright in a Post-Racial Imaginary* (2014). He is currently completing a book-length study on American Modernism and radicalism entitled *Reinventing Persuasion: Literary Journalism and the American Radical Tradition, 1900–2000,* and is coeditor of the forthcoming *Routledge Companion to American Literary Journalism*.

Douglas Field lectures in twentieth-century American Literature at the University of Manchester. He is the author of *All Those Strangers: The Art and Lives of James Baldwin* (2015), and he is the cofounding editor (with Dwight McBride and Justin Joyce) of the *James Baldwin Review*. He was the coeditor (with Rich Blint) of a special issue on Baldwin for *African American Review* and the editor of *A Historical Guide to James Baldwin*. He is a frequent contributor to the *Times Literary Supplement*.

Kathy Roberts Forde is Associate Professor of Journalism at the University of Massachusetts Amherst, and a US journalism historian with research interests in the First Amendment, the African American freedom struggle, literary journalism, and the history of the book and print culture. Her book *Literary Journalism on Trial: Masson v. New Yorker and the First Amendment* (2008) received the Frank Luther Mott-KTA and the AEJMC History Division book awards. Forde is working on a second book, a publication and reading history of James Baldwin's *The Fire Next Time*. She has twice received the AEJMC Covert Award for her journal articles.

Timothy McGinnis is a writer from Charlotte, North Carolina. He received a Master of Philosophy at the University of Oxford in Economic and Social History, where he studied colonialism in Africa and co-convened a weekly seminar on the works of James Baldwin at the Rothermere American Institute. His thesis, "The Uses and Abuse of Amputation: A Social History of Violent Amputations in the Congo Free State, 1885–1908," is cataloged at the University of Florida Smathers Libraries in addition to those of Oxford. He attended Deep Springs College and finished his BA in Anthropology at Princeton University before working in global health. Tim currently lives in Cambridge, Massachusetts, where he is a student at Harvard Medical School.

Isabelle Meuret is Associate Professor at the Université libre de Bruxelles, Belgium. She teaches media in English, British and American cultures, and narrative journalism. She was a Visiting Professor at Universiteit Gent (2012–16), where she created a course on literary journalism in the Master Program in American Studies, and then at Fordham University (2014). Her research interests are comparative literature, narrative and medicine (*L'Anorexie créatrice* (2006); *Writing Size Zero* (2007)), literary journalism, photography and reportage. She has published articles in *Literary Journalism Studies* and was the guest editor of a special issue devoted to the French-speaking world (Fall 2016).

James Miller is Senior Lecturer and Course Director for the MFA in Creative Writing at Kingston University. He was educated at Oxford, UCL, and Kings College London, where he took his PhD, "A Warning to America: History, Politics and the Problem of Identity in the Fiction and Non Fiction of James Baldwin." He is the author of the novels *Lost Boys* (2008), *Sunshine State* (2010), and *UnAmerican Activities* (2017) as well as numerous short stories. His articles on James Baldwin have been published in the *Journal of American Studies* and the *European Journal of American Culture*. www.jamesmillerauthor.com/@jmlostboys.

Bill V. Mullen is Professor of English and American Studies at Purdue University. His books include *UnAmerican: W. E. B. Du Bois and the Century of World Revolution* (2015); *W. E. B. Du Bois: Revolutionary Across the*

Color Line (2016); *Afro-Orientalism* (2004), a study of the interethnic anti-racist alliance between Asian and African Americans; and *Popular Fronts: Chicago and African American Cultural Politics 1935–1946* (1999). He has edited five other books in collaboration with Sherry Lee Linkon, James Smethurst and Fred Ho. He is currently at work on a biography of James Baldwin.

Claudine Raynaud is Professor of American Studies at the University Paul Valéry, Montpellier, France. She has taught in Birmingham, Liverpool, Michigan, Northwestern, and Oberlin. A Du Bois Fellow (2005), she headed the nationwide African American Studies Research Group (2004) and works at the CNRS. She is the author of *Toni Morrison: L'Esthétique de la survie* (1996) and numerous articles on black autobiography. Her publications include two essays in Cambridge Companions (2004, 2007) and an article in *Afromodernisms* (2013). She has edited *La Renaissance de Harlem et l'art nègre* (2013), *Diasporas, Cultures of Mobility, "Race"* (2014, 2016) and translated *Truth's Narrative* (2017).

Robert F. Reid-Pharr is Professor of the Studies of Women, Gender, and Sexuality at Harvard University. A specialist in African American culture and a prominent scholar in the field of race and sexuality studies, his major works include: *Conjugal Union: The Body, the House, and the Black American* (1999), *Black, Gay, Man: Essays* (2001), *Once You Go Black: Choice, Desire, and the Black American Intellectual* (2007), *and Archives of Flesh: African America, Spain, and Post-Humanist Critique* (2016).

Tyler T. Schmidt is Associate Professor of English at Lehman College, City University of New York (CUNY), where he also co-coordinates the college's Writing Across the Curriculum program. His book *Desegregating Desire: Race and Sexuality in Cold War American Literature* (2013) investigates cross-race writing, interracial sexuality, and queer identity in post–Second World War American poetry and fiction from 1945 to 1955. His critical work has appeared in *African American Review*, *Women's Studies Quarterly*, and *Radical Teacher*. His current project focuses on a little-known circle of writers and visual artists based in the Midwest in the 1950s and 1960s.

James Smalls is Professor of Art History and Theory and Affiliate Professor of Gender and Women's Studies and Africana Studies at the University of Maryland, Baltimore County. His research and publications focus on the intersections of race, gender, and queer sexuality issues in nineteenth-century European art and in the art and culture of the black diaspora. He is the author of *Homosexuality in Art* (2003) and *The Homoerotic Photography of Carl Van Vechten: Public Face, Private Thoughts* (2006). He is currently completing a book entitled *Féral Benga: African Muse of Modernism*.

INDEX

CPSIA information can be obtained
at www.ICGtesting.com
Printed in the USA
LVHW030204180820
663422LV00011B/284

9 781501 367571